And Bid Him Sing

And Bid Him Sing

A Biography of Countée Cullen

Charles Molesworth

The University of Chicago Press
Chicago and London

Charles Molesworth is coauthor of *Alain Locke: The Biography of a Philosopher* and the editor of *The Works of Alain Locke*. He writes a regular art column for the quarterly *Salmagundi*.

The University of Chicago Press, Chicago 60637
The University of Chicago Press, Ltd., London
© 2012 by Charles Molesworth
All rights reserved. Published 2012.
Printed in the United States of America

21 20 19 18 17 16 15 14 13 12   1 2 3 4 5

ISBN-13: 978-0-226-53364-3 (cloth)
ISBN-13: 978-0-226-53366-7 (e-book)
ISBN-10: 0-226-53364-6 (cloth)
ISBN-10: 0-226-53366-2 (e-book)

Library of Congress Cataloging-in-Publication Data

Molesworth, Charles, 1941–
    And bid him sing : a biography of Countée Cullen / Charles Molesworth.
      pages ; cm
    Includes bibliographical references and index.
    ISBN 978-0-226-53364-3 (cloth: alkaline paper)
    ISBN 0-226-53364-6 (cloth: alkaline paper)
    ISBN 978-0-226-53366-7 (e-book) (print)
    ISBN 0-226-53366-2 (e-book) (print)
    1. Cullen, Countee, 1903–1946. 2. African American poets—20th century—
Biography. 3. Harlem Renaissance. I. Title.
PS3505.U287Z75 2012
813'.52—dc23
[B]

                                                        2011050825

♾ This paper meets the requirements of ANSI/NISO Z39.48-1992 (Permanence of Paper).

This book is dedicated, with anticipation and love, to
Brittany and Alexandra

"And so with a pint or two of ink,
With paper by the quire and ream,
She soberly sat down to think,
To bite her pen, and dream and dream."

Contents

Acknowledgments

I would like first to thank three people whose expert assistance and generosity helped make this book possible. Lee Hampton, the director of the Amistad Research Center at Tulane University, where the Cullen archive is housed, has graciously granted me permission to consult and quote from the archive. Christopher Harter, the curator of the Cullen archive, never failed to assist me in finding material and was most hospitable when I visited the Amistad. Thomas Wirth, director of the project to put Cullen's correspondence online, has diligently and successfully located many records of Cullen's early years and has most kindly shared them with me. I hope that future Cullen scholarship will be able to profit from the assistance of these three gentlemen as thankfully as I have.

A number of librarians were helpful in supplying copies of correspondence and other materials from various archives. I thank especially Diana Carey of the Schlesinger Library at Radcliffe, Micah Hoggart at the Houghton Library at Harvard, Andrea Fisher of the Artists Rights Society, Mary Beth Hinton of the Syracuse University Library, Leah Jehan and the staff at the Beinecke Library, Danielle Kovacs and the staff of the library at University of Massachusetts–Amherst, and the staff at the Givens Collection in the University of Minnesota Library. Hillina Seife was most kind in sharing her research on the Ethiopian students with me.

I also own a debt of gratitude to Mr. Robert Pinsky, who offered sound and useful advice on a matter of some complexity.

Fred Kaplan, my longtime friend and colleague, was once again a strong pillar of support and graciously read some of the earlier drafts of this book.

My wife Carol listened to stories, rumors, and woes—some of them Cullen's and some of them mine—with a remarkable patience that fully deserves repayment.

Introduction

A black man. A poet. One whose "chief problem has been that of reconciling a Christian upbringing with a pagan inclination." These three strokes can constitute a reasonably accurate portrait of Countée Cullen. They sketch the public figure and the inner man. The public identity of Countée Cullen, the result of a complex fate, is bound up with his emergence as the leading African American poet of his age. In turn, this poetic identity was mingled with that of a prodigy, a highly gifted but rather unassuming, gentle man. The reputation of Cullen was built on genuine public affection, and it stayed relatively high even after his prodigious output of lyrics tailed off and he went on to other labors. Among these other labors were ten years of teaching in a public school and attempts to write for the stage. As for the inner man, everyone remarked on his reticence, and its cause was seldom explained, even to his close friends. It may have resulted from being an orphan, or from his sexual orientation, or—more cryptic yet—simply his temperament. He left behind no autobiography or extensive journals, though his correspondence with several people gives a full account of his inner life: his values, his experiences, and his longings.

It was Duke Ellington, most gifted of all the nation's composers, writing in his first published article in 1931, who positioned Cullen in a place of high honor: "The history of my people is one of great achievements over fearful odds; it is a history of people hindered, handicapped and often sorely oppressed, and what is being done by Countée Cullen and others is overdue in our music."[1] From the time this praise appeared, however, Cullen subsequently went on to write only one more book of lyric poetry. True, he was productive in other ways. People nevertheless expect poets to be born and not made, and so they are expected to go on singing no matter the time or circumstance. This falling off in productivity can perhaps explain why there has been no full-length critical biography to help contextualize and illumine the poetry. In turn, some of the poetry has been neglected, while other parts have become canonized to the point where they, too, are undervalued.

A proper evaluation of Cullen is not readily achieved. From the point of view of high romantic poetry, many judged that he fell short of greatness. As far as his inner life developed, he was weighted with the conflicts that involved his deepest longings and widest horizons: race and religion, inevitable death and unrequited love, spiritual transcendence and earthly ambition. Just to have dealt with such serious issues—and Cullen was indeed serious, even as he greatly enjoyed art and dance and Paris—is to have kept faith with his considerable poetic gifts. What he was able to reveal of his inner life and character won him many readers, though they tended to praise most heartily his sense of race consciousness and the African American experience during the last decades of Jim Crow. Few readers and only a handful of later academic critics realized that Cullen's inner life was on display in his work in the tradition of the love lyric. Though some of his longer poems are of exceptional interest, it is his shorter poems and sonnets on themes of carpe diem, the inconstancy of love, and the vanity of human wishes that make up the main part of his poetic corpus. Most frequently, however, his reputation flourished when he wrote directly about the experience of race and its injustices. While it is easy to see that his poems on racial issues would more likely attract attention, evaluating Cullen's poetic stature means attending to all the parts of his poetry.

As all the evaluative scales by which poets are measured can be adjusted, it is possible to turn the framing context in a different direction, from African American music and the struggle for rights focused on by Ellington's encomium to a rather different set of terms. Here is a latter-day estimation of Cullen, by Darryl Pinckney, as seen in the context of another tradition he loved, that of high English romanticism:

> Cullen wanted to be known as a "Poet," not a Negro poet, but we remember him only because he was black. . . . Since his death, interest in him has tended to rest in the contradictions of his example, that of a modern black writer attempting to reconcile his identity with the tone and style of a nineteenth-century British poetic tradition. . . . One can find in Cullen so many diverse echoes—Swinburne, Dante Gabriel Rossetti, Stephen Crane, Housman, Dickinson—because his work is itself an anthology devoid of a strong single personality. . . . The sadness of his career lies in his inability to claim as his own the tradition he admired, to conceive of it as something to be inherited and added to. He borrowed it and handed it back, like a poor relation careful to show his painful good manners.[2]

This lays out what stands as the fullest case against Cullen, and by beginning with race and ending with a polished subservience, the paragraph might seem little but a caricature. Many people, however, in the biographical and critical writing on Cullen would share at least some of its attitude. Somewhere in between the two views—Ellington's sense of his greatness and Pinckney's image of him as a "poor relation"—lived a flesh-and-blood writer, an individual with some uncommon awareness about human experience and emotion, and a frequently embattled figure who struggled to fulfill his vocation according to his own lights.

Cullen's sexual orientation added to his inclinations for concealment, for there was no easy way to be an openly homosexual African American in the first half of the twentieth century in America. In a way, it magnified the sense of being a "problem"—that disorienting sense that W. E. B. DuBois pointed to as the fate of the Negro in the twentieth century. Rumors about Cullen's being homosexual were rife but whispered throughout the years of the Harlem Renaissance and beyond. Complicating this aspect of Cullen's experience is the role his adoptive father, the Reverend Cullen, played in his life. Gossip circulated throughout Harlem that the renowned preacher was effeminate and made use of his wife's makeup and clothing. Some have even suggested that the preacher may have had homosexual longings for the young Cullen when he was adopted into the parsonage at an early age. But there is no documentary evidence to support such speculation, and in any case it would hardly provide an overall or monocausal explanation for Cullen's much-noticed reserve, even secrecy, about his early years.[3] Still, while there is in his correspondence no explicit record of any homosexual relationship or encounter, or any direct acknowledgment by Cullen of his homosexuality, the circumstances surrounding his relations with a number of his male friends make it obvious.

But like the other African American writers—Langston Hughes being the most notable example—who used any number of guises to conceal their sexuality from the public scorn it would certainly have suffered, Cullen went to similar lengths. Later generations have simultaneously understood and regretted these guises. This led to a paradox in the later critical assessments of Cullen's poetry, which was honored for its skill but belittled for its lack of daring and innovation. (In short, "an anthology devoid of a strong single personality.") A later style of critical commentary saw Cullen as homosexual regardless, and so reinterpreted his poetry in that context, often making it read as the covert record of unacknowledged desires. This meant, not exactly a poetry against expression, but one wary of it. Such an approach, and other circumstances, meant that Cullen's life was more or less known to us but not always clearly, for by virtue of his occluded poetry he told us all that he could. So his once laureate-like reputation declined, and a fuller picture of the life and the work became less and less sharply etched.

As a result of the absence of details about his life, and hence a fuller consideration of his poetic vision, we have almost lost sight of Cullen's other writings. Though limited in quantity, his prose columns, written for *Opportunity* under the heading "From the Dark Tower," now garner little notice. His editorial efforts resulted in an important anthology, *Caroling Dusk,* but it soon became outdated. His novel was well received when it first appeared. His translation—the first by an African American—of a Greek tragedy continues to be seldom staged or explored. His children's books are admired, but almost never enter into a full picture of his sensibility. And his musical finally reached the Broadway stage, but only after his death, at the young age of forty-two. However, each of these writings has genuine merit and something to tell us about Cullen. Using these other works to illumine the poems will not be taken amiss, since it is easy to think that Cullen would not mind being considered first and last as a poet. All writers cobble together a set of measures and urgings by which they can know how accurate it is to refer to themselves as writers. For Cullen this happened early, in his teenage years in fact, and the later circumstances of his life didn't make it very easy to answer to his own high standards. Still, he was a writer who believed in availing himself of the desk, and he never sloughed off the demand for excellence and skill. A wise man once said, when he heard a young poet complaining of the travails of the lyric vocation, "Just remember, you volunteered." Cullen would agree.

What has happened to Cullen in the wake of his diminished reputation is typical of what happens in many such cases. He has come to be known only (or chiefly) on the basis of a small number of poems or lines from poems. In Cullen's case there are two such passages, from "Incident" and "Yet Do I Marvel." The first ends with the lines describing an insult and a response:

> he poked out
> His tongue, and called me "Nigger."

> I saw the whole of Baltimore
> From May until December;
> Of all the things that happened there
> That's all that I remember.

The second is the last line of "Yet Do I Marvel," the first half of which presents less an insult than a bedazzlement or a curse, and its attendant response in the second half, in this case an ironic exclamation. It says, puzzling over God's plans, that some fates are more than difficult: "To make a poet black, and bid him sing!" Both poems have a similar mixture of tones, chiefly one of reserve, but an artistic reserve that hopes to intensify the emotion it would seem to repress. Such lyric poetry believes that a proper reserve invokes and sustains an otherwise invisible strength; it therefore uses a tone that stops short of condescension, lest that turn into vitriol or coarse satire. Readers have extrapolated from this mix of tones to create a persona, and eventually a personality, for Cullen. He was by many accounts personally reserved, even secretive. He carried throughout his life a thoroughly shrouded childhood, one that he concealed from nearly everyone. He owed his general welfare to a beneficence that was not "cold as charity" (as it often is), but was, nevertheless, a beneficence that made him feel obligated beyond the ordinary keeping of accounts.

Cullen's readers are not completely mistaken when they revert to this standard view of his personality and his work. But the standard view had its predictable omissions. Cullen was less reserved in his poetry than he was in his life. He was more angry and frustrated in his life than he was in his poetry. His early success, in mastering the art of verse and in receiving a level of recognition that gave him self-assurance, led to polished poetry. His dutifulness, derived in large measure from that parsonage where he grew to manhood, induced him to write on a regular basis, so sometimes his poetry—in its ideas and its melodies—misses the highly original note. But by keeping faith with the higher callings of poetry—the full immediacy of feeling, the self-scrutinizing attempts to go one step further toward the truth—he left behind a body of work that has as its main subject the fate of love, and as its stylistic marker, a mix of tones that are reserved and revealing.

He felt bidden to sing, and he did.

1

Persons and Places, 1903–1922

The date and place of Countée Cullen's birth cannot be known with complete certainty. Research into these questions, however, has turned up pieces of information that can be assembled into something like a broken mosaic. Briefly told, the poet was born in Louisville, Kentucky, in 1903, of a woman called Elizabeth Lucas and a man named John, or John Henry, Porter. Presumably because he was born out of wedlock, Cullen remained quite reticent about the details of his birth and early life. Sometime in the early years of the twentieth century, however, the boy apparently was brought to New York City, where he would spend the major portion of his remaining years. In the 1910 census for New York City, the official record shows a family named Porter—this was the name Cullen went by for the first fifteen years or so of his life—living in Manhattan, and this particular family's head was listed as Henry Porter.[1] The female in the household was called Amanda, and there was one child living with them, named "County," the phonetic version of the name the census taker must have heard. The census taker also assumed that Amanda was Henry Porter's wife. However, later evidence establishes that Amanda Porter was in fact Cullen's grand-mother, not his mother. All three were listed as black, and all were born in Kentucky. Many years after the census was taken, Cullen confirmed to Harold Jackman, his closest friend, and to Ida Cullen, his second wife, that his birthplace was Louisville, Kentucky.[2] The census listed the boy "County" as being eight years old, which would make his birth date 1902 or 1903—and when he was an adult Cullen himself consistently listed the latter date on various applications and official forms; he also repeat-edly named New York as his place of birth. The census taker entered Mr. Porter's occupation, cryptically, as "Theatre," and years later faint rumors mentioned his work as a doorman or porter at one of New York's many flourishing theaters. So, on this evidence, the poet's date and place of birth can be fairly well established, though no document, such as a birth or baptismal certificate, validates the story further.

Beyond these frail facts, however, little can be discovered about Cul-len's first five or six years. Probably the family was poor, maybe even des-perately so. The Porter family did seem to change their New York resi-dences often. Records of the young boy's earliest schooling, all of which was conducted in the New York Public School System, complete the pic-ture of transience. Inquiries sent to the board of education in New York back in 1960, and answered by Claire Baldwin, an assistant superinten-dent, record his earliest years as a student.[3] He attended several grammar schools: he went to the first grade at P.S. 27 in Manhattan, in February 1908, and stayed at that school until June 1911. Then he was enrolled for a year each at P.S. 43 and P.S. 1 (the latter in the Bronx), followed by two years, also in the Bronx, at P.S. 27, from which he graduated.[4] Only spec-ulation could answer why he, and presumably his parents or grandpar-ents, moved around so often. Assistant Superintendent Baldwin, how-ever, supplied a clarifying address for the period when he was enrolled in P.S. 27 in Manhattan: 668 Third Avenue. This is the same address listed on the 1910 census. The documentary record slowly becomes clearer. His grammar schooling culminated in his admission to Townsend Har-ris Hall, a preparatory high school run by the City College of New York, where the grades on his exams were commendably high. His registration form from there lists several more pieces of information. His father's name is given as John Henry Porter; he was sent to the School of Com-merce in January 1917; his residence is listed at 190 West 134th Street, as the family settled in Harlem; and his date of birth is given as May 30, 1901 (though the final two digits are hard to read.) Some accounts had mentioned that Cullen attended Townsend Harris for one year, though none mentioned the marginal note on his transcript, namely, that he was transferred to the School of Commerce for a short period prior to his going to DeWitt Clinton. Thus, slowly and piecemeal, some of the early facts about Cullen's life are established.

What is tentatively drawn out from this picture, however, in certain ways conveys less than the settled fact that Cullen himself chose not to record many of these details. After he became a well-known poet and cultural figure, he might readily have recorded his biographical information on the various applications he completed and in numerous interviews he gave to newspapers. But he chose not to, and for reasons he kept equally to himself. For several decades after his death, people recounted or speculated on what was mainly a missing record: his birthplace was listed at different times as New Orleans, Louisville, Baltimore, or New York City. Even his birth date was never definitively established, for while May 30 was cited, the year varied from 1900 to 1903. An undated issue of a short-lived Harlem newspaper of limited circulation and reputation, called *Headlines and Pictures,* adds some details.[5] It tells of Cullen's mother (more likely his grandmother) being obese, so much so that she was often embarrassed to leave her house. She supported herself by taking in foster children, presumably after her husband passed away. All in all, there were possibly features of Cullen's childhood, not least the frequent changes of residence, which could fairly be called Dickensian.

Among the large number of records, letters, and documents that Cullen kept throughout his life, a unique item stands out. This is an oval portrait, either a photograph or done with considerable skill in pencil and measuring twenty inches high and fourteen inches wide. The subject, a young boy, is clearly Countée Cullen. Staring straight out at the camera, his face conveys a mixture of innocence and self-possession. Ida Cullen, in her reminiscences, says that the portrait is of Cullen, and that he brought it with him when he returned from Kentucky, where he had gone to attend his mother's funeral.[6] Adding to the portrait's importance, a small reproduced photograph, about one-and-a-quarter inch square, has been taped to the lower left part of the oval. This depicts Cul-

1. A photo of Cullen as a young boy, which has his Harvard graduation photograph (dated January 1927) attached to it. Cullen brought it back with him to New York from Louisville, where he attended his mother's funeral.

len's graduation from college, as he is shown wearing the traditional cap and gown. It seems quite likely that Elizabeth Lucas was somehow given the oval portrait and kept it with her in Louisville. She very probably clipped the small graduation portrait of her son and taped it to the larger picture (see figure 1). When Cullen brought the picture back to New York after his mother's funeral, it was one of the rare times when he retrieved and kept a physical memento of his childhood.

Elizabeth Lucas died on October 25, 1940, aged fifty-five, and was buried in Louisville. A close friend and neighbor, Mrs. Martha Fruits, notified Cullen, who asked her to arrange everything according to his wishes, namely, that she be buried from her home, without any church ceremony. The funeral director, Mr. R. G. May, sent Cullen a bill for $218 to cover the funeral services, which Cullen paid in cash.[7] (This also indicates that he went to Louisville for the burial.) Written in either Cullen's or Ida's hand is a note on the back of the envelope that contained the bill: "Important Mother's funeral bill." Later research would lead to interviews with people living near Elizabeth Lucas, and they confirmed that she had had a son, that "he worked as a teacher in New York and that he was writing books," and that he sent her a monthly check.[8] (Since the mailing address for Elizabeth Lucas is written in Cullen's small phone directory that he carried in the 1930s, this last point gains further credibility.)[9] The people in Louisville remembered Cullen's arrival and his gentle and diligent efforts to arrange the details of the funeral, which was delayed until he could reach the city by train. He expressed his thanks to all of those who assisted him throughout what was obviously a moving experience.

There are two more documents, however, that tell a great deal: death certificates that are likely his grandfather's and his grandmother's.[10] On January 22, 1917, at the age of fifty-two, John H. Porter died in New York City of "acute lobar pneumonia."[11] According to the certificate, he had lived in the city for fourteen years—arriving just around the time of Cullen's birth. What strongly indicates he was Cullen's grandfather is that his address is given as 190 West 134th Street. (The character of the premises is shown as "tenement.") Nearly a full year later, at Manhattan Harlem Hospital, on December 8, 1917, Amanda Porter passed away. Her address is likewise listed as 190 West 134th Street, the same as that given on John Porter's death certificate and on Cullen's Townsend Harris Hall registration form.[12] The certificate also says that she was forty-eight years old and had lived in New York City for eighteen years. This means she came to the city, from Louisville most likely, at the age of thirty, in 1900. Perhaps she preceded Henry Porter to New York and was later called on to help raise her grandson.[13] It is perhaps the case that Countée's father remained in Kentucky, but then, without wedding Elizabeth Lucas, decided to send his son to the city where Amanda had taken up residence. But things are far from certain.

It was, in any case, first in late 1917, and then for the nearly thirty years following, that Cullen—now an orphan—resided with the Reverend Frederick Ashby Cullen, the pastor of the Salem Methodist Episcopal Church, one of the largest in all of Harlem. From then on, his life records become clearer and clearer, though his early childhood remains largely visible only in outline form.

Because Cullen never corrected the uncertainty about when and where he was born, it makes the reconstruction of his first years difficult, but not impossible. The absence for many years of such a reconstruction has nevertheless influenced, if only to some extent, the critical reception of Cullen's poetry. Among critics and scholars the sense began to dominate quite early that he was withdrawn and secretive. Added to the questions of his place and date of birth, there is the problem of a comparative lack of diaries or autobiographical accounts or essays that could help create a more finely etched portrait for the early years. In similar cases where life details are missing, critics and scholars have turned to the works of the author—the obvious case is Shakespeare—to satisfy the reader's appetite for more knowledge. Even here there is some frustration, for Cullen's poetry is not ostensibly autobiographical. His earliest poems date from around his fifteenth year, but they don't revisit or reminisce about his previous experiences or thoughts or dreams.

Looking ahead to a moment in 1925 when Cullen published a poem called "Fruit of the Flower," he left a highly symbolic picture of his father and mother. Though it is impossible to tell if he speaks of his natural or his adoptive parents, what he says unveils a great deal about his attitude toward parentage and filial ties.

> My father is a quiet man
>   With sober, steady ways;
> For simile, a folded fan;
>   His nights are like his days.
>
> My mother's life is puritan,
>   No hint of cavalier,

> A pool so calm you're sure it can
> > Have little depth to fear.

The poem at first praises the parents' solidity, but then goes on to picture both parents as perplexed by their child's "wild sweet agony." The drama in the poem could be read as a stereotypical verse about a young man's rebellion, while nevertheless reasserting the true ties that bind parents and their offspring. The poem ends on a definite note, though in the form of a rhetorical question, which allows Cullen to strike a balance between rebellion and acceptance.

> Who plants a seed begets a bud,
> > Extract of the same root;
> Why marvel at the hectic blood
> > That flushed this wild fruit?

By picturing a child who at one and the same time rebels against his parents and insists that they should accept him—indeed, accept the responsibility they incurred by having him—the poet claims the energy of his autonomy even as he professes the stability of his birthright.

The first fourteen or so years of Cullen's life, outside of his school records, remain largely a blank as far as any vivid eyewitness account goes. Of course, these years were not a blank to him. This means that, given the absence of his own testimony, he went to some considerable effort to conceal from everyone, and in part from himself, just what those years signified to him. The persistent air, not of secrecy exactly, but of an exaggerated reticence entered into many of the later psychological images of Cullen. This is not altogether unheard of in the case of lyric poets, who after all spend much of their literary effort revealing some of their deepest and most closely watched emotions, but only through the strict mediations of artistic form. One of the most obvious facts about Cullen is his race, and all the attendant emotions and values that come with it. What precise strategies he might have developed early on to deal with the affronts and wounds of racism can only be guessed at, though clearly he couldn't proceed carelessly. His intelligence was manifest early, as was his love of musical words and a fascination with stories out of books. As with any memorable lyric poet, the song may be the truest account of the self, even as the life offers its own lights and shadows.

After the first fourteen years or so of his life, however they transpired, Cullen grew plainly and visibly planted in New York City, and more pointedly in the section called Harlem. His poetry, however, possesses few marks of urban life in its harshest aspects. Rather, he had the cosmopolitan's sense of the city, a place where the art and culture of previous centers of civilization are profusely and variously available. Dressed constantly as an adult in his three-piece suits—just like W. E. B. DuBois and Alain Locke, mentors for Cullen and widely respected "race men"—he added the elite touch of his Phi Beta Kappa key and chain across his vest. New York appealed to whatever sense of the theatrical Cullen allowed himself, and there are stories of his great zest and talent on the dance floors of many Harlem parties.

Whatever the unknowable circumstances of his birth and early childhood, Cullen possessed certain traits that occasionally made him seem unhoused. Later in life he would travel summer after summer to Paris and parts of Europe. Paris became like a second home, and he praised its ways intensely. He also wrote children's books, as if to circle back and supply himself with a source of comfort otherwise denied him in his first years. Rather late in life he retreated to Tuckahoe, New York, in Westchester County, north of New York City, to escape the wear and tear of Harlem and what had become the megalopolis, perhaps in answering a call to some early pastoral memories. Many of his poems, especially the early ones, speak of loss and departure. These supply standard subjects for lyric poetry, but Cullen may have known more of their lineaments than other people did. One of his most famous poems, "Incident," recounts visiting a new city, confronting racial hatred, and having it erase all the positive thoughts that he might otherwise have enjoyed.

If his birth year is taken as 1903, this meant Cullen entered the world the same year W. E. B. DuBois published *The Souls of Black Folk*. This synchronicity appears innocent to some, but the question of timing would stay with Cullen. He entered his adopted home around the time America entered the Great War, and his teenage years saw the extensive migration of African Americans to New York City, and furthermore to Harlem. In his early twenties he published his first book of poetry, in 1925, the same year *The New Negro,* that eponymous anthology, appeared. He passed away just after the Second World War ended. Throughout his life he encountered the segregation that had seemed only to intensify since the beginning of Jim Crow laws. Whatever he learned from adults and childhood friends about how to face and respond to the notions that lie behind white supremacy, his studiousness led him to be capable of both forbearance and defiance.

Though the young Cullen was unhoused from his original birthplace, he found secure lodgings by the time he was fourteen. In late 1917 or early 1918 he entered into the home of the Reverend Cullen, who within a year would become the boy's adoptive father. (Rumors circulated among some that the adoption was never formally legalized.)[14] The reverend, born to slave parents in Maryland, began life in deep poverty.[15] He attended the State Normal School before going on to Morgan College, an all-black institution in Baltimore. While enrolled there he experienced a strong religious conversion. For two years he taught at an elementary school in nearby Fairmont but soon decided on the ministry. This led him back to Morgan, where he obtained a divinity degree and was ordained an elder in 1900. After serving as the pastor in several small Maryland churches, in 1902 he was sent by the Methodist Episcopalian hierarchy to New York City. His assignment was at the Salem Methodist Episcopal Church, which was then a branch (the official term was *mission*) of another, larger church, St. Mark's. It was on Fifty-Third Street that St. Mark's sat and enjoyed its position as the largest African American church in town. But the black population, drawn by cheaper rents and more stable housing, had already begun the move uptown to Harlem. So it made sense that the reverend would become the assistant to Dr. William Brooks, whose pastoral and preaching duties were conducted at the mission on St. Nicolas Avenue and 122nd Street. At this location the Salem Church consisted of little more than a storefront. The collection taken up the day the reverend preached his first sermon amounted to only nineteen cents. It wasn't long, however, before the congregation began to outgrow even this arrangement. In his first year at Salem, the reverend moved the church into a larger building on 124th Street.

The Salem mission became an independent church, separating itself from St. Mark's, in 1908, but it then acquired an impressive building—

this time it was six private houses joined into one structure—on West 133rd Street. The purchase price was fifteen thousand dollars, paid for by the New York City Missionary and Church Expansion Society, an arm of the United Methodist Episcopal Church. It was in this imposing structure that Cullen's life took a major turning. He was a young boy of thirteen when he came to the attention of James Gowins, a serious and considerate officer of the Salem Church. (Some say it was Gowins's wife who first took notice.) Gowins frequently observed the pious youngster at Sunday School and spending time at the local hospital visiting an ailing woman. No one was sure then if the woman was Cullen's mother or grandmother; contemporary accounts differ, though the death certificate of Amanda Porter now makes it clear it was his grandmother. In any case, Gowins was impressed with the boy's dutifulness and shy sensitivity, so he spoke to Reverend Cullen about him. After an interview with young Countée—then still called Countée Porter—the reverend decided he could see his way to take the boy into his house and care. Years later, as an accomplished poet and public man of letters, Countée spoke of his being raised "in the conservative atmosphere of a Methodist parsonage." (He went on to say of himself, that his "chief problem has been that of reconciling a Christian upbringing with a pagan inclination.") The church, meanwhile, would help to defray any expenses involved, and Gowins had been adamant that Countée would eventually merit a college education. It all seemed a sound investment. And so, without any formal adoption papers being recorded, eventually, and it would appear easily, Countée Porter became Countée P. Cullen.

The Reverend Cullen took quick advantage of the extra space in his newly expanded church. Important speakers were invited to shape and stir the civic mission of the church, and a Salem Crescent Athletic Club was founded. There was a Floral Society, a Benevolent Society, a Boy Scout troop, and a Phyllis Wheatley Club. The latter held formal teas as a fund-raising effort. To everyone's surprise, the reverend began to edit a newsletter, called the *Announcer,* to keep his parishioners well informed and fully committed. His young adopted son was probably dazzled by the reverend's furious energies. With his privately published autobiography, completed in the early 1940s near his death, and entitled *From Barefoot Town to Jerusalem,*[16] Frederick Cullen added another chapter to the many stories of American success. For the next thirteen years after buying the

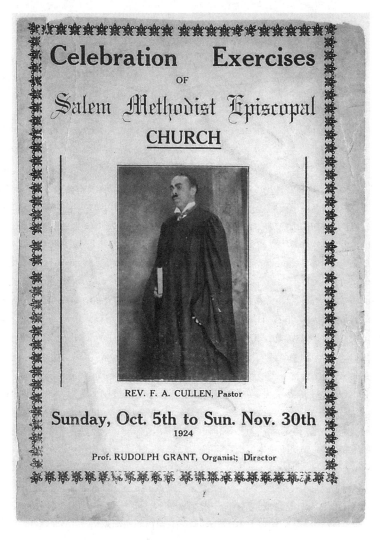

2. The booklet for the anniversary celebration of the Reverend Cullen's twenty years of service. Many of Countée's friends participated, including Alain Locke.

133rd Street building he steadily continued to expand his congregation, and then took yet another culminating expansive step forward. In 1924 he purchased the white-owned Methodist Episcopal church at 129th Street and Seventh Avenue (now Adam Clayton Powell, Jr. Avenue) for the impressive sum of $258,000. The fog of Countée's early mysterious years had by then dissipated, and his new family had conferred on him a very public, very proper cast.

The impressive expansion of Reverend Cullen's church in physical terms was more than matched by his growing sense of a civic mission. The formative and sustaining role of the church in the black community, as has often been said, is hard to overstate. For the reverend the Sunday stroll up the broad spaces of Seventh or Lenox Avenue constituted more than "outreach." It served as a part of his daily existence and clerical identity. The story circulated that he would play marbles with children along the avenues, befriend them, and eventually lead them and their families to join his church. Countée saw his adoptive father as an all-commanding figure, though such prominence as the reverend began to enjoy brought with it a measure of gossip, some of it salacious. Whispers about the use of his wife's makeup and undue attention to the choirboys persisted for years. It remains impossible to prove or disprove such rumors, or even to decide how much they were the result of speculations about Countée's own struggles with his sexual orientation.[17] A clear gregariousness and an assured ego accompanied the reverend in all his pastoral chores and public duties, however. The shyness of his adopted son could have intensified in reaction to such traits. Whatever private experiences Countée had in the confines of the home and parsonage, his father fully occupied the role of a race leader. When the young man's literary talent began to flourish, it would be joined to a shy interior life that had nevertheless managed to look with some equanimity on the challenge of public speaking.

Reverend Cullen was not in the least content to exercise his powers of persuasion only from the pulpits on 129th and later on 133rd Street. He became increasingly visible and active in fighting against racial bigotry and the Jim Crow laws that continued to stunt the civil rights of his parishioners. He was elected president of the Harlem branch of the National Association for the Advancement for Colored People. The Niagara Movement had swelled the numbers of people urgently committed to racial equality. Serious organizational work began for the movement in 1910, which was the founding date for *Crisis: A Record of the Darker Races,* one of the most important and influential of all African American publications. In fact, the reverend carried the organizational tide forward and saw to it that the Harlem branch of the NAACP sent a delegation of its members to represent colored people at the League of Nations in Geneva. Just who might lead such an important delegation presented a crucial question. The reverend steered things so that it was W. E. B. DuBois—the editor of *Crisis* and by now fully formed as the most notable race leader of his age—who was chosen to act in that capacity. DuBois later became one of Cullen's most important mentors, as well as a major supporter of his artistic gifts.

Other occasions arose where the reverend's organizational and persuasive skills proved effective. The race riot in East St. Louis provoked a "Silent Protest" march, in July 1917, of ten thousand people, the children dressed in white, filling the uptown avenues in Harlem. Reverend Cullen acted as one of the march's organizers. Then, a month later, a race riot in Houston, Texas, resulted in thirteen black soldiers being convicted of a capital crime, namely, illegally firing their weapons; their sentence was carried out on December 11, 1917, without any chance for appeal to the secretary of war or the commander in chief. The reverend joined a group of four spokesmen—one of whom was James Weldon Johnson—to visit President Woodrow Wilson and convince him to grant executive clemency for fifty-six other soldiers, five of whom were sentenced to hang while the others faced very long prison terms. The group traveled with a petition signed by twelve thousand New Yorkers. Wilson agreed to commute some death sentences and affirmed others, and those serving long terms had their sentences reduced as a result of further pressure by the NAACP. Countée could hardly have failed to be impressed by his adoptive father's role in these highly visible events.

Ferment in Harlem took the form of many political demonstrations, movements, and newspapers. In March 1916 the arrival in the city of the remarkably charismatic Marcus Garvey and his United Negro Improvement Association added to the social energy that was also being driven by an increasingly radical press. The socialist ideas advanced by the *Messenger* stirred many readers, and *Challenge*, referred to as the least restrained of the new outlets, gave both programmatic and unprogrammatic form to the unrest. The young Countée witnessed much of this and would eventually add his voice to a new generation of calls for greater racial justice and autonomy. Meanwhile, he would take his place in a somewhat exceptional setting, one that shaped his unique gifts and brought them to more visible notice: a public school with elite aspirations.

Shortly after the end of the war, Cullen entered DeWitt Clinton High School, by general consensus the best public school in the city. He thus inaugurated his lifelong ties not only with educational institutions but also with the New York Public School System. His entry into DeWitt Clinton came soon after the death of his grandmother and in the midst of the social unrest among Harlemites after the war. The school likely seemed more a haven to the young man than a place where discomfort or boredom overrode all other reactions. During the last fifteen years of his life he would be a teacher at Frederick Douglass Junior High School in Harlem, the expert on subjects he had pursued more than two decades earlier at DeWitt Clinton. In 1919, Cullen's first full year there, DeWitt Clinton was located at Tenth Avenue, between Fifty-Eighth and Fifty-Ninth Streets, having moved to that location from an earlier spot in Greenwich Village. It was a beautifully designed, massive building, of red brick and considerable stone trim and details. Shortly after Cullen's time there it became what was reputed to be the largest high school in America, with twelve thousand students. It was an all-boys school, and overwhelmingly white; seldom was there more than a handful of blacks in any of Cullen's classes. Situated next to Clinton Park, the school taught its students to start and maintain a community garden in the park, the first in the city. The school shone as one of the gems of the city's system, with its roster of famous graduates that included musicians, artists, politicians, and business leaders. Cullen was in the class of 1922, which included Edward Bernstein, later to become the first president of the International Monetary Fund. The class also included Jan Peerce, the famous tenor who starred at the Metropolitan Opera. Behind Cullen was the abstract artist Barnett Newman; ahead of him by one year was Lionel Trilling, who served with Cullen on the editorial board of the *Magpie,* the school's literary magazine and later enjoyed national renown as a critic and English professor at Columbia. Charles Norman, who went on to publish several books of poetry and a critical study of Ezra Pound, was also at Clinton, as most of the boys called it.

3. A class photo from DeWitt Clinton High School. Cullen, the only African American in the group, is second from the right in the first row of standees.

Cullen's first discovery in high school, in terms of personal growth and public notice, was poetry, or, since he had already written poems, it was the power of poetry to bring its author widespread approval. It was actually at Townsend Harris Hall, which he attended just before entering Clinton, that he first uncovered the way. He wrote a poem, called "To the Swimmer," for one of his teachers, George Cronyn, and it showed up, to Cullen's great surprise, in an 1918 article that Cronyn published about the high skill of his students. This represented for Cullen a rather obscure triumph, as the poem was in the pages of the *Modern School*, a journal devoted to progressive ideas about education. The main point of the poem, however, ends with a rhetorical question: "Is your heart as true as your arm?" The poet in effect wonders if the inner strength and character of anyone's exertions truly matches his or her physical strength. A certain skepticism, and an attention to a conflict of the spirit (it is the poet's spirit that formulates but doesn't speak the poem's concluding question), mark the poem as striking, especially considering that its author was only fifteen years old. The language and images of the poem are straightforward, almost realist in flavor, like the paintings of the Ashcan School then flourishing in New York City.[18]

Cullen faced his high school environment as one where he was clearly marked out by his race, but also by his talent. Like his later friend and mentor Alain Locke, who spent four years as one of the very few black students at Central High in Philadelphia, Cullen soon became conscious of the intersection of racial identity and its cultural expression. Every one of his artistic achievements, and there were many, brought up the idea, difficult to resolve, or even formulate, that his talent either came through, or came despite, his being black.[19] Still, he would proceed with a strong sense of direction no matter what questions lay in his wake. One classmate would later recall thinking Countée was a year or two older than his classmates since he gave the impression of being worldly. Another, who lost the oratorical contest to him, asked if it was any wonder why Cullen triumphed. Some teased him over what they saw as the affectation of his insisting on pronouncing his name as "Count-*tay*," not "Count-*tee*." Some school publications listed him by his nickname: "Tay."[20]

He joined the Inter–High School Poetry Society, attempting to bring citywide recognition within his grasp. His oratorical victory in a school competition was secured with a speech entitled "God and the Negro." The school produced a newspaper, called *Clinton News,* and Cullen's writing impulses further displayed themselves when he became its editor. The editorship of the *Magpie,* the school's literary magazine, also increased his impressive extracurricular résumé. In his second year it featured a poem of his with the lines,

> Poet, poet, what do you ask
> As pay for each glad song?
> Thy thanks will pay me double well,
> And last my whole life long.

Every young poet begins by being at least partly enchanted by the prospect of fame. Here Cullen transforms one form of payment into another, more ethereal but also more enduring. But payment for his singing ability soon materialized in a quite different form. The Federation of

Women's Clubs sponsored a citywide contest that garnered considerable notice, and it was Cullen's poem that took first prize. It was also the first time that his poetry received more than an ordinary amount of attention, and the winning poem became one that characterized Cullen's talent for a number of years.

This prize poem was his "I Have a Rendezvous with Life," which ran in the *Magpie* in January 1920. Like "Renascence," the Edna St. Vincent Millay poem that won a contest and brought her considerable notice, Cullen's lyric has at its center an uplift that has always been attractive to readers and judges of poetry. The background of the poem lends it gravitas as well. An American soldier-poet named Alan Seeger published a poem entitled "I Have a Rendezvous with Death" that was much reprinted. Ironically, Seeger, who had joined the French Foreign Legion, would in fact meet his death during World War I. However, Cullen was able to counter the gloomy and fateful Seeger lyric with a poem that turned to a very different outlook as a way to confront the contingencies of life. The poem ends:

> Sure some would cry it better far
> To crown their days with sleep,
> Than face the road, the wind and rain
> To heed the calling deep.
> Tho' wet nor blow nor space I fear.
> Yet fear I deeply too,
> Lest Death should greet and claim me ere
> I keep Life's rendezvous.

This poem would strike most readers as a mature, though sentimental, expression, and measurably more so given that the author was only eighteen years old when it first appeared. (It later was printed in *Current Opinion,* a national publication, in 1924.)

Conventional in its images and quite safe in its rhymes, the poem still contains a sense of a divided self—"Yet fear I deeply too"—who can assume a fearless stance that carries only so much perseverance. But the center of the poem registers a tone that would sound repeatedly in Cullen's work, a note of strong moral judgment that some would say verges on condescension toward those who are felt to be wanting. Add to this that Cullen has elliptically referred to another poem, and so borrowed its resonance for his own purpose, and the sum of talent displayed by the high school student is considerable. Perhaps it is not claiming too much to say that the poem also reflects what was the mood of calm pride in the national achievement represented by America's victory in the war. In any case, the poem followed Cullen as only certain early works can follow an artist. Prize winning became almost habitual for Cullen in the years following his "Rendezvous" poem, and by having it published three years after the Federation of Women's Clubs singled it out, Cullen testified to his satisfaction with the work and the notice it brought him.

However transformative were Cullen's struggles with the larger issues of life, and the especially troubling aspects of race, religion, and personal identity, it was through his literary sensibility that he mulled over and shaped his values. This sensibility was itself formed quite intensively at Clinton. On the basis of their shared love of literature, Cullen formed a lasting friendship with one of his classmates, William Fuller Brown, Jr.[21] Brown had to leave Clinton when his family relocated before his junior year. He was a year ahead of Cullen in school, but even after he left New York he maintained a regular correspondence with him. The letters that survive are mostly from Cullen, and they are full of gossip about grades and academic matters and poetry; Cullen often sent Brown copies of his poems and would even ask Brown to send some back after several months, since Cullen sometimes misplaced his own copies.

Brown, a year younger than Cullen, was born in Lyon Mountain, a small town in the remote northern reaches of New York State, about twenty miles west of Plattsburg. It was to Plattsburg that the Brown family moved in 1918. Brown's father was a doctor, and perhaps he returned upstate to practice in a town where he may have had relatives. In any case, Brown, an eager and excellent student, won a scholarship to Cornell, where he graduated in 1925. He taught for a few years in North Carolina, and eventually took a PhD in physics from Columbia 1937. After a very successful career in business and education, he died in 1983. He kept Cullen's letters, as well as the drafts and finished versions of the poems that were included with them, and donated them all to the University of Minnesota, where he had been professor emeritus since 1973.

Brown and Cullen indulged their love of learning by writing parts of their letters in Latin, and later—shortly after Cullen started studying it—in French as well. The use of language was fairly rudimentary: *"Sumus in Nova Yorka. Schola hodie incepit . . . Noster Latinus magister est optimus"* begins the earliest epistle. After a paragraph or two the writer reverts to English. The gossip deals with the relative merits of having class in the main building rather than the annex, and how "second termers" aren't truly noticed, they're just tolerated. Cullen worked diligently at his grades and assignments, since his job keeping the books at the reverend's church proved to be time consuming. He gladly relayed the news to Brown that he, Brown, had left behind the highest average among his class members when he moved upstate. Brown had scored 95.5, and Cullen was just behind him in second place, with a 95.0. Meanwhile, Cullen wanted to know all about the "rustic" school where Brown studied, though judging from his courses—in algebra, Latin, and Greek, among others—he probably attended a private school.

In January 1919, Cullen was placed in fourth-term English class instead of third, and he began to study French in the fall term; like any number of Harlem's "talented tenth" he could comfortably converse in it rather soon. His concern about a Regents Scholarship began to build early, so he made a point of taking Regents courses, the exams for which were statewide and especially rigorous. Before long, however, geology would become a bane, as Cullen regrettably had no aptitude for the hard sciences, often managing no more than a C in such subjects. In the spring term he was, however, the top scorer out of 240 boys in the history exam: "I do not consider 94 so good, yet it pleases one to be first." He also bragged about having "risen a step on the ladder of fame" when his poems appeared in the school magazine as well as the paper. And he instructed Brown to be sure to put the accent on the first *e* in Countée, now that he was taking French.

Though the letters to Brown are more playful than intimate, Cullen clearly felt very fond of his absent friend and often expressed a wish to have him visit in New York City. At one point he went a step further: "I have not met another boy whose friendship I so desired to keep as yours, especially a Caucasian. I used to detest and despise them all." In the same letter Cullen confessed, "It may interest you to know that I am determined to be a writer and poet. . . . Do you still want to be an editor?"

He then added an account of his "defense" of a classmate, Moses Bloom, who was insulted by an article in the school newspaper, perhaps as a result of anti-Semitism. Cullen defended Bloom in front of the student assembly and was judged the victor as Bloom got his apology, though one of the boys claimed the jury was partial to Cullen. Along with Brown, Cullen had befriended a boy named Arnold, and the three of them referred to themselves as the "triumvirate." Cullen busily imaged adults roles for them: "You [Brown] a famous editor and a man interested in Latin research; Arnold a famous, but very peculiar inventor; and I a poet contributing to 'Snappy Stories' or some other magazine of equally high repute." Even as he began his summer vacation in 1919, Cullen committed himself to translating Caesar in order to be better prepared for the fall term.

One classmate reported that Cullen worked on his poetry every day just to increase his fluency. All forms appealed to him. He published two Lewis Carroll imitations in the *Magpie* in which he demonstrated his satiric bent, as his version of the "jabberwocky" style employed the names of various teachers at the school. He tipped his hat to Carroll's notoriously inventive wordplay by calling the efforts "Facultywocky." He contributed an early effort at the short story, entitled "Frenchman's Bath." There was a review of *The Three Mulla-Mulgars*, Walter de la Mare's nursery story about three motherless monkeys, and an appraisal of Amy Lowell's early literary history, *Tendencies in Modern American Poetry*. Cullen treated this latter book with respect, recommending it be read by one and all, and only barely revealing his personal taste by suggesting that the imagist poets (of whom Lowell was one) were "perhaps" of limited interest. Here his mistrust of free verse asserted itself.

His Latin teacher spotted Countée's talent early and enlisted him in a program that had older students act as mentors for younger ones. This was known as the "Help Classes Association," and Cullen became one of its officers. Avid for all things related to poetry, he happily discovered the work of Paul Laurence Dunbar, and also wrote a series of verses in homage to a number of poets, such as Byron and Longfellow. The one to Dunbar addressed the older poet as "heart's brother and blood brother," making his racial allegiance clear. Writing verses that paid homage to his fellow poets was a literary tradition in which Cullen took pride. His studiousness, however, did not hamper his popularity. Instead of the usual choice of an athlete, his classmates chose him as class vice president. Most important, perhaps, is that in his senior year he received news that he had been awarded a New York State Regents Scholarship, which would help fund four years of college.

As Cullen began his second full year at Clinton, he was elected to the editorship of *Magpie,* the literary magazine. In his poetry he was willing to address large subjects, sending Brown these two quatrains from a thirty-two-line poem he called "The Fool Hath Said":

> With scientific reasoning
> > And ruthless unbelief
> He rents in twain what godly men
> > Have left us as our fief.
>
> And yet how man doth contradict,
> > And give himself the lie;
> They must His pow'r acknowledge
> > Who would His being deny.

Cullen, speaking self-protectively perhaps, told Brown that "I had some object [in] mind, but having read the poem, I cannot find the object." As a schoolboy, he addressed the task of writing poems with just that sort of approach. He continued to speculate about poetry, saying that "the most used topic of all is the rose," and then proceeded to send along a ten-quatrain poem about that very subject.

> One morn the chaste white roses
> Fresh from a bath of dew
> Beheld my Love in her beauty
> A nymphean dance construe.

When the poet identifies his love as "Eternal" the white roses blush "a crimson red." As commentary Cullen averred, "there is not an atom of truth in that poem," adding, however, that when people look for truth we "lose the beauty and glamour of things, for Truth . . . is really ugly and fearful." This early observation formed part of Cullen's aesthetic stance throughout his life.

Cullen continued to fill his letters with poems, asking Brown for advice while suggesting the background or weakness of each effort. He referred to some of them as his "poemites," a word of his own coinage.[22] One poem dealt with the wreckage caused by alcohol, while another retold a newspaper article about an Illinois senator who suggested using whiskey as an antidote to influenza. He even mentioned that a poem devoted to the charms of "Jean" was written on order for a friend of his to celebrate his girlfriend's sixteenth birthday. Yet another verse, this one devoted to "Mary," went to Brown, and he was urged to substitute any other appropriate girl's name, as Cullen wasn't "familiar with feminine appellations in Plattsburg." He also conceived of a plan where he would write song lyrics—"All they need is a swing and a rhyme"—that Brown would set to music. His motive was largely mercenary, and he began to scour magazine advertisements that featured help with smoothing out one's verses for a modest fee and a small percentage of any royalties that might ensue. For the next few years Cullen pursued this project avidly, sending Brown countless lyrics, raising his musical talents, and hoping for a major achievement. From his seventeenth year on, Cullen's poetry would always be entwined in various ways with musical accompaniment and ideas.

All his fluent and sometimes glib versifying activities were capable of being refocused, however. In March 1920 the city school system formed the Inter–High School Modern Poetry Circle. Here Cullen could truly shine, even though his English teacher said she felt he was too mature for the circle. All of his spare time was spent "poring over volumes of poetry," and Cullen feared he would "develop into a poetry maniac." In one letter to Brown, he included seven poems, among them one "written merely to get the form of a 'roundelle'" and two others that were "little pieces of conceit." All this happened in the same year Cullen was first allowed to wear long pants. The new sartorial mode was stipulated when he was elected to the "Datey Squad," which was charged with disciplining the younger students in the school. The Reverend Cullen also acknowledged the boy's emergent manhood, but added that long pants would be acceptable only for wearing to school. Cullen told Brown that he wore them "with as much sangfroid as if I were born in them."

If Cullen's dress was strongly ruled by nineteenth-century standards,

4. The Reverend Cullen, the poet's adoptive father and pastor of Salem Methodist Episcopal Church, one of the largest in Harlem.

so, too, on occasion was his poetic language. He clung to rhyme and explored standard forms as if he were an avid hobbyist, and he added to his adolescent yearnings a penchant for high-minded sentiment. Of all the poems he sent Brown over the years, perhaps the one that most displays this is "In Memory of Lincoln." Cullen read it before the student assembly, to resounding applause as he told Brown, on the Friday before Lincoln's birthday in 1921. Later awarded second prize in a citywide poetry contest, and written in octets, with alternating tetrameter and trimeter lines, it resembles an obvious attempt to capture some civic prize by recounting patriotic themes. However, Cullen turned to the question of slavery near the poem's conclusion. This clearly identifies its speaker as an African American, and bases much of its praise for its subject on emancipation:

> He came with pity, love, and pow'r;
> Revoked the ancient ban;
> As deep we drank of freedom's show'r,
> The slave became a man.

The first-person speaker of the poem, though sometimes specifically African American, sometimes stands as inclusive of all Americans. As for Lincoln, he is sometimes described in the third person, sometimes addressed in the second. But the last lines of the poem reach for a heroic romanticism that offers religious echoes and the tropes that turn political figures into something like a natural force.

> To us the years that tireless go,
> But make thee more sublime;
> True gratitude doth whisper low;
> "Thy memory ends with Time."

Combining the sublime and the eternal was a redoubtable feat, even if the sixteenth president's stature had already risen to such heights in the popular mind.

By the end of 1920 Cullen's unflagging work on his poetic talents led to one of his more important early recognitions, when his "Rendezvous" poem took first prize. The details would surely impress Brown: he and eight other high school students (drawn from twenty-six different schools) read their poems at the splendidly elegant Astor Hotel. But in writing to Brown about this triumph, he also mentioned another award: election to the school's academic honor society, Arista. Having amassed a stellar record, he was given a "Grade A Certificate," with a 94 average, the third highest on the Honor Roll. Success in poetry and in academics proceeded on the same upward curve. Later his poetic spirits were almost crowded out by the demands he placed on himself in terms of study and the need to achieve high marks.

Cullen's spent his last full year at Clinton in 1921, and it held a number of prizes, but he was denied one for which he worked very hard. Taking as many Regents courses as he could, he had primed himself for a college scholarship. At first his eyes were set on Columbia. He even urged Brown to apply as well, so that they might attend school together once again. Columbia offered him admission, but with no supporting funds. Briefly, he shifted his attention to City College. Eventually, of course, he went to New York University, where he received a full scholarship. As for prizes, he added a special one to all that his poetry had brought him. This was the prize for oratory, named after Douglas Fairbanks and given as the culmination of a public contest held at Clinton with due fanfare. Though the contest could not be attended that year by its namesake, the boys were reassured he would be there in spirit.[23] The subjects of the five finalists were, as one might expect, full of civic high-mindedness and spiritual uplift. Milton Bergerman, who took second place, spoke on "The Function of Government," and others offered "American Ideals," "Honesty, the Cornerstone of Democracy," and "Ancient Barbarism and Modern Humanity."

Cullen chose a formidable subject that would persist as one of the central concerns of his life: "God and the Negro." It was a brief oration, not much more than 250 words. But Cullen filled it with deep feeling for his race, and managed to skillfully touch on a number of arguments and themes that not only animated and guided African American cultural values of the time, but for several decades afterward. The speech begins with 1619 and the onset of the Atlantic slave trade. Immediately the dense and dark immersion in American history dominates the fate of the Negro: "There has been no era in American history in which he has not figured, no battle in which his blood has not flowed." Cullen in one brief paragraph sketches a picture that extends "down to the present time." The Negro asks for his rights as a citizen: "He desires no more; he will be content with no less." In the typed copy he sent Brown, Cullen strikes out against Benjamin Tillman of South Carolina, a rabid white supremacist and exterminationist, firmly to deny any call for emigration. Cullen asks, "but to where? Africa? The American born Negro is no more intimate with the banks of the Niger than white Americans . . . are intimate with the banks of the Loire or the Volga or Po" rivers. He also rejects "amalgamation," proclaiming that the Negro has "no desire to purchase his citizenship by losing his identity in a fusion with his fairer brother."

Cullen ends on at least a putatively triumphalist note, insisting that the Negro "intends to fight to success, but in a method peculiar to himself." In what is perhaps the speech's boldest stroke, Cullen, anticipating a latter day's multiculturalism, says that the Negro has as his "comradein-arms" a figure known by different names: "Some call Him Jehovah, some Allah, and some Christ." The struggle will continue, "until the pigment of the skin will no longer stamp a man as unworthy and character and efficiency will evoke a just judgment and right will prevail." Many of Cullen's later themes—such as his relationship with Africa, the stress on character over color, the spiritual burdens of doubt and belief—were adumbrated here at the start of his career as a writer speaking to a public. Though he would more than once take a stand that was contradictory or paradoxical, these issues ceaselessly drove his art and his identity.

Whether Cullen drew from sources he heard constantly in his adoptive father's church or whether he had drawn more heavily on history lessons at Clinton, his speech met with considerable approval. He was able to repeat it some weeks later, at Boys High School in Brooklyn, on April 29, as he was chosen to appear and compete with nine other students from the region's high schools, in a "Prize Speaking Contest" sponsored by Hamilton College. When it was announced that Cullen would be given the second prize, the audience hissed their disapproval that he had not placed first. A while afterward, the sponsors invited Cullen to travel to Hamilton, in upstate New York, but a teacher at Clinton declined the offer on his behalf.

The summer before his final term at Clinton, Cullen garnered more honors, a number of which pleased him intensely. He was chosen as the class poet to offer a poem at the coming commencement to be held in January 1922; "I shall not attempt a Pindaric Ode. It is too difficult," he admitted to Brown, but sketched out for the effort an involved rhyme scheme. He was also elected president of the Arista Society and named editor of the school's newspaper. He continuously suggested to Brown that their efforts at songwriting would eventually bear monetary fruit. The fall term heard him deliver a speech to the Arista Society, which went along with fifteen new poems, some editorials for the newspaper, and a short story, the merits of which he could not vouch for. The September 16, 1921, issue of the *Clinton News* carried his name as editor on the masthead. One of its key items was a story on the recently held graduation ceremony (which took place at the end of each semester, in June and January), listing Cullen's gold medal for the Douglas Fairbanks oratory contest and boasting of Clinton's largest graduating class ever—four hundred men, who "solemnly march up upon the platform and received their diplomas, and an encouraging handshake from Dr. Paul." Cullen would follow in their footsteps just a few months later.

Able to graduate from DeWitt Clinton in the January 1922 ceremony, he was there fulsomely bedecked with laurels. Earning an overall 92-point average in his courses, he placed among the top twenty-five students in a class of six hundred. He gathered Honors in five areas, including a sixth in General Honors. Whether it was through work habits fostered by the reverend or by an instinctive disposition, and most likely it was both, Cullen excelled at academic efforts. Whether he was called precocious or a prodigy, he had found in learning an activity—writing poetry—that brought him favor and satisfaction. In later years, despite tensions between the sometimes twinned and sometimes contrastive activities of writing poetry and intense academic study, he left behind a record that struck many as easeful and mature. To bolster this point, it should be recalled that at least two of the poems Cullen published as a high school student were subsequently to appear in his books of poetry: "Under the Mistletoe," from *Copper Sun,* first published in the *Magpie* in 1921; and "The Poet" in *Copper Sun,* first appearing in the *Magpie* in 1920. The *Southwestern Christian Advocate* published the latter, with a revised and religious ending, in November 1923. Poetry was at one level a school exercise; at another level, it would be a source of identity and attainment.

So for three years Cullen had gone back and forth between two large buildings, two impressive social institutions. The path between the Reverend Cullen's church and DeWitt Clinton High School connected two sets of values. Both sets promoted self-discipline and raised the banner of service to others. But one was religious and made transcendent demands that involved strict behavior and eternal rewards, derived from a constant urging toward humility. The other presented art and self-fashioning, a way to gain attention, even fame, calling for skillfully lyrical emotional expression. Cullen ended his time at the high school apparently having managed both sets of values with laudable success. But he was also facing, during his daily round trip between the buildings, what would increasingly become a personal tension: how could he articulate artistic values that honored spiritual ones? Complicating this even further was the question of race. The two buildings were set apart in this regard, one occupied almost completely by white people, the other by

5. Mrs. Cullen, wife of the Reverend Cullen. She sang in the church choir and generally managed the manse.

black. They were both versions of home, replacing the one that was lost earlier. And they both were built with the notion that you eventually had to learn how to leave them.

Because he had entered Clinton in January, thus becoming a "second termer," Cullen would graduate in the same month, in his case, January 1922. In the summer of that year he ambitiously took enough courses to advance his class standing and so was able to graduate from college in the spring of 1925, having compressed four years of study into three and a half. The beginning of 1922 would bring significant changes in Cullen's outlook on many issues. More years of academic work and even more considerable dedication to literature, as both a student and writer of lyric poems, lay ahead. At the same time a larger social world would open to him. His career, by then brief but impressive, merited a flattering notice in the *Crisis,* one of the most prestigious of African American magazines, complete with an account of his prizes and a photograph, wearing his signature bow tie and a modest downward gaze.[24] A larger community waited to see what would become of him. Though he was almost twenty years younger than Alain Locke, and thirty-five younger than W. E. B. DuBois, race leaders and cultivated thinkers whose lives would cross significantly with his, like both of them Cullen breathed in the air of the academy without hesitation, a trait that was evident at least as early as his years in high school. To his academic achievements he would continue to add poetic laurels, finding himself unsettled as to the exact shape of his vocation, yet increasingly committed to facing persistent artistic and racial questions.

2

Higher Education, 1922–1925

When Cullen graduated from DeWitt Clinton in January 1922, he entered the Jazz Age and the first years of his full adulthood. By the time the decade was completed, the Depression had settled on America and was spreading to the rest of the world, and he had published three books of poetry and an important anthology of poems by African Americans. The years following the Great War would be marked by a large influx in the African American population in Harlem, and with it an increase in group consciousness that, among other things, energetically took on cultural issues. Cullen, dedicated as he was to his own higher education and his poetry, added considerable talent to this emerging new social landscape. Even as his adoptive father's church moved into an elaborate edifice in 1924, Cullen moved further and further into a network of literary and cultural figures. There were, however, almost predictable signs of trouble: tension within his heart about the doctrines of the Reverend Cullen's religion and a more dedicated sense of purpose in relation to his own art. In one signal instance he became a spokesperson for what he saw as a movement among younger blacks, away from conservative ideas about religion and toward a greater desire for more education. Everywhere prospects for new ideas began to appear, partly as the society itself shifted about him, and partly as his sense of growth and direction sought out new markers.

But his most immediate prospect meant more study, this time at New York University, where he earned his bachelor of arts in 1925. He worked hard at his studies, driven by a sense of duty but also by an ever-increasing commitment to the realm of the aesthetic. Teachers influenced him profoundly, and most of all a teacher named Hyder E. Rollins, who taught him about the poetry of John Keats. Deeply engaged in other poets, such as Edna St. Vincent Millay, he discovered as well French novelists like Gustave Flaubert. The attraction to French literature produced mixed reactions. He admired Flaubert so much that he joked he should reconsider his dislike of realism, but he also found other French novelists too overrefined in their late romantic styles. Despite many tempting aesthetic possibilities, his approach to poetry was already quite firmly set. By the end of 1925, however, he was increasingly drawn to African American literature and his place in it—a place that was to be won by talent and hard work—and he would publish *Color,* his first book of poetry. This brought him to the attention of many in the African American community and conferred on him notice and acceptance equal to his ambition. Cullen grew toward his high status as a significant poet in the first half of the decade of the twenties, even as he greatly widened his literary experiences.

But his place in the world grew increasingly complicated. He made a number of important friends, some of them lifelong, and yet he often floundered socially, even as he righted himself in terms of ambition and a sense of self. The choice and challenge of a vocation remained a looming challenge, and he needed to settle on a position, if not a vocation. He at one point planned to take the test for competency as a high school teacher in the New York Public School System, even though he had no definite plans to be a teacher. Most of his references to the pedagogic profession hammered away at its portion of boredom. His ability to win prizes in poetry contests continued unabated, and he won important recognition in every one of the three years after he entered New York University. Gradually, he sensed his commitment to poetry needed a sense of justification, a sense of the way the poetic meanings he might discover were, not accidental or winsome, but complex issues in need of clarification. This meant a consideration of race and beauty and the social values that rested on these two concerns.

His attendance at New York University took place at the uptown campus at 180th Street and Burnside Avenue, in a then-pastoral area of the Bronx known as University Heights; Cullen described it as "a place of verdure and blossom, well worth firing a poet's imagination." By attending summer classes one year, he was able to make up for the lag caused by his entering in February, and thus he was able to graduate in three and a half years. He majored in English, with a first minor in French and a second in philosophy. He took a number of courses with Hyder E. Rollins, a popular professor who began by studying medieval ballads but had recently shifted his interest to the English romantic poets, chiefly John Keats. The most important course, the one devoted to an in-depth study of Keats, stretched over the two terms of the academic year 1923–24. Rollins's influence on Cullen's literary taste was hard to overstate, though it was also the case that Cullen was more than prepared to absorb the special music of Keats.[1] The idealized status of the poet—the sensitive soul who longed for transcendence even as he bravely faced his own mortality and the tragic betrayals of the limits of human love—struck Cullen with a force that remained undiminished for years afterward. This special aesthetic sense was in part a form of medievalizing that looked back to the Middle Ages through the lens of early nineteenth-century England, threatened with the harshness of an industrialized, urban society. But Cullen was not completely given over to the past, as he also came to admire the poetry of Edna St. Vincent Millay, whose extreme popularity—she was the first woman poet to win a Pulitzer Prize—concealed a partially modernist sensibility that needed irony and acerbic wit to bring her vision into focus. When he graduated on June 10, 1925, he did so having submitted his senior thesis on "The Poetry of Edna St. Vincent Millay: An Appreciation."[2]

As he began his college years, his poetic efforts remained persistent, various, and increasingly complex. He and Brown continued to trade poems in their letters, Brown offering at one point a translation of Catullus and a pantoum, the formalism of which pleased Cullen. For his part, in the fall of 1922 Cullen would start working on a long poem in the ballad form, inspired perhaps by the influence of Rollins. This would become "Ballad of a Brown Girl," which he described as "a gruesome affair with no less than three murders in it. It is founded on an old song which every colored Kentuckian knows." The *New York Times* had accepted two poems, and "I Have a Rendezvous with Life" eventually appeared in three metropolitan newspapers. He continued to try and keep up Brown's hopes that they would sell a popular song, and he even thought that one day they would craft a stage musical together. He worked on translations of Horace's Odes, even sending Brown his version along with one of the same poem (book 1, ode 8) by Louis Untermeyer. He was, however, not done with his strong streak of medievalism, pronouncing "A Life of Dreams" his favorite recent effort. It begins,

> My life is woven all of dreams
> Like some rich patterned tapestry,
> Whose shift and change and subtle gleams
> Are parts of pagan pageantry . . .

He continued fitfully to work on a novel, trying to coauthor it with a friend, but gaining little traction. Meanwhile, he had plans for a novel of his own.

He sent William Brown a summary of the plot of this novel, asking him to suggest a satisfactory ending. He also cautioned his friend to put aside his prejudice, since he had expressed his disdain for mixed-race marriages. The story dealt with passing, and its main character was a light-skinned Negro female. She finds it difficult, given as she is to honesty in her dealings with people, to conceal her mixed parentage. While aspiring to a career on the stage, she meets and becomes engaged to a young man who is prejudiced against Negroes. In order to change his mind, she takes him to the "city's colored sections, its cabarets, churches, etc." He becomes intrigued by what he sees and decides to write a play set in this area, though his play needs a female lead, and he convinces his fiancée to take the part. The play mirrors the situation of the couple, and so the actress is living out her life in reality and on the stage at the same time. Such narrative doubling has roots, of course, in medieval literature, but it is a trope used by modernist writers as well.

The appearance of the actress's dark-skinned brother complicates the plot, and so the playwright flees to Europe, unable to accept the situation. When he returns three years later he confronts the actress at "a reception [of] the Drama League"—and there Cullen became divided in his compositional will. He was unable to decide whether to have the lovers reconcile and marry or to have had the playwright find a wife while overseas. Brown's suggestions for the ending, if any, were not recorded by Cullen, though Brown asked after the writing of the novel, which Cullen pursued for several months. The Harlem Renaissance would see a number of novels written about the subject of passing, but Cullen's efforts fell short for one reason or another. He did tell Brown he was having a difficult time with the writing and had even started on the final chapter as a way to gain momentum. By February 1923 he lamented that he "had put my novel aside until I get more of a philosophy of life. When I sit down to write I realize how little I know about most of the things I have written." Several times previously he mentioned that the short story was not his "métier," and it would be several years later that he would finally publish a novel. His poetry, meanwhile, came much more freely.

Whatever models existed for the role of a public poet were dominated in large measure by the rhetorical exigencies of the nineteenth century. For Cullen, as a college student in 1923, such models were public and hard to avoid. In February he was witness to a performance by two of the most famous poets in the country, both women, and both winners of the Pulitzer Prize for poetry. The first was Leonora Speyer, now little known, but at the time quite famous. She enjoyed the glamour of being a concertizing violinist whose portrait had been painted by John Singer Sargent. Though native born, she and her English husband had returned to America in 1919, driven from England in large part because of their pro-German views. Her poetry exuded romanticized excitation: "Pan, blow your pipes and I will be / Your fern, your pool, your dream, your tree!" Cullen, alert to dramatic gestures, told his friend Brown that "she has never forgotten that she is a Lady, however, you should see her use her lorgnettes!" On the program with her was none other than Edna St. Vincent Millay, whose texts Cullen absorbed thoroughly. But her performance he was able to resist. "The poetry was good, but she spoiled it by her reading. She read like a Tragedy Queen." (Of Speyer he observed her reading was better than her poetry.)

As he had done at DeWitt Clinton, Cullen took his appointed place on the school's literary magazine. In the case of New York University, this was the *Arch,* a reference to the landmark arch in Washington Square

Park, near the downtown campus of NYU. Over the next three and a half years he published eight poems in the *Arch,* as well as poems in a handful of national magazines, such as the *American Mercury,* the *Nation,* and *Vanity Fair.* Among these were versions of poems he had written earlier, back in DeWitt Clinton, while others were freshly composed, and some were even to find their way into his first published book of poetry. This particular pattern of composition and publication was a distinctive feature of Cullen's way of working: he was able to keep at the polishing of a poem so that it might appear years after its first version, and he could recycle versions, rewriting them extensively on occasion, so that his body of work increased slowly, even cautiously. While he labored to ensure freshness in his rhymes, he was also willing to abandon poems that never quite clicked.

Poetry remained a chief focus of Cullen's work and study, but he also turned his talents to public speaking on occasion. One of the most notable such occasions occurred at Town Hall in New York City on April 29, 1923. The topic of the speech, known as "The League of Youth Address," was the emergence of the new generation of writers and leaders among the African American community.[3] Matching and qualifying some of the important ideas that he had incorporated in his earlier talk on "God and the Negro," it was a bold speech, especially considering that Cullen was only a college sophomore when he delivered it. Most remarkable among its features is the way it touches on some of what would become the most disputed and important themes in the Harlem Renaissance, especially those related to race and culture. The opening salvo announces "a spiritual and an intellectual awakening." Widespread as the awakening has become—Cullen mentions the German Youth Movement, for example—he concentrates on the movement's adherents among African Americans. Less ostentatious though it was in the black community, it was no less intense. Segregation and discrimination were problems that such a movement could be called upon to solve. Education will provide the spearhead of the movement, even though "it may be that this increased respect for education is selfish in the case of each individual without any concern for the group effect." Still, education must be prized and sought after because eventually it "is working a powerful group effect." This became one of the main arguments in the Renaissance, as various leaders (Alain Locke and W. E. B. DuBois prominently among them) insisted on the need to raise the rates of education and literacy in order to realize the social promise and possibilities so far stunted by racist ideas and policies.

Equally important as a Renaissance topic—and point of considerable contention—was the role of the black church in the development of social and civil liberties. Cullen might have been expected to take a conservative stand on the issue of religion, as all knew he shared the home of a religious leader. But Cullen spoke out against the stereotype of the young Negro who was pictured as "liking nothing better than to be slapped on the back, and to be called a 'good fellow'—and to leave all to God." But religious dependence "breeds stagnation, and passive acquiescence, where a little active resistance would work better results." Moving ahead from this question, Cullen pointed out that racial misunderstanding was "not one of sections," since in the South it was no different from the North except by degree—the prejudice of the North was "sly and crafty and cloaks itself in the guise of kindness and therefore more cruel," indicating for the first of many times how relentlessly Cullen spoke out publicly against racism. Taking aim at the feud between the science of evolution and the retrograde turn to simple-minded fideism, Cullen said, "We have not yet reached the stage where we realize that whether we side with Darwin or with Bryan we all spring from a common progenitor." Cullen's attitudes, as reflected in this speech, are clearly opposed to any trace of racial superiority, while trusting in the individual's responsibilities and efforts to alter the system. "There is such a thing as working out one's own soul's salvation. And that is what the New Negro intends to do."

Reliance on one form of balance after another marks the entire speech. The youth movement is not widely visible, but it is strong. Pious religion can be disabling, but true spiritual striving redeems people. Darwin and Bryan speak from utterly different principles, but the human race has a biological unity. Racial discrimination comes in forms blatant and covert, but it is always unenlightened. Cullen's commitment to education, of course, was a belief that didn't require balance, as he was to spend much of his life as a teacher, one who "realizes [education's] potentialities for combating bigotry and blindness." By his use of the term "New Negro," Cullen signals ahead of the events that he will be active in as a contributor to the Renaissance. He seldom returned to the kind

6. Young Countée, probably around 1925, with an inscription to James Weldon Johnson.

of forum represented by Town Hall, and later his prose would be much more often addressed to artistic rather than political or social questions. Still, he had a taste of the air in which controversy and political activism would happen. Jessie Fauset, then serving as assistant editor at *Crisis*, attended the speech and asked Cullen to send it to her for publication. Meanwhile, he told Locke that some of the newspapers had taken notice, but Cullen was afraid what they quoted "will get me an unsavory reputation among 'respectable' people."[4] The space Cullen traveled between "God and the Negro" and "The League of Youth Address" is considerable and tells a great deal about how his attitudes toward race and religion would eventually be complicated to the point of paradox, if not outright contradiction. The latter speech, meanwhile, was able to extend its audience when it was published in the August 1923 issue of *Crisis*.

The sentiment in the "Address" resonated deeply in Cullen's writing at the time. There was worldwide disillusion on the part of the younger generation (as was evident in Cullen's allusion to the German Youth Movement) in the face of the failures of the leaders of the civilized world who took so freely to mass slaughter in the Great War. Cullen himself followed up the "Address" with a poem about the relations between "youth" and "age." When he first sent the poem to Brown, he spoke of it as like all "made-to-order" poems, namely, "very bad." Called "From Youth to Age," the poem was never reprinted by Cullen. One of the stanzas conveys the bombastic edge in the high-minded exhortations.

> To War and Hate that sever friends
> We pay no further youthful toll,
> But, armed with love, we aim to cleanse
> The inner altars of the soul.

Here the poet clearly desires his pious images to ward off any suggestion that he rebels against militarism in any but a Christian, or at least religious, context.

But he took to the subject again, and this time he felt that he had done some justice to it. The poem was called "Wisdom Cometh with the Years." This was a poem that he would later include in his first volume of poetry, but only after changing the final stanza. A comparison of the two versions shows just how Cullen's feelings had shifted between when he wrote the poem in 1923 and when he published it in 1925. The last quatrain of the first version, included in a handwritten draft to Brown, read:

> I must rise soon and lie down late
> And shed my futile tears;
> Not even I may shun the fate
> Of changing with the years.

The published version displays a different set of tones:

Let me be lavish of my tears,
And dream that false is true;
Though wisdom cometh with the years.
The barren days come too.

The published version abandons the acute plangency and self-dramatization of the first, but not completely. Instead a sense of self-conscious self-deception ("Let me ... dream that false is true") shows through and is followed by a world-weariness that seals the compact between the generations. Age comes to all, and each generation must negotiate that inevitability as best it can. Even though he might feel, as he said about his novel-writing attempt, that he needed to "get more of a philosophy of life," his poetry was gaining gravity.

Jessie Fauset, besides soliciting his "Address" for publication in *Crisis,* was one of several people who attentively sought to advance Cullen's reputation. Born in 1882 in New Jersey but raised in Philadelphia, Fauset had deep aesthetic longings and would eventually publish four novels and many essays. Her commitment to higher education—she had earned a master of arts degree from the University of Pennsylvania and attended classes at the Sorbonne—and her refined taste shaped the characters and plots of her elitist fiction. Hughes once quipped that when people mentioned "Florence" at one of her parties they were referring to Italy, not Alabama. Moving to New York City in 1919, she became the assistant editor at *Crisis,* where she did much of the soliciting, selecting, and editing of the contributions, working very closely with DuBois. She stayed on at the *Crisis* until 1926, after which she married and moved to New Jersey, where she lived for the remainder of her life. Though her journalism is undervalued, and her novels only recently more closely studied, she played a key role in the Renaissance for a writer such as Cullen, with whose tastes and literary ambitions she was thoroughly sympathetic. Her editorial and creative work contributed significantly to forming the audience of African American readers who would lionize Cullen. Her decision to publish Cullen's "The League of Youth Address" was one of the first steps in this direction.[5]

Cullen, in part through the sponsorship of Fauset, knew many people associated with both *Crisis* and *Opportunity.* The editors of these two journals, W. E. B. DuBois and Charles S. Johnson, respectively, would in various ways champion his work. Through the notice he received from the various prizes his poetry earned, he was sought after by many people in Harlem, especially those who traveled in literary and cultural circles. Sometime around the summer of 1923 he met Yolande, the only surviving child of W. E. B. DuBois. Her father knew the Reverend Cullen well from their various protest activities. She was born as Nina Yolande DuBois in 1902, named after her mother. Near Cullen's age, she would soon enter Fisk University in Nashville—the same place her father had studied—and she graduated in 1926, afterward taking up a long career as a teacher, especially of drama and English. Clearly having absorbed some of the cultural predilections that were part of those people her father defined as "the talented tenth," she worked hard to maintain a sense of academic commitment. Her school record, however, did not place her in the top 10 percent, nor give her a sense of mission as a leader. After her graduation from college she settled in Baltimore, often traveling home to Harlem to visit her parents. Eventually, she became the drama teacher at the Paul Laurence Dunbar High School in Baltimore, and in the later decades of her life her father settled in that city for several years. Rumors circulated that she was shy and naive, but her correspondence reveals other character traits. When it came to Countée—she always addressed her letters to him with the accent on the first *e*—there was a clear and energetic purpose.[6]

Cullen felt attraction to the young woman—she would later begin to sign her letters to Cullen as "Lady"—during that first summer of their acquaintance. He called on her a number of times and recorded his impressions in his letters to his friend, Harold Jackman. "She pleases one without any reservations. No, she is not beautiful—but one is drawn to her by some indefinable magnetism of refinement and soulful honesty." Her family would naturally be a point of cultural status, but there were also aspects that Cullen couldn't help but notice. "A man like her father could do a great deal for her with a little more attention. It is a common point of comment, though, that he is interested more in other people's daughters than in his own. The pity of it." Cullen's rather analytic sensibility returned when he saw her several days later. "I had an opportunity to study her at close range. My delight in her increased fourfold." A singular trait that he most noticed especially drew them close together: her frankness. "Candor can always enthrall me," he said. Yet at this point he was a long way from being committed, even suggesting to Jackman that the "way lies open to you." The next week Cullen took Yolande out dancing in Atlantic City, which produced an "unconcealed and absolutely depraved delight" as they listened to jazz, and Cullen unblushingly said that he "lived more poetry last night than I ever wrote." He felt he and Yolande "were inexpressively well matched." The language of his reactions and the description of the events convey a strong sense that for the two this was a passionate summer affair. Perhaps separation and the return to school on both their parts would cool things. But it did not.

Yolande first wrote to Cullen in December 1923, while she was attending classes at Fisk. Seeking to revive the summer's interest, she began coquettishly, "Surprised? . . . thought you would be." Her announced occasion was a chance to congratulate him on winning the Witter Bynner Prize, the event having come to her notice through an article in the *Nashville Tennessean*. Proclaiming that "we forgive geniuses most any thing," she went on in affectionate terms. Quoting the description offered by one of her friends, she praised Cullen's "tender eyes and the delicate shyness of [his] hands." They had obviously revealed their feelings some time earlier, for he had told her—using a line from Yeats—that she should "tread lightly," and she agreed to do that, "so as not to mar the wonderful fabric of your dreams." Their correspondence often sounded this romantic note, and Yolande described one of Cullen's letters as being "prose poetry." She was rather burdened by her studies—later dispraising herself as "dumb as a beetle when it comes to Psychology and History"—but she worked hard at them. She also found time to enjoy college life, and, more than once, attendance at a football game—usually one against Howard—resulted in postgame parties and night-long dancing. Cullen would read his poems to her when they were together, and she consented to have him dedicate a sonnet to her. Constant requests from her to Cullen that he correspond more frequently apparently produced few results. For her part she wrote often, quick to answer his latest letter, saying that "if I wait much longer you'll never speak to me again and that would be tragic." But through various misunderstandings and jealousies, petty and serious, their relationship began to develop.

Cullen spent his summers in the mid-1920s away from the university, but not away from his delving into various forms of literary works. He and his adoptive parents routinely went every summer to Pleasantville, New Jersey, where the reverend had a vacation home. A few miles west of Atlantic City, the town was a favorite of African Americans; the 2000 census shows that the population was over 50 percent black. Cullen spent some of the time, too much to suit his eager appetite for reading, at a job as a busboy working in the Traymore Hotel in Atlantic City. The people he waited on at the resort hotel were far from impressive; as to the atmosphere of the whole scene, "my bourgeois soul receives it as one takes an emetic." Adopting the defense of the third-person speaker, Cullen modeled his experience into an especially crafty set of figures in "Atlantic City Waiter."[7] His twenty-year-old sensibility could not tolerate the middle-class style, and, using Jackman as a sounding board, he proclaimed, "I am not at all a democratic person. I believe in an aristocracy of the soul." Even allowing for the special intolerance of youth, Cullen was marking out a theme that he would never abandon, since for him any transcendent art would always shrink the importance of everyday pursuits, even those of idle pleasures.

He thought constantly about his friendship with Harold Jackman,[8] who started at New York University—at the downtown branch—two years ahead of Cullen. Graduating in 1923, Jackman went on to Columbia for a master of arts degree. Interested in becoming an educator, he eventually taught in the New York Public School System for decades. His friendship with Cullen was based on their shared aesthetic interests, and it was a love of literature that most likely brought them close together. However close they were at the university, the summer separation brought in its wake an intense correspondence. Jackman was born in London in 1902, but came to America as a young child. Intellectual and aesthetic in equal measure, he would go on to become an important patron of the arts, especially those of a dramatic sort. Cullen remarked on how successfully he supported the artistic endeavors of others, while never producing any writing of his own. But he and Cullen went to the theater together often, and Jackman made it his overriding vocation to collect theater memorabilia for the rest of his life. His collecting impulses extended to all manner of things artistic, and his donations of literary and artistic material before and after his death went to a number of libraries. An impeccable dresser, Jackman possessed a striking profile and an aristocratic bearing. He knew everyone in Harlem, and everyone there was impressed with him. Jackman had recently met Claude McKay in New York, shortly after the Jamaican poet came to New York, and he began to correspond fitfully with him for the next several years, during which time McKay was often abroad. When McKay inquired about Jackman's background the answer was fairly detailed.

> You want to know something about me as you say. Well, (a typical American beginning, n'est pas?) I was born in London of a West Indian mother (from Barbados). My father was German (white) I came here when I was three. Three years ago I received a degree from New York University —of this city, and at the end of this summer I hope to have an M.A. from Columbia. Of course I consider myself an American (I am a citizen but I mean as one born here) but Eric Walrond likes to think of me as English. The connection? None, just that some other people like to consider me foreign. At present I am teaching at a public school in Harlem. No, I don't expect to do that always. Yet Lord knows (and I am twenty-five and getting gray fast) I don't know what I want to do. I am still groping. It is sad, isn't it. I hope I land somewhere one of these days.

The cosmopolitanism of this letter typifies Jackman's insouciance, even as it displays how alert he was to the role of one's image in the public eye. Later in the same letter Jackman spoke of being "passionately fond of music especially modern music and literature is second nature with me."

Before the summer was over, Cullen's friendship with Jackman had greatly intensified. Considering his general shyness, Cullen might all too easily have been drawn to Jackman simply because the social aplomb Jackman showed would attract any number of admirers. But while still beginning to court Yolande, the poet started to reveal more and more of his feelings to his friend. The letters he sent Jackman in 1923 set out a relationship that would deepen and endure, and would often be expressed in high-minded terms. Cullen saw Jackman as "a friend to whom [I] feel free to reveal the mystic rites which take place on the inmost altars of [my] soul." By the beginning of 1924 he had arranged for Locke to meet Jackman—a sure sign of Cullen's serious attachment, and an extension of the homosocial ethos shared by all three men—and he was very keen to know the resulting impression. "Caring as much for him as I do, I am very anxious to know your reaction to him . . . I want to know how [he] will stand up under your scrutiny." He took pains to let Jackman know that he was not simply lost in vague affection: he pointed to the "distinction between a friend and an appreciative friend." Cullen sensed that there was a creative spirit in Jackman, but he told him that it needed something "to light your altar fires." Finding things in both Jackman and Yolande that he needed, Cullen would often turn to a language of devotion that elevated and aestheticized the two relationships. Whether it was Yolande's naive frankness or Jackman's cultural sophistication, his two new confidants impulsively stirred Cullen's imagination.

Cullen's own aesthetic taste was changing in a complex process, which, given his admiration for French literature, could be seen as his sentimental education. Turning to Jackman for advice and approval on matters professional and personal, Cullen relaxed into what became his deepest and longest lasting friendship. In the summer of 1923 he teased Jackman about his middle name, addressing the letters to "Harold Denzil Jackman." When Jackman objected, Cullen tweaked him further, saying the name sounded like that of a Russian duke or an aesthetic poet. Then, as a mock peace offering, he volunteered that occasionally he was chagrined to receive letters addressed to "*Miss* Countée Cullen." But the banter was often mixed with serious reflections and questions. Reading *Madame Bovary* at Jackman's suggestion, Cullen was intrigued with Flaubert's realism, even though for him "the word realism generally has a distasteful connotation." He was planning to go on to Prevost's *Manon Lescaut* and Gautier's *Mlle. De Maupin.* He willingly declared *Blue Bird,* a play with a fairy-tale basis, by the Belgian Nobel laureate Maeterlinck, a "masterpiece by an exotic soul." Later in the summer he would feel that Gautier had "too much beauty of word and phrase," and it "has sickened me." He found it hard to steer a middle course between realism and romanticism.

Plans for future writing centered some of the literary discussion. Alain Locke had come over from Washington, DC, for a short visit, bringing along some suggestions. Having received national recognition when he was the first African American to win a Rhodes Scholarship in 1907 and having graduated with a Phi Beta Kappa key from Harvard the same year, Locke had already become one of the most exquisitely educated men of his generation. A year at Oxford and another in Berlin studying philosophy only further enhanced his reputation as an elitist;

he was to become popularly known as "the Proust of Lenox Avenue," an allusion to his refinement and his sexual orientation. Locke was often eager to induce his literary friends to move and develop in certain directions. In this instance it was to urge Cullen to write a play that could be included in an anthology of Negro drama that he and Montgomery Gregory were planning to publish. The play should have folk material as its base. Later in the summer, Cullen confessed to Locke that he had abandoned his idea of writing a play based on a "black Pierrot." He had, he said, exchanged it for the figure of a "black Christ," which he would use in a "miracle play" (and would, over a decade later, use in one of his most complex poems). Cullen turned to Jackman and asked him to send him two books: the plays of William Butler Yeats and a book on African folklore. The books dutifully arrived and Cullen set to work reading them, though no play or any other composition resulted directly. He excused himself in part by telling Jackman that the reverend insisted he spend more time on his studies, and Cullen complied. But meanwhile he read *Camille,* and Langston Hughes increased his reading list by recommending Somerset Maugham's *Rain.*

Perhaps because he read so much and so was tiring of the symbolist and late-romantic styles, Cullen suggested that "French authors go too far." Then he reflected and retreated slightly: "I suppose I am [puritanical]." But the mixture of aesthetic tastes and sexual orientation persisted as a topic of curiosity and analysis. Donald Duff, a white friend from the university, was a close friend of both Jackman and Cullen, and—according to Jackman—he was homosexual. Cullen pointed out to Jackman that Duff had previously accused him of being puritanical; this led Cullen to defend himself and change the subject slightly by asking, "do you two [Jackman and Duff] like each other better, or worse? That sentence reads queerly, but you know what it means." Cullen's romantic and sexual desires led him to constant formulations and searchings. He asked Jackman, "Tell me more of Yolande DuBois. Is she in any way brilliant?" He confessed to his reluctance and confusion about heterosexual couples. "Few beautiful women are worth the clay and spittle which were mixed to make them," going on to describe the arrangement of Adam and Eve as one of God's "fiasco[es]." But he felt the weight of expectations. "And yet some woman will probably make me eat an apple someday without any thought at all of the consequences." Further ambivalence showed when he said he couldn't appreciate George Moore's *Confessions of a Young Man*—recommended to him by Langston—perhaps because the autobiographical novel dealt too extensively with the particulars of artistic longing in a bohemian existence.

As much as Cullen treasured the intimacy with his contemporaries like Jackman and Hughes, he also found very gratifying the support of older friends who could give advice and professional guidance. Locke was one such who played this part most compellingly. Cullen first came to know Locke when the younger poet—he was born eighteen years after Locke—approached him seeking a reference for his application for a Rhodes Scholarship.[9] Cullen's letter, dated September 24, 1922, set the respectful tone one would expect: "you are our race's sole representative as a Rhodes scholar." With that honor fading into his background, Locke was now somewhat unhappily ensconced at Howard University in the philosophy department, though he had recently been turning his thoughts to various cultural and aesthetic questions and their relationship with race and race consciousness. His response to the young poet was immediately warm and generous. Thus began a friendship that Cullen, for his part, always hoped would involve an academic as well as an aesthetic component. But the friendship was complex and in many ways complicated, as the men were both mentor and student as well as intimate confidants. Locke had lived through social adjustments and developed a wariness that enabled him to intuit Cullen's frame of mind. In November of 1923 Cullen told Locke: "With you, I feel freer than with any of my friends, because whereas most of my friends are sympathetical [*sic*] on notice, you are the only one for whom I am not compelled to wear a placard on my back." The relationship between social concerns and aesthetic expression would strengthen the bonds between the two men. While many considered each of the men as insufficiently political in his activities, neither writer treated aesthetic values as completely otherworldly. The aesthetic was a realm that one entered through certain exertions of idealism, but it was a realm from which one returned, often bearing messages of practical consequence. The question of a cultural and artistic renaissance—one that would engage them both for years to come—was a question that necessarily had to be addressed in public terms.

As a poet, Cullen accepted and pronounced his social concerns, though not always in partisan terms, however. When he gave his "Address" at Town Hall in 1923, using the term "New Negro," he boldly said he himself represented this movement, marked as it was by a commitment to higher education and a sense of self-shaping. Some of the ideas in that speech may have echoed things he heard from Locke, but in any case the two men were thinking many of the same thoughts. Cullen's preoccupation with questions of identity, as well as his strong sense of scholarly duty and a devout sense of obligation to his adoptive parents, and perhaps most of all a love of high aesthetic ideals, all provided points of friendship with Locke. Both men constantly dealt with racial issues, refusing to back away from the demands and promises of race pride, while at the same time seeking and believing in a realm of universal aesthetic values. By the winter of 1922–23 the two had met in person, and Cullen visited Locke in Washington on occasion, even as Locke continued to come quite often to New York, where he rendezvoused with Cullen, among others. In a letter apparently written in 1923, Locke offers Cullen a full measure of advice and reveals something about himself as well:

> I do not want to claim any special breadth of view—but I must say a propos of your remark that one's intimate confidences often seem foolish even to the best-intentioned confidants. I think I may assure you of but one standard of judgment,—and that is the law of a man's own temperament and personality. But one cannot often discover this, especially if there are convention-complexes[,] except through confessional self-analysis. I have always thought that the wisest institution of the Catholic church was the confessional. Its only drawback is its moralistic background and condescension. If I were inventing a religion I would try to work out some beautifully ritualistic mode of reciprocal confession and make all conception of punishment and reward psychological and self-inflicted.

Though he was a closeted homosexual throughout his life, Locke strove never to lie to himself. He rather gloomily opined that "a few of us surely may outrun the slowly inevitable," by which he meant to suggest that too often convention tended to ossify sentiment. He added that his "listening ear is as kindly as it is acutely receptive." Cullen heard in this letter an approach and a tone that he responded to eagerly.

The correspondence between the two men remained warm and even intimate, as they shared their fears, hopes, and experiences. As winter turned to spring in 1923, Cullen wrote often to his new mentor. Keen to share Locke's aspirations and private ideals, he angled to join his private circle. Locke had earlier told him that he wanted a "most professional reaction" to one of his, Locke's, poems; he described his sending them to close friends as "an exchange courtesy which I have been following . . . now for a number of years." Cullen, in turn, would occasionally submit one of his poems to the older man's stern judgment. Cullen had already considered the appearance of his poetry in book form, and he fretted over such a signal event. This led him to bring up the subject often with Locke. He promptly took up the older man's recommendation and read Edward Carpenter's *Ioläus,* the discreet anthology of gay writing that presented itself as a book about male camaraderie through a wide range of literature, from the Bible and the classics to modern times. Cullen felt its revelatory force; "I loved myself in it," he said. Frankly full of desire, he mused to Locke, "I suppose some of us erotic lads, vide myself, were placed here just to eat our hearts out with longing for unattainable things." The two discussed other books by Carpenter in their correspondence, using the material to refer to their discussions of homosexual issues with an idealizing vocabulary of "perfect friendship," in part adapted from Greek classicism.

In March 1923, Cullen wrote that his father had given him permission to spend the Easter holidays with Locke and that he was looking forward to meeting Georgia Douglas Johnson and visiting her salon. Cullen excitedly described Langston Hughes, a new friend who was beginning to establish himself as a published poet, in the most glowing terms. In New York, he and Hughes had gone to see the Moscow Players' production of Gorky's *The Lower Depths,* and Hughes had promised to write Locke and send along some of his poems. In April, a letter from Cullen included two poems of Hughes's, with a note asking Locke not to send them out for publication. Meanwhile, Locke had given one of his former students, C. Glenn Carrington, Cullen's address and urged him to correspond with Cullen. Carrington, a social worker and Cullen's contemporary, was a graduate of Howard and greatly interested in the performing arts; he had been socially initiated into Locke's circle of gay friends, and Cullen began a long friendship with him.

Advice and descriptions of new friends, all of an artistic bent, flowed in both directions between Cullen and Locke. The two men avidly shared their idealization of Hughes, but they also opened their private lives to one another in ways they did not usually employ with other people. Cullen once referred to Locke's "spiritual and mental anguish" and went on to say: "By all means keep a racial heart if you can do so without injury to yourself. But this cannot always be done." This came in a letter that also expressed Cullen's happiness that Locke and Hughes had begun to correspond. Cullen suggested to Locke that Hughes might accompany him on an upcoming trip to Egypt that Locke had planned. "Oh it would be wonderful if he could go with you this summer . . . each of you will be such inspiration to the other." In a letter of May 31 he offered to step aside where Hughes was concerned and let Locke take over in Hughes's affections. "I would be willing to make the sacrifice could it ensure your happiness," he said. But the cycles of shifting affections and changing plans were always in operation. In July, Cullen and Hughes spent four days together in Manhattan, and Cullen reported to Locke that some misunderstanding had occurred that caused some unexplained alienation: "He [Hughes] is probably unaware of what he has done, and, doubtless, blames you." Perhaps Hughes's coyness with Locke caused signals to be missed, or Cullen was too open in his homosexual attraction to Hughes, and Hughes may have put this down to Locke's urging Cullen to be more self-accepting. Despite the closeness, even intimacy, of the relations among the three men, misunderstandings could occur.

Cullen chose to celebrate his twentieth birthday with Georgia Douglas Johnson in Washington, DC, which he was visiting for the first time. She was well known in the nation's capital as a promising poet and ran a literary salon there that attracted illustrious and various attendees. She and Cullen conversed intensely; "she really has the soul of a poet," he testified to Locke. Meanwhile, Scribner's had rejected his book of poems, but a promising offer from Boni and Liveright was on the table. Cullen saw his commitment to pursuing the Rhodes Scholarship begin to fade, and he meant instead to concentrate on his poetry, as the lifelong tension between the two commitments was troublingly felt. In the summer he announced some important news to Locke: "Recently I met Yolande DuBois and I am near the solution of my problem. But I shall proceed warily." This last remark is especially ironic, since it would be almost five years until Cullen married Yolande in an ill-fated union that did nothing to lessen the difficulties Cullen faced about his own sexual orientation. This letter remains one of Cullen's most direct references to his sexual orientation, and at the same time it provides evidence of his trust in Locke.

In the fall of 1923 Cullen continued to befriend writers and artists. Jessie Fauset, working as DuBois's secretary at *Crisis,* would occasionally relay news from Locke and others. By one account, it was Fauset who introduced Cullen and Hughes, having been able to get their addresses from the poems they submitted. When she first approached Hughes, she told him that readers of *Crisis* often wrote to the journal praising his poems. The gossip between Harlem and Washington, DC, was carried, if not trumpeted, in both directions, as black bourgeois and artistic circles thrived in each city; in fact, Fauset and Locke were good friends at this time, as their families had known one another in Philadelphia. Taking note of Hughes's return in 1924 from his trip to Africa aboard a tramp steamer, Cullen enthusiastically observed to Locke that Langston was "looking like a virile brown god." Equally enthusiastic was his mention of the trip to Jackman: "Think of being in Africa!" He added that Hughes was considering going to Howard, though the absence of any scholarship support soon ended that plan, and after a short stay at Columbia University, Hughes took to the sea.

Whether they were introduced at a party by Fauset, or met at the public library, as another account has it, Cullen and Hughes formed a strong friendship in 1923.[10] Like Cullen, Hughes had begun having success getting his poems published and noticed, but the men had utterly different attitudes toward the use of academic training in the aid of poetic inspiration. This difference became more marked as things unfolded. Hughes at the time had dropped out of Columbia, frustrated by the academic approach to things. He wrote to Cullen from what Cullen referred to as "some place called Las Palmas," adding in a note to Jackman that Hughes was "really squeezing life like a lemon." Ready to travel widely at any provocation, Hughes first spent his time in Mexico with his father, whom he came to dislike intensely, and had then shipped out rather casually as a deckhand on working vessels. He found a job in late

1923 on a rusty ship, called the SS *Hassayampa,* that was moored at Jones Point, on the Hudson River north of the city and across from Peekskill. The navy had put several ships there when they were declared unseaworthy. For Hughes it was a cramped but livable space, and he wrote poems at a good clip; he said he always wrote best when he was sad or lonely. It was from this ship that he mailed poems to Cullen and sometimes came ashore to join his new friend at one play or musical or another. Cullen was still pursuing his studies at New York University, of course, but Hughes had little difficulty convincing him to cut class in favor of a stage production. Harlem at the time was teeming with new musical and theatrical talent, and Hughes possessed very broad tastes when it came to popular entertainment. Cullen had only a few years to go before he would be known as the poet laureate of Harlem. Hughes, for his part, came to enjoy being referred to punningly as the "poet low-rate." This period took on a halcyon feeling later, when the poetic theories of the two men—regarding the role that racial identity plays in artistic responsibility—caused them to drift apart.

The earliest days of the friendship between Cullen and Hughes brought both of them into a deeper sense of their own poetic practices and the different ways to advance and justify them. Hughes began with an exceptionally generous gift: he mailed Cullen a packet of thirteen of his poems, written out in longhand, with a cover sheet that said, "To a fellow poet, these unpublished poems."[11] These were a gift, a bond, and a request for comments and reactions. Unfortunately, Cullen's reactions to the poems are lost, perhaps a result of Hughes's footloose disposition at the time. Cullen, however, responded in kind, sending Hughes some poems that elicited very thoughtful responses. The packet of poems was a mix of free verse and rhymed poems, all of them short. Hughes was not expert at rhyming, and many of the poems are discordant in terms of how the rhymes support the stanzaic structure. Three of them deal with the figure of Pierrot, whom Hughes uses rather sentimentally, to charming but slight effect. One more resonant poem is titled "Gods":

> Yet the ivory gods
> And the ebony gods,
> And the gods of diamond-jade

> Are all but silly puppet-gods
> That the people themselves
> Have made.

This is answered to some extent, by Cullen's poem "Heritage," where he says:

> Quaint outlandish heathen gods
> Black men fashion out of rods,
> Clay and brittle bits of stone,
> In a likeness like their own.

However, the speaker of this poem then adds,

> I belong to Jesus Christ,
> Preacher of humility;
> Heathen gods are naught to me.

The poem goes on to explore in considerable and ambiguous depth the role of African culture in the minds of Renaissance poets. Cullen also dedicated "To a Brown Boy" to Hughes, who was flattered. Hughes, perhaps mockingly, asked Cullen to recite one of the poems, "Syllabic Poems"—a Dada-like exercise, one of whose lines says "Ay ya! Ay ya!"—at a public reading the two had scheduled at the Harlem library, and which Hughes could not attend. Hughes saw his experimental poem as part of "an era of revolt against the trite and outworn language of the understandable." This marked another, perhaps most important, point of difference in sensibility between him and Cullen. About gods and dada, the two poets differed.

One exchange provided a singular occasion to illustrate their different sensibilities. Cullen sent Hughes a "suicide" poem, called "Suicide Chant," which ended with a quatrain:

> Pull up the weed;
> Bring plow and mower;
> Then fetch new seed
> For the hand of the sower.[12]

This was meant as a response to Hughes's own poem on the same subject, called simply "Suicide," and written in a blues idiom:

> Ma sweet good man has
> Packed his trunk and left.
> Nobody to love me:
> I'm gonna kill myself.[13]

Hughes felt strongly that "people are taking [the poem] . . . all wrong. It's purely personal, not racial. If I choose to kill myself, I'm not asking

7. Langston Hughes, 1924, the main claimant for the honor of African American poet laureate. Though very different in style and temperament, he and Cullen remained friends.

anybody else to die, or to mourn either. Least of all the whole Negro race." Hughes's reaction to Cullen poem was quite negative, and he spoke bluntly about his reaction to it, feeling the rhymes were trite and the horticultural imagery all wrong. Though more or less on the same subject, the two poems could hardly be more distinct, exemplifying as they did the difference between the two poets.

This early exchange of poems and opinions was near the time when Hughes was expanding his own poetic sensibility. He had recently met René Maran, whose novel of African tribal life, *Batouala,* won the Prix Goncourt, and a colored prince named Kojo Lovalon. When reporting how often interracial fights between American and French sailors resulted in the use of fists and knives, Hughes crowed, "Let the white world tear itself to pieces." Clearly, both poets were trying to comprehend their own quite different experiences. Hughes mentioned how Locke "frightened me stiff," and he was afraid to meet the professor "because I know he'd find me terribly stupid." Cullen, of course, courted Locke's mentoring and felt much more nearly his intellectual equal, at least potentially. Meanwhile, Cullen studied hard at NYU and polished his poetic skills. Hughes boarded a tramp steamer and sailed for Africa, reaching Nigeria by July of 1923—his sixteenth port of call—and described to Cullen the oarsmen ninety miles up the Congo, as "gorgeously naked save for a whisp [*sic*] of loin cloth." He turned homeward when he left Sierra Leone in October, "Just a little bit homesick for New York." Within months, however, he had reached New York and then set out once again across the Atlantic, only this time to jump ship in France with just nine dollars in his pocket. The summer would come and he would meet Locke, finally, and live a Bohemian existence for several months before finally coming back to see the publication of *The Weary Blues,* which appeared just months after *Color.*

Cullen added another mentor for the sake of advice about poetry, one quite different from Locke. By the spring of 1924, Cullen had arranged for the imagist poet Witter Bynner to write the introduction to his first book of poems. Bynner was an aesthete, devoted to the writing of sonnets and much enamored of the poetry, and the person, of Edna St. Vincent Millay. A Harvard graduate, he was twenty-five years older than Cullen, but Cullen wrote to him animatedly, alerting him to the impending arrival of the manuscript and seeking his approval in the form of editorial selection as well as an introduction to his poems.

The manuscript is on its way to you; it contains not all my work, but those pieces which I should like to have published. Please let me know if you think any of them so bad that they ought to be omitted, also if any are too frankly imitative. You see, I don't want to give the critics too much opportunity to mention how many poets my work recalls. It seems to me that most of my poems can be grouped under one of two heads: the purely racial, and the purely lyrical.

If I do succeed in having my manuscript accepted by a publisher, there are several poems which I want to dedicate to some of my friends. Would you mind if I dedicate my ballad to you, as it is through that alone that I came to know you in this personal way that has meant so much to me?[14]

Cullen's concern about how his poetry would be accepted already possessed nuances, but the question of race and its dynamics of reception and identity in poetry was there from the beginning.

It was in the poetry contest named after Bynner that Cullen took some of his earliest prizes; this is what led to their meeting. It also opened up the question of what audience for his poetry Cullen should be addressing. Access to white-owned publishing houses and outlets would be a major concern for authors during the Renaissance. Figures like Walter White had come to the attention of white editors and published books that sold well. The younger generation of authors—like Cullen, Hughes, Toomer, and McKay—relied, sometimes chafingly so, on the benevolent watchfulness of older figures. Locke, for his part, was eager to serve as a mentor to Cullen and Hughes, and despite many differences along the way, he was able to offer them both various kinds of advice and support for the next two decades. Despite his accomplishments, however, Locke could not readily supply access to white publishers. Cullen, by virtue of his prizes and his earlier publication in national magazines such as *American Mercury,* was in some ways well enough placed to bring his poetry to a wide readership.

But because of his concerns about propriety, ambition, and racial sensitivity, Cullen could not take casually the problem of garnering an introduction to his first book. He wrote to Locke that he "would much prefer to have you do the introduction, unless you think there would be more point to one outside the race." Locke may well have felt slighted by Cul-

len's choice of Bynner to help launch his poetry. Locke nevertheless offered advice in a professional tone and let Cullen know that an article he,
Locke, was coauthoring with DuBois for *Crisis* would have to be adjusted
accordingly:

> As to the matter of the preface, I appreciate your attitude, but I have no
> suggestion to offer as long as Bynner has a mind to keep the agreement.
> I only thought he had defaulted and wanted to know whether to hold
> back some things from the article on "The Younger Generation." As this
> will not be finally edited until early November, you can keep me posted
> as to developments: as it is, I will write out the paragraphs and include
> or cut as the occasion requires. You should by all means see his preface
> before deciding. A preface beyond one's first volume is I think undigni-
> fied and not exactly "comme il faut."

In fact, Bynner felt several of the poems Cullen wished to include in the
volume were not of sufficient quality, and Cullen suggested to Locke that
he might use this as a way of removing himself from the agreement with
Bynner. Eventually, however, the volume would appear without an introduction by either Locke or Bynner.

A few months later Cullen received back from Locke a poem he had
sent him for comments. As Cullen read it he realized that Locke had "corrected" it in a way that was too severe. He complained to Locke: "Very
few people can reach you. Do bend down a little." Locke firmly believed
that black writers should use their racial identity in their art, drawing
on a tradition rooted in folk culture and yet still strive to attain a universal meaning. For Cullen, the burden of being a lyric poet was enough
at times; adding to it a strict responsibility for group expression struck
him as excessive. Much of the interest of his poetry, on the other hand,
comes from his attempt to include both perspectives. He also complained
to Locke that things were not going well with Yolande and that Hughes
had fallen for a young English girl in Paris. This news was accompanied
by Cullen's heartfelt declaration: "I have come quite definitely to the conclusion that I shall never again love any one with all my heart and soul.
If I must be a libertine in order to preserve my health, my sanity, and my
peace of mind, I shall do so; I shall make no further sacrifices." His letters
to Locke during his years at New York University were dotted with ex-

pressions of frustration and fatalism. Though Cullen would occasionally use words like *libertine* and *pagan,* he seldom publicly declared or acted out extreme emotions. Despite what seems a vow to indulge his sensuality, he continued to remain very discreet about his private life, and in this he and Locke were also sharing an important common experience.

In the winter of 1924 Locke had occasion to visit Cullen at the parsonage of his father. The reverend had gone out before Locke arrived and was "nearly furious" when he came back to discover that he had missed a chance to be introduced to the professor. Cullen and the reverend resolved to make sure a meeting would be arranged. So, later that fall, Locke took advantage of an invitation from Cullen to come and speak at his father's church, which had grown to be one of the largest in Harlem. At the same time, Cullen, anxiously awaiting news from the Rhodes committee, felt his interest revitalize in the prestige and support such a prize offered. With such revitalization came a concern for gathering letters of recommendation from people whose national stature would be self-evident and yet whose worth Locke would certify. The plea to Locke was heartfelt: "If you have any strings to pull, do tug away with all that's in you," Cullen wrote, sending along his list of references, which included DuBois, John Farrar (editor of the *Bookman*), and H. L. Mencken, among others. In addition to placing a poem in the *Nation,* Cullen secured from its socially progressive editor, Oswald Garrison Villard, the promise of a letter of recommendation to the committee. Cullen himself was fully aware of how such awards were often decided on the basis of one's letters of reference, and, in the wake of the misunderstanding about having sought Bynner's introduction to his poems, he was keen to have his mentor approve his procedures.[15]

Along these lines, he suggested to Locke that a potentially influential letter might come from John Haynes Holmes, a committed social reformer and Unitarian minister who served for many years as the vice president of the NAACP and assisted in the founding of the American Civil Liberties Union. Holmes, whom Cullen probably knew through his work with the reverend, was no casual acquaintance. Eventually, some years later, Cullen would write a sonnet, "Millennial," in honor of Holmes's twentieth anniversary as the pastor of the Community Church at Park Avenue and Thirty-Fourth Street. The sestet was unchecked in its praise:

Once in as many years a man may rise
So cosmopolitan of thought and speech.
Humanity reflected in his eyes.
His heart a haven every race can reach,
That doubters shall receive a mortal thrust.
And own, "This man proves flesh exalts its dust."[16]

The reference to race signals how Cullen admired those who were brave enough to see beyond racial prejudice, especially if they were strong enough to "thrust" their beliefs into society in effective ways. The poem also allows Cullen to exercise his unabashed approval of high purpose, for him one of poetry's main functions. But still the Rhodes committee rejected his application in December, before Holmes could supply his letter of recommendation.

Cullen's reputation as a poet had grown considerably by late 1924, and Llewellyn Ransom, like Glenn Carrington a student of Locke's from Howard, began a serious study of Cullen's work. Cullen was a bit apprehensive about this and wondered if Ransom were sincere. Several letters from Cullen to Locke contain cryptic references to a "L.R.," apparently Llewellyn Ransom, and hinting at a sexual relationship. Cullen would, however, make Ransom's name public, so to speak, when he dedicated one of the poems in *Color* to him. It is highly probable that Ransom and Cullen were sexually intimate shortly after they met, and though they subsequently remained friends for some time, their intimacy cooled.[17]

As for Glenn Carrington, he was interested in the dramatic arts, as was Jackman, and he likewise amassed a large collection of memorabilia, which now rests at the Moorland-Spingarn Research Center at Howard University. Carrington first wrote to Cullen in the spring of 1923, urged to do so by Locke. Cullen found the letter "very pleasurable and complimentary," and despite a warning that he, Cullen, was "no conversational giant and . . . unspeakably ignorant of current affairs," he promised to correspond. What happened next was a variation on the social network and exchanges typical of Locke, Cullen, and many others who were active in the Renaissance. From his summer house in New Jersey in late July, Cullen sent Carrington a letter of introduction to Jessie Fauset and urged him to visit Fauset at the *Crisis* office. At the same time, Cullen wrote Jackman, then working at the 135th Street library, and asked him to introduce Carrington to Eric Walrond, another member of the circle. Five weeks later Cullen let Carrington know that things had gone well; "Jessie Fauset and Harold Jackman have both been very profuse in their praises of you." Cullen went on to suggest that next there should be meetings with Jean Toomer and with Georgia Douglas Johnson, who were, by virtue of living in Washington, DC, already close in distance to Carrington, as he was still pursuing his studies at Howard. Cullen also shared with Carrington that he was enjoying a visit from Jackman, that he was deciding to go to Europe (despite parental disapproval), planning to seek help from Walrond in arranging the trip, and hoping Hughes would go with him. So the network was drawn and the gossip and news began to circulate.

Cullen's energy and the delight he displayed in introducing the different writers and aesthetes of the Renaissance to each other were modeled to a large extent on that of Locke. However, the social code was commonly followed and produced in its wake not only reams of gossip but emotional support and professional guidance. In any case, Locke and Cullen always enjoyed sharing friends, and Cullen's view of his mentor was deeply appreciative on both aesthetic and personal grounds. Months earlier he had said, in regards to Locke and Hughes, that "I am deeply happy at your friendship for one another and proud to be its instrument." As for Cullen and Locke, they would work together as poet and critic, though perhaps less closely as friends, throughout the Renaissance years. Carrington and Jackman would both develop deep and meaningful friendships with Cullen that lasted throughout the poet's life. The circles revolved around the issues of art and race and homoerotic friendship, and most of the issues generated affectionate pride and delight in a way that each man treasured.

Though his friendship with Locke was more complex, and the one with Hughes more problematic, Cullen began a valuable lifelong friendship with Carl Van Vechten sometime in the mid 1920s. Witter Bynner knew Van Vechten well, and he may have encouraged an introduction, but it could also have been through Eric Waldron that the friendship began. Any number of Harlem figures may have introduced the two at a party thrown by James Weldon Johnson, who often socialized with Van Vechten. In any case Van Vechten recorded in his daybook for November 11, 1924, that he met for the first time, not only Cullen, but Hughes and DuBois as well.[18] Cullen wrote to Locke in late November 1924 to

8. Alain Locke, circa 1925. Cullen's most influential mentor, Locke advised Cullen on matters poetic and personal.

say that he and Walrond had recently had dinner with Van Vechten. Van Vechten, of course, had by then won his somewhat notorious reputation as a bon vivant and patron of the arts. He was most noted for attending closely to all the latest developments in African American culture, perhaps especially those connected with the poets. His years-long correspondence with Hughes, for example, is full of play and bonhomie and incessant and measureless gossip.[19] Van Vechten would soon offer to help Cullen publish his first book and nearly two decades later would enlist Cullen in his work at the Canteen, a sort of USO refuge for soldiers stationed in New York City during the war. With his usual enthusiasm, Van Vechten took up Cullen, and the friendship meant admittance to Van Vechten's circle of homosexual friends. At the center of their relationship, gossip served as root and branch. In the period just before Cullen went to Harvard in the fall of 1925, he wrote to Van Vechten from his summer retreat in Pleasantville.

> Just a line o' type or two to let you know that I have my friends in mind, although I am enjoying a luxurious rest that is making me lazier than usual. I haven't the slightest idea of what is going on in Harlem, but you, with your excellent entrée to all social functions of color, must know more about Lenox and Seventh Avenue gossip than even Eric Walrond. I envy you; although it is fine to be knee-deep in June and mosquitos in a country place, I think it is better to be Charleston crazy in New York, even if it is hot enough there to cause many religious conversions by way of anticipating hotter times promised by my father's profession. If you have time to drop me a line, won't you tell me all the dirt?[20]

Between Jackman and Van Vechten, Cullen was supplied with gossip throughout all his days. Judging from most of his letters, however, Cullen was more a dedicated consumer than a producer of the latest information about the cultural and social scenes then actively underway in Harlem. There was, however, no doubting his eager engagement with the entire range of goings-on.

Color

Graduation from New York University, deepening friendship with Jackman, Locke, and others, and movement toward a more serious courtship with Yolande: all of these 1925 landmarks and developments did not outshine the singular event of the publication of his first book of poetry. The appearance of *Color* gave clear evidence of what Cullen's poetry meant to say, and of what forms it would use. Drawing on an African American tradition begun by Phyllis Wheatley, he turned to the high art traditions of European verse. Such verse was marked by elevated diction, a belief in universal truths, and sentiments of transcendent longing. This stood in contrast to the alternative tradition of idiomatic vocabularies and folk motifs, best shown in the dialect poems of Paul Laurence Dunbar, and brought to a high point by Langston Hughes. Many readers have appreciated the influence of John Keats and Edna St. Vincent Millay on Cullen, but there are also clear traces of Horace and other Latin poets who

9. Photo of Cullen, which is dated February 20, 1925, in the inscription to Carl Van Vechten, around the time of their first meeting. Cullen disagreed with Van Vechten on several issues, but their friendship was long and steady.

used epigrammatic forms. *Color* contains a number of short poems with alternately rhymed lines in four-line stanzas. This is the so-called ballad rhyme scheme. Cullen employed it as it was inflected by the model of the lyrical ballad, which meant a stylized and expressive lyricism that borrowed from, but also psychologically deepened, the material of the anonymous folk ballad tradition.

The key to such poetry is to make it appear natural, even easy, while ensuring that its symbols and arguments have a universal resonance. The subject matter is often love, and more specifically unrequited love, and the related subjects of despair and death. When the memorization and recitation of poetry as a public event was common in the African American community, as it was in the 1920s and 1930s, these poems were similar to song lyrics and—along with a number of his sonnets—led to a considerable reputation for Cullen as an accomplished and public poet. Later these poems were read in a different way, as evidence of Cullen's conflicts over his sexual orientation or his self-questioning psychology. Such poems demand a ground of tension, a sharp emotional conflict—though one that is eventually resolved, harmonized—in order to animate the short form and the polished diction. Here is a fairly typical example, called "If You Should Go":

> Love, leave me like the light,
>   The gently passing day;
> We would not know, but for the night,
>   When it has slipped away.
>
> Go quietly; a dream,
>   When done, should leave no trace
> That it has lived, except a gleam
>   Across the dreamer's face.

The speaker of the poem magnifies and sharpens his identity by speaking for "the dreamer," an abstract person whose emotional experience is both illustrative of natural processes ("like the light") and delicately resolved ("except a gleam"). It is the illusion, carefully crafted, of calm mastery that shows through in these short poems. The poem also faintly echoes the line from Yeats—"tread lightly because you tread on my dreams"—that Cullen and Yolande had quoted to each other. However, Cullen could also demonstrate his skill in a longer verse form as well.

It was the longest poem in *Color* that offered Cullen his most striking chance to mediate European forms and African American subjects. "The Shroud of Color" stands as one of Cullen's most ambitious poems, because of the way it is energized by the mediation of race and art and because it draws on such broad and deep traditions that it faces risks that would intimidate lesser writers. Its closest model is the romantic quest poem, such as Keats's "Endymion" or, more distantly, Shelley's "Alastor." Millay's "Renascence," published a few years earlier, may also have been a model, though contrasts with "The Shroud of Color" (for example, the use of race in Cullen's poem) are also telling. These poems all involve a speaker who recounts a quest—partly an agonized introspection, partly an allegorical search for ultimate meaning—which dramatizes longing and despair and transcendent hope. The poems often end ambiguously; this is not surprising given their highly spiritual subject matter.

Cullen had been hard at work on the poem as early as the spring of 1924, and he sent an early draft of it to Locke.[21] At the time Cullen had entitled the poem "Spirit-Birth." This was the title under which H. L. Mencken published it in the November issue of *American Mercury*. The poem's immediate biographical origin arose from a ruptured friendship with someone Cullen referred to only as "K." Writing to Locke, he tried to console himself with a sense of irony and paradox. "Depression seems to be good for my verse, but it is terribly telling on me." Apparently, the poem had already been accepted by the *Mercury*, and so Cullen told Locke he must return it so Cullen could mail it off by the tenth of May. He admitted to Locke that the editorial suggestions made by the older writer were good, but he wasn't able to incorporate them, as he felt the poem was a settled affair. He also received some comments on it (which do not survive in full) from his friend Brown, and to them he responded both defensively and strongly:

> Your objection to my portraiture of divinity is, in itself, within reason, but your reason for the objection pains me. You don't like the picture because it seems "inconsistent with the conventional and accepted conception of God and Christ." Guillaume, that sounds rankly conservative,—not to like something because it does not tally with the accepted

conception. Didn't you mean that you didn't like it because it was incon-
sistent with *your* conception? I hope that's what you meant.[22]

"The Shroud of Color" remains one of Cullen's boldest poems, and it
shows him in both his darkest and his most resolute moods.[23]

Cullen's version of the romantic quest warrants close reading, since
it takes its form from English romantic poetry, but its content from the
Christian tradition of redemptive suffering. The young poet—Cullen was
only twenty years old when he wrote the poem—shows considerable
mastery of literary models, form, and vocabulary. What most surprises,
however, is less his poetic mastery than his deep psychological agony.
"Shroud" calls for a close and repeated reading since its innovative approach to the questions of race and racial identity generates for the poem
an original position in African American literature. It is the struggle for
identity that the poem seemingly concentrates on, but it also contains
both a historical and social dimension. This elevates the poem above the
experience of a single person, but does so by asserting and enacting for
its singular speaker powers of suffering and redemption that are vatic,
even prophetic.

The poem commences in deep hopelessness, a state that is due to the
poet's color: "forewilled to that despair / My color shrouds me in." His
racial identity binds him to despair and, more to the point, is the very
source of that feeling. The poetic tradition doesn't permit Cullen to spec-
ify how and why race, even racial prejudice, forms the details of his existence. But the despair causes him to long for quietude, even surcease.
"Shall breath and being so inveigle me / That I can damn my dreams":
facing such self-destructive prospects, the quester nevertheless decides
to praise the power of life and its gifts. Such praise, however, becomes
but a prelude to death: "To dream still pure all that I loved, and die." In
this very low moment, the poet surrenders only to discover his first vi-
sionary moment: "Below, above, to left, / To right, I saw what no man
saw before." This is the great prophetic gift, the ability to see into the
nature of things. What the poet sees is the life force, the desire of all
mortal creatures to cling to life, and so his first great anxieties are resolved. The almighty can now be heard: "*The key to all strange things is in
thy heart.*"

But possession of this key turns out to be less than a complete resolution. The life force he saw earlier reappears now under the aspect of evolutionary destruction:

> I saw
> Evolve the ancient fundamental law
> Of tooth and talon.

(This echoes his allusion to Darwin in the "League of Youth Address.") The poet must admit that his "heart was still a pool of bitterness." Here Cullen displays his poetic ambition in a startling way. He uses the next stage in the quest to recapitulate the fall of the demon angels, and indeed shows Lucifer as almost winning the first struggle of good and evil. But rather than allow this epic struggle to capsize the poem, Cullen turns to a second conversion. He hears in his blood "a strange wild music," which is the "note / Of jungles, primitive and subtle." Calling up, without specifically naming it, his African ancestry, he claims that the entire race speaks through him. "The cries of all dark people, near and far /Were billowed over me." Though different from the resolution of "Heritage," this invocation of Africa serves as one of Cullen's touchstones. This second conversion means that he has "no further claim to urge / For death," and his "spirit has come home, that sailed the doubtful seas." The poem concludes with the image of "the rising sun." The struggles have concluded, and there is the promise of more life, and more light.

Read in the context of then contemporary expectations for African American poetry, "The Shroud of Color" stands as a very important and complex poem. Those expectations were manifold, but a clear sense of them can be gathered from what Charles S. Johnson, editor of *Opportunity,* said about the awards his magazine was to give for literary efforts.

> It [the contest] hopes to stimulate and encourage creative literary effort among Negroes; to locate and orient Negro writers of ability; to stimulate and encourage interest in the serious development of a body of literature about Negro life, drawing deeply upon these tremendously rich sources; to encourage the reading of literature both by Negro authors and about Negro life, not merely because they are Negro authors but because what they write is literature and because literature is interesting, to foster a market for Negro writers and for literature by and about

Negroes; to bring these writers into contact with the general world of letters to which they have been for the most part timid and inarticulate strangers; to stimulate and foster a type of writing by Negroes which shakes itself free of deliberate propaganda and protest!

Cullen obviously saw "The Shroud" as part of "the serious development of a body of literature," that is, as fitting into—perhaps inaugurating a new branch of—a literature that would address the issue of race. The force of the poem's narrative plot does not argue for replacing one idea of racial supremacy or prejudice with another, though a slack reading of the poem might lead some to see it that way. Rather, what the symbolic and allegorical meanings point to is a decision, a resolution, to take up the burden of race as a form of destiny. Racial identity can be imagined or experienced as a source of despair, a burden that clouds the views that would otherwise accept and love the universe and its orders. However, it can also—and much more fruitfully—be mediated with a vision of the life force and an ethical understanding in such a way as to render unmerited suffering as redemptive.

The poet added to the orthodox belief of Christian suffering a new and distinct dimension, one that invoked a distant land and a submerged history. Cullen may well have heard various professions of a racial ideology that stressed the roots of the African American experience in its purely African origins. These professions often went beyond mainstream Christian teachings, yet in the black community of Harlem in the 1920s they were heard frequently. Reverdy C. Ransom, an early activist in the Niagara Movement, professed such ideas.[24] Ordained a bishop in the AME church, he was known to have believed that "God brought naked barbarians from Africa, put them upon the anvil of American Christianity and Democracy; under the white heat of denial and persecution, He is fashioning them with sledgehammer blows into a new pattern for American civilization." In May 1923 Ransom published a poem, called "The New Negro," in the *New York Amsterdam News*. It began with these lines:

> He is new, he is old as the forests primeval.
> Stark in the nakedness of limb,

His forebears roamed the jungle and led the chase.
Crystallized by the heat of Oriental suns,
God made him a rock of undecaying power,
To become at last the nation's corner stone.

The allusion to the nation and its founding clearly took the issue of white supremacy and turned it around, trumping racial inequality with historical transcendence. History held a further strength, as Ransom said of the New Negro in the closing lines of the poem,

The Oriental sunshine in his blood
Shall give the warming touch of brotherhood
And love, to all the fused races in our land.

While living inside the ambience of his adopted father's church, Cullen would have seen such a claim as one more way of mediating the experience of Jim Crow and the oppression of African Americans with the high-minded claims of social equality dominant in American democracy. Ransom's "sledgehammer blows" were in a way the rhetorical equivalent of Cullen's "shroud of color."

While "The Shroud of Color" can be read as Cullen's reflections on racial identity in its most transcendent form, "Heritage" addresses the issue in the context of a much more fundamental way. The theme of Africa as the ground of an African American's birthright animated many of the works of Harlem Renaissance writers, and though some, like Wallace Thurman, would treat it satirically, most spent considerable aesthetic energy exploring its ramifications. Cullen's poem—with its famous opening line, "What is Africa to me?"—did as much or more than any other work to keep the issue near the forefront of Negro aesthetics.[25] "Heritage" gained a currency in the Renaissance roughly equal to that of "Incident" and "Yet Do I Marvel" and the later "From the Dark Tower." Since then it has become a standard anthology piece, though it hasn't expunged the hollow charge that Cullen was somehow less racially conscious than he should have been. Seldom has the poem been read in an autobiographical context, even though its central ambivalence reflects Cullen's prose formulations about the relationship between the universals of high romantic poetry and the particulars of individualized racial experience. "Heritage" is a poem definitely written out of knowledge gained from books, but it also records a mindfulness rooted in a racial identity. Here the imagination of Africa, especially in its more aggressively romanticized aspects, gave onto a larger prospect than that of mere national sentimentalism.[26]

The poem also stands as one of Cullen's most modernist, if modernism is characterized by the use of ironic structures as well as details. The striking rhetorical question that begins the poem opens the possibilities of extensive significance and meaning. The poem continues, awash with imagery that owes more to aesthetics than anthropology.

> What is Africa to me:
> Copper sun or scarlet sea,
> Jungle star or jungle track,
> Strong bronzed men, or regal black
> Women from whose loins I sprang
> When the birds of Eden sang?

The invocation of Eden rests on the ancient notion that temporal priority equals moral authority. Cullen's use of it, however, also suggests that a Christian morality might eventually emerge in the poem, as it does, but not before Africa is personified. The voracious and feminized continent awakens in a dream world drawn out of an imaginary text:

> Africa? A book one thumbs
> Listlessly, till slumber comes.
> Unremembered are her bats
> Circling through the night, her cat
> Crouching in the river reeds,
> Stalking gentle flesh that feeds
> By the river brink . . .

The struggle between "Quaint, outlandish heathen gods / Black men fashion out of rods" and the "Jesus of the twice-turned cheek, /Lamb of God" causes Cullen to "play a double part," aiming at a reconciliation or a consummation that can only be oneiric. Operating at both imagistic and highly symbolic levels, the unsettled self-knowledge of the poem recalls DuBois's well-known definition of the Negro as having a double identity; at the same time Cullen's lack of a clear knowledge of his actual parentage becomes an avenue, in this instance at least, to freely imagine himself as sprung from distant sources. Cullen's civilized self appears to win out in the struggle for a moral identity. Using italics to emphasize the self-instruction he needs, however, he ends on a decidedly ambivalent note:

> *One thing only must I do:*
> *Quench my pride and cool my blood,*
> *Lest I perish in the flood,*
> *Lest a hidden ember set*
> *Timber that I thought was wet*
> *Burning like the driest flax,*
> *Melting like the merest wax,*
> *Lest the grave restore its dead.*
> *Not yet has my heart or head*
> *In the least way realized*
> *They and I are civilized.*

The threatening possibility that the "grave restore its dead" turns the Christian myth on its head, and that ironic twist circles around the notion that Cullen is, in fact, civilized, though these strange atavistic stirrings keep him from realizing it. Of course, most often the poem is read without a fully ironic sense, so that the "Nor yet" means that his heart and head have not "yet" realized "in the least way" their civilized status because they haven't fully achieved it.[27] At this level of semantic ambiguity the poem catches up, at a greater or lesser remove, many of the tensions that run throughout Cullen's poetry: the debate over whether or not to write in the mode of uplift; whether one's identity as a poet must be racialized; what audience, white or black, is it most proper to address. Cullen would borrow an image—"copper sun"—from the opening of "Heritage" to serve as the title of his next book of poems. The tensions would continue there.

Cullen's time at New York University was successful by virtually every measure. His classmates later remembered him as quiet but talented, easily moving among the various aspiring poets and writers as one of the few African Americans in the university. He continued his prize-winning ways when he captured the Witter Bynner Award for poetry three years running, 1923–25. The first Bynner-winning poem was called "The Ballad of the Brown Girl"; the second was "Spirit-Birth" (later retitled "The Shroud of Color"). In both of the first two years he was the second-place winner. In the third year it was the pleasure of the first-place honor that came his way, for two poems: "Heritage" and "To John Keats, Poet. At Springtime." Near the same time, the John Reed Memorial Prize, as Harriet Monroe explained in her letter, "has been awarded to you by the editorial staff of *Poetry,* because of the general quality and promise of your work, evidenced especially by your poem of last May, 'Threnody for a Brown Girl.'" The poem appeared in the May 1925 issue in *Poetry;* "To One Who Said Me Nay" appeared the same month in *Opportunity,* having taken second prize in that magazine's first literary contest. Not to be outdone, the *Crisis* awarded Cullen the Amy Spingarn Prize for "Two Moods of Love." In March he had been elected to Phi Beta Kappa, an award that he told the *Pittsburg Courier* was "an exceptionally fine one," even though he said he hadn't "set my cap for it." The accuracy of this last claim may be forgiven for programmatic modesty.

Cullen also mentioned his Phi Beta Kappa key to his new friend: Carl Van Vechten. After the two had met at the November party hosted by James Weldon Johnson, many notables had gathered at Happy Rhone's, a Harlem speakeasy that was available for rent on special occasions. Fletcher Henderson's orchestra played, and Alberta Hunter sang.[28] Such unfolding festivities were common in the period, and Van Vechten would often not arrive back home until five in the morning. At first Cullen's status as a student probably mitigated any such nocturnal carousing, and Van Vechten saw much more of Hughes and Walrond. However, Cullen was able to tell Van Vechten within a matter of months about his Phi Beta Kappa key and also the news in March of the impending publication of *Color.* Van Vechten had earlier offered to place Cullen's book with his own publisher, but Cullen demurred. Cullen instead relied on Frederick Lewis Allen, recently employed by *Harper's* magazine as an editor and unofficial agent for the publishing house of Harpers and Sons, at the annual celebration held by the Urban League. It was through Allen's effort that the young poet gained the contract for *Color.* But it would be Van

Vechten who opened up a frenetic social world for Cullen, which must have struck the college senior as altogether scintillating.

Van Vechten was perhaps at the height of his socializing frenzy, where his lavish apartment on Fifty-Fifth Street was replete with bathtub gin, Gershwin songs played by Gershwin, and nighttime gatherings of every sort of cultural and entertainment figure. But he sincerely appreciated Cullen's poetry and decided to promote its acceptance. The June 1925 issue of *Vanity Fair* featured some poems by Cullen, selected and introduced by Van Vechten, who averred, "All his poetry is characterized by a suave, unpretentious, brittle intellectual elegance." Cullen and Van Vechten often agreed on what counted as elegance, but there were differences as well. In 1925 Cullen was at times swept up in Van Vechten's all-encompassing circle, dining with him and others, like Jackman, Walrond, and Jean Toomer. In February Cullen even treated Van Vechten to a display of his talents at dancing the Charleston. On another occasion Cullen brought along Henry Liscomb, who had recently published a now-forgotten novel, *The Prince of Washington Square*. Van Vechten, however, found Liscomb too shy and remarked that he even declined to dance the Charleston.

In June Van Vechten attended a more sober party, this one to honor Reverend Cullen, where the guest list included Zora Neale Hurston, Paul Robeson, Jackman, Walter White, and Charles S. Johnson. In August, at the Renaissance Casino, *Crisis* handed out its awards for the arts, and again many of the Harlem stars attended. It was in the wake of this party that the title of Van Vechten's novel occurred to him: *Nigger Heaven*. This scandalous novel was written in short order in the first part of 1926, and though his editor didn't particularly like it, Van Vechten went on to publish it to considerable negative reaction, and some praise as well. Around this time Van Vechten was trying to sort out his judgments about the proper audience for Negro literature, prompted in part by his response to the widely noticed *Crisis* questionnaire, "The Negro in Art: How Shall He Be Portrayed?" He rather rakishly suggested that Negroes themselves had better engage literary treatment of the more racy aspects of their culture before white authors preempted them.

Trying out the new title for his novel throughout many months, with both his white and black friends, Van Vechten delighted some and offended others. He nevertheless withstood criticism and disapproval well. When it came Cullen's turn to hear the title of Van Vechten's soon-to-be-notorious novel, his opinion was far from favorable. In a diary entry for November 27, Van Vechten recorded Cullen's reaction to the proposed title: "Countée Cullen comes in & we talk about my title *Nigger Heaven.* He turns white with hurt & I talk to him."[29] Only a day later the issue returned, as Van Vechten again recorded it: "At 3 o'clock Countée Cullen came in & we had another long argument about the sensitiveness of the Negroes. He leaves at 5:30 & returns to Harvard tomorrow." When Cullen returned to New York from Harvard for the Christmas holidays, Van Vechten attended another party for Cullen, one where Paul Robeson sang and dozens of Van Vechten's friends and acquaintances celebrated; the occasion was very likely the appearance of *Color.* In any case, Cullen and Van Vechten went on as friends for the next two decades.

As casual and delightful as Van Vechten's social world may have seemed to Cullen, the young poet remained concerned about issues that the older man took up with insouciance. When a senior figure in the Renaissance, such as James Weldon Johnson, spent considerable time with Van Vechten, it could serve as an imprimatur. On the other hand, DuBois's review of *Nigger Heaven* was excoriating, as he advised his readers to throw the book into the gutter. Hughes felt the novel was amusing and defended it, although somewhat guardedly, considering how close he grew to Van Vechten. If Van Vechten had not recorded Cullen's blanching at the mention of the title, it would be hard to intuit his reaction; even now, it remains unclear what he thought of the novel beyond its title. The questions about the white readership of African American authors did not usually reach the finer points: Were the only (or main) white readers people with progressive views who would appreciate that certain "lower class" characters did not stand in for all African Americans? Was the use of Negro material by white authors just a fad that would soon pass, as some less concerned readers might think? Was Hughes's position urging a laissez-faire approach by African Americans to their own experience (a view shared to some extent by others, such as Locke and even Cullen himself) likely to bring about the best chance to produce broader and "truer" writing? Was the social mixing of black and white individuals in the settings dominated by people like Van Vechten a necessary step in opening larger audiences for more various representations of African American experience and values? The *Crisis* symposium offered no clear consensus on such issues, and in his ambivalence Cullen might have been more representative of such experience and values than some of his contemporaries.

In the midst of these social flurries and accolades the intermingled questions of race and art appeared with profound force. Interviewed by Margaret Sperry for a newspaper article, Cullen confronted the intermingling with a series of remarks that forecast many of the struggles and contradictions he would face for decades:

> If I am going to be a poet at all, Mr. Cullen began, "I am going to be POET and not NEGRO POET. That is what has hindered the development of artists among us. Their one note has been their concern with their race. That is all very well, none of us can get away from it. I cannot at times. You will see it in my verse. The consciousness of this is too poignant at times. I cannot escape it. But what I mean is this: I shall not write of negro [sic] subjects for the purpose of propaganda. That is not what a poet is concerned with. Of course when the emotion rising out of the fact that I am a negro [sic] is strong, I express it. But that is another matter.[30]

The remarkable shift in tones here conveys much of Cullen's deepest sense of his race and his aesthetic: moving from the very firm (those capital letters), to a bit of insouciance ("That is all very well"), to reserved bitterness ("too poignant at times"), to a final reserve that sounds almost haughty ("that is another matter"). Cullen was only twenty years old when he gave this interview.

In "The Shroud of Color" he had poeticized and allegorized the "hurts," and many of the poems in his first volume were on the subject of race, especially "Heritage" and "Incident," which would become his most frequently anthologized lyrics and touchstones of African American poetry. The first of these poems confronted the racial origins of African Americans, asking "What is Africa to me?" It ends with something like a boast and a burden:

> Nor yet has my heart or head
> In the least way realized
> They and I are civilized.

The second tells of a racial insult suffered at the hands of a young boy. It ends,

> I saw the whole of Baltimore
> From May to December;
> Of all the things that happened there
> That's all that I remember.

Both poems tell of the persistence of racial questions, and the way that persistence becomes a chief factor in one's consciousness; however, one relies on mythic material and the other on personal experience. Clearly Cullen wanted to address the subject in both kinds of discourse.

All of the prizes and the public notice eventually reached a critical mass and so brought about one of the major events in Cullen's life, the publication in 1925 of *Color* by Harper's, a major "white" publisher. The book contained over seventy poems and was reviewed by more than forty magazines and newspapers. Seven New York City papers reviewed it, as did black newspapers in Pittsburg, Nashville, and Los Angeles. Shortly after he graduated Cullen was given one of the most prestigious recognitions of all: the Harmon Award in Literature, which carried a prize of four hundred dollars and a gold medal. George Haynes, the Race Relations Secretary for the Federal Council of Churches, had administered the contest. The summer after graduation from NYU also bought new delight when his portrait, by Winold Reiss, graced the cover of the July 1925 issue of *Opportunity*. The pleasures were compounded in August, as W. E. B. DuBois notified Cullen that he had won the Spingarn Prize of fifty dollars, sponsored by *Crisis* and named after the wife of one of the founders of the NAACP. Meanwhile, the reverend must have rejoiced at Cullen's admission to Harvard University. Cullen confessed to Harriet Monroe that it was indeed the reverend's insistence that made him pursue the advanced degree, even as he told her that he would balk before going for a PhD.[31] Harvard would prove a solid bridge to further education, and the pleasures of Cambridge somewhat surprisingly worked to broaden his social efforts as well.

3

The Renaissance and Its Issues, 1926–1927

By the time 1926 arrived just about everyone agreed there was a New Negro Renaissance in full flower. Until then many sporadic gestures helped formulate the term and enliven the spirit. Ranging from an anthology published in 1900 that contained Booker T. Washington's essay, called "The New Negro for a New Century," to *The New Negro* (1925), the collection of writing in various genres edited and introduced by Alain Locke: the milestones were being carved, it seemed, day and night. Years later some even suggested that the appearance of Cullen's *Color,* at the end of 1925, was the sure harbinger of much that followed. Cullen himself, finishing his year's work on a master of arts degree at Harvard at the end of the spring 1926 term, pointed out that "the new movement in Negro literature is certainly being hogged by the young people." This signaled that generational authority was at stake. Slowly, an African American readership was developing, and white readers and publishers eagerly took notice. Within a few short years the Renaissance gathered considerable momentum and was being not only touted but reflected upon by senior spokesmen. One of these was Wal-

ter White, whose novel *The Fire in the Flint* was a part of the literary productivity. In *The Negro's Contribution to American Culture* (1928), with its
aggressive subtitle, *The Sudden Flowering of a Genius-Laden Artistic Movement,* he assessed the state of the culture:

> one runs no risk of overstatement in saying that there is nothing which
> is doing more to change the stereotyped American concept of the Negro
> as a buffoon or criminal or childlike and subservient "befo' de wah" type
> than the work which Negro writers, painters, singers, actors and ac-
> tresses are doing. Where one's environment has led him to harbor preju-
> dices which no amount of reasoning can change, often those preconcep-
> tions have been swept away under the magnificent beauty of the voices
> of . . . Roland Hayes or Paul Robeson, or the frequently gifted lines of
> Negro poets such as Countée Cullen, James Weldon Johnson or Langs-
> ton Hughes.[1]

There was also talk of the time being ripe for support for a Negro novel,
and though Cullen decided not to join the competition just yet, he wondered who would be the winner: Jessie Fauset, Walter White, or Eric Walrond.[2] Meanwhile, his own ambition and the temper of the times melded
into the forces that would keep him highly recognized as a poet.

At Harvard the academic year 1925–26 held many gratifying encoun-
ters for Cullen, especially in the spring semester. Like Alain Locke two
decades before him, he arrived at Harvard with a sterling academic record and bearing some of the responsibility for the "talented tenth," Du-
Bois's famous phrase delineating the African American leaders of progressive forces. Though aware of carrying the hopes and aspirations of
many African Americans with him, Cullen more than balanced his academic pursuits with some considerable pleasures. Even before beginning
classes, he wrote to Jackman about the texture of life as he was to enjoy
it for the next nine months.

> This letter is for your private consumption, inasmuch as it may contain
> confessions and descriptions of things that might not be approved by
> more orthodox minds. In the first place, I slept in silk pajamas last night.
> Talk of the thrill that comes only once in a life time, that was one; taffy-
> colored silk pajamas. You see, one of our brothers gave a small party to

celebrate my coming to Cambridge, and the celebration was so strenuous and so lasting that it was out of the question for me to think of going back to my rooms. Hence, the silk pajamas. And a splitting headache all this blessed day. Now, don't you get the idea that I am up here running wild; fact is, classes don't begin for me until Friday.

The reference to the "brothers" meant the national black fraternity, Alpha Phi Alpha, which Cullen and Jackman belonged to at NYU and which Cullen tried to get Hughes to join when he enrolled in Lincoln University. This was Cullen's first extended time away from the strictures of the reverend's home, but he had, not only his fraternity ties to ease the transition, but also his place in the web of academic affiliations.

Cullen's favorite teacher from New York University, Hyder Rollins, was in the process of moving from New York University to Harvard, but he took courses with a number of other professors instead. There was a course in "English and Scottish Popular Ballads" from George Lyman Kittredge, a legendary teacher who helped define the field of ballad studies and was himself the teacher of Rollins. In his last year at New York University, Cullen received a gracious letter from Kittredge praising him for his use of the ballad form in his prize-winning "The Ballad of a Brown Girl." Bliss Perry, another Harvard luminary, taught Cullen the ins and outs of the "English Critical Essay," while Irving Babbitt offered the "English Romantic Movement." Robert Hillyer, an established poet, offered a course in poetry writing in which Cullen labored, and he eventually befriended Hillyer, who at first was not altogether impressed with the young man's talent. Frederick Lewis Allen, Cullen's editor at Harper's, tried to arrange for Cullen to take a course with "Copey," Charles T. Copeland, the Bolyston Professor of Rhetoric and Oratory, but it seems not to have happened. The combined force of these professors, most of them widely recognized as experts in their field and all active as scholars and writers, further reinforced the literary values of Cullen's education. While reviewers and critics routinely noticed the influence of poets like Keats and Millay when commenting on Cullen's poetry, the deep effect of his Harvard teachers has been somewhat slighted. Even when an old friend reported many years later that Cullen had complained of the "stuffy atmosphere" in Cambridge, the gathered force of his year as a masters-level student is hard to overestimate.[3] The experience lasted only nine months, but it intensified and extended Cullen's sense of tradition, especially in a genteel and even Anglophilic tone.

The twenty-two-year-old poet meanwhile wasted little time in adapting to an energetic social schedule. Many evenings featured parties with his fraternity brothers at Alpha Phi Alpha, most of whom were eager and capable of arranging female companionship for him. At one dance, quick to display his skill moving to "the most tantalizing music," he had to sit out most of the evening—"like a Knight of the old order"—because his companion sprained her ankle at the start of the festivities. He was invited on several occasions to dine with William Stanley Braithwaite, who for many years had been the book reviewer for the *Boston Evening Transcript*. Braithwaite was very well known among African American writers, so much so that even the young Cullen had written to him as early as 1921: "For the past four years your anthologies have inspired me and my greatest ambition is that someday I shall have a poem worthy of a place in them."[4] At the same time, some of Braithwaite's contemporaries, and the younger writers, faulted him for contending that race should not play a large part in the writing and comprehension of poetry, if any. However, he won the NAACP's Arthur P. Spingarn Award in 1919 for his contributions to literature. His annual anthologies of poems were his singular contributions, collections that brought him to the attention of readers far beyond Boston. After the Depression reduced his means considerably, he took a teaching job at Atlanta University and there for the first time experienced segregation in the South, and he subsequently became more forthright and activist on racial matters. In 1925 he mentioned Cullen in his annual "Yearbook" of American poetry, calling him "an intensely racial singer." The young poet returned the favor when, soon after arriving in Cambridge, he asked Braithwaite to contribute to the special issue of *Palms*, a well-regarded poetry magazine published in Mexico, that he was to edit.[5] Cullen also demonstrated his feeling for the older man's guidance and support when he dedicated his anthology *Caroling Dusk* to him. The two men shared a belief that confrontation and the depiction of disreputable or decadent characters only worsened interracial relations. But at the same time they both held somewhat nuanced views about race and art, wishing to use cultural expression and aesthetic values to improve such relations, without going so far as to preach merely the need for racial "uplift."[6]

Being wined and dined in grand Boston fashion, Cullen found Braithwaite's supply of wine "prodigious," and the entire Braithwaite family
treated him royally. A chance for the young poet to meet the older man's
firstborn child, Fiona, added to the feeling of being cosseted. In fact he
was "subjugated," as he put it. Fiona was just the type that interested
him, "slender, dark, a bit foreign looking, with a thin ascetic face." But
he told Jackman, "I fear my trials are harder than yours, for my passion
is not concentrated, but divided between Miss Sydonia Byrd and Miss
Fiona Braithwaite," adding that he felt like a "sheik" for the first time in
his life.[7] Relations went along warmly for several weeks. He celebrated
his birthday at the end of May with Fiona and her sister, whose birthday
was the same as his. The Braithwaites graced him with books, and he also
got a telegram from Carl Van Vechten and a number of cards. By early
spring he could tell Jackman that "I sincerely believe I am really in love at
last," but teasingly didn't mention with whom, though he seems to have
meant Fiona. The end of May apparently brought the revelation: "Fiona
is a darling and sends her love to the future *best man*." However, things
were not completely clear; his choice wasn't Fiona, but rather Yolande.
At the beginning of June he commissioned Jackman, who was to visit
Baltimore, to "run by to see Yolande," but added a diplomatic burden:
"Don't mention Fiona to her." Though he had on more than one occasion voiced his displeasure over Yolande's behavior with her male companions, he had no desire to complicate the matter. Jealousy ran in both
directions between the two. So while he may have enjoyed the attentions
of Fiona—and was delighted that she and Yolande were daughters of
well-known writers—his commitment slowly turned to Yolande.

In February Jackman wrote to Cullen about his, Jackman's, having
fallen in love, though as only Cullen's response survives it is not possible
to know if it was with a man or woman. In any case, Cullen was quick
to offer sympathy and support. "You must not worry," Cullen advised,
"I passed through a stage that has all the ear-marks of that described
by you. . . . My philosophy of life is hardly the same from day to day."
Their postadolescent confusions served as one of the common experiences that drew the two men together. It was hard to be certain, even
of one's own feelings, in "a world as strange and shifting as this," Cullen
lamented. He was on occasion not completely clear about his feelings
when an attentive woman was involved. One instance of this was his

friendship with Ruth Marie Thomas, a woman his own age who came to
know him in Pleasantville and kept up a correspondence for a number of
years. As Cullen went off to Harvard, he received a letter from Thomas,
then working as a teacher at Hartshorn College in Richmond, Virginia.[8]
She inquired about his poetry and praised her copy of *Color,* saying that
all her fellow teachers were "most enthusiastic over it." After Cullen took
the editing job at *Opportunity,* their correspondence continued, with her
complaining that his letters were always too short. He dedicated "Sonnet to a Scornful Lady" to her and would include it in *Copper Sun.* In
this rather stilted poem, laden with medieval and courtly imagery, the
speaker is "a suppliant on gory knees," whose requests to the lady are
met with scorn. "Lean with my passion's hunger, I / Lay bare the bruises
of my heart," the poet cries, even as the lady melodramatically refuses to
spare his life. It is one of the last poems in which Cullen employs such
excessively archaic language and incidents, as if he'd become conscious
of how ineffective it is in conveying his present-day emotional states.
In 1926, Thomas moved to Lawrenceville, Virginia, after taking a job at
St. Paul's School there, and urged Cullen to come and visit her over the
Christmas break. "There are so many things going on in Harlem," she
said, adding that a class she was taking in "Negro Literature" was using
The New Negro as the textbook.

In his first days at Harvard, Cullen had written to Thomas, mentioning that he was in love with someone, thus strengthening the supposi-
tion it was with Yolande, as he had not yet met Fiona. Yet Thomas remained persistent: "Even if you are in love, do you think it necessary to
forget an old friend?" She also has access to Harlem gossip and took a
certain delight in coyly relating the news about his relationships. "Someone who has been spending the winter in N.Y. says that you have been
showering poetry on a little damsel. Go to, Countée," she teased. Eventually Cullen needed to confess that he was engaged to Yolande. Thomas
wasn't able to remain completely placid; "To be unaware of your engagement might have caused me much embarrassment. . . . I did deserve the
whole truth." Despite this ungentlemanly incident, the two continued
to write back and forth, though with less frequency and fewer warm
feelings. Four years later Thomas was teaching at Wilberforce College in
Ohio and took a moment to characterize Cullen, perhaps with more than
a touch of frustration about his reticence: "You take things in, never

say a word, and then later one receives a surprise." Still, years later, she would see him briefly in New York in 1944 and graciously referred to him as "the same old friend."

Such confusion extended beyond affairs of the heart. Cullen, despite treating him as a friend and fellow poet, had become wary about the growing reputation of Langston Hughes and needed Jackman to reassure him. Hughes, and the discussion and friendship from the previous year, remained very much on Cullen's mind. Referring to a poetry reading of Hughes's that Jackman had recently attended, he asked, "Has he [Hughes] platform presence, and were the poems well received? I understand he is going to Lincoln University. Does that mean *colored* Lincoln?" Anxiety found many other objects as well. Jackman's taste and aesthetic refinement helped provide an anchor. Cullen praised his friend, saying, "through you music comes to have the fine meaning I now find in it." There was also the unburdening in relation to religious belief and its felt obligations. "I went to Chapel yesterday morning (I go every Sunday, being, sometimes, I fear, more of a model son than is good for me.)" Clearly, social pressures to conform and excel were at work on several fronts, and they led to any number of resolutions, the kind a "model son" would adopt.

It was not a simple case of absence making the heart grow fonder, but the letters back and forth between Cambridge and Baltimore drew their own bonds between Cullen and Yolande. They became formally engaged that spring of 1927, perhaps during a trip he made to Baltimore the first week in May, but declined to tell many people, even though they had already settled on Jackman as the best man. Yolande's appearance was markedly different from Fiona's, but apparently the separation— with Yolande in Baltimore teaching and Cullen in Cambridge studying— had given them both the freedom to be more open about their feelings. They seemed at least implicitly aware of how their marriage would be the cynosure for many in Harlem and beyond. DuBois himself visited his daughter in Baltimore in early June, and that may have been when she explained her plans. Yolande was delighted, but also a bit scared that Cullen had already told his mother of the engagement; "I still fear her disapproval," the nervous Yolande admitted. But the next twenty months or so would see a flurry of furniture buying, parties with the future bridesmaids, and various entanglements with the African American press over

10. Yolande DuBois, in cap and gown. She graduated from Fisk University in 1926.

when to release the news. Briefly, in the spring of 1927, there was talk about a wedding as early as Christmas of that year, but eventually an April 1928 date was chosen. It was a relatively long engagement, and there were indications all along the way that, despite much affection, the two had temperamental differences.

Meanwhile, Cullen was alternately basking in the pleasure and renown that the reception of *Color* had brought him and anxiously looking for reviews and new chances. He had been asked to edit a special "Negro Poets" issue of *Palms,* the small magazine run by Idella Parnell and coedited by Witter Bynner. Many special favors were called for in order to enrich the issue: he asked Locke, for example, to write a review of Hughes's *The Weary Blues* from page proofs, as the book wouldn't appear until after the special issue. He also wanted to include some of Locke's own poems, but the professor demurred. There was also a contract, signed in December 1926, for Cullen to edit an anthology for Harper's, and he was hard at work on it. This would be *Caroling Dusk,* a collection devoted to African American poets that appeared late in 1927. He mentioned to Yolande that he was contemplating taking a PhD in French, but he obviously changed his mind, and the question of a vocation jostled with that of seeking a position. He made plans to take the New York Public School's competency test for high school teachers, even though he had no immediate plans to teach. Back in 1924, however, in his interview with Margaret Sperry, he expressed his desire at the time: "I shall teach literature if I can. I prefer to stay in New York. Here I can see things. Be with people who know a little of what I am trying to do." He asked Jackman to nominate him for the Harmon Award in literature, explaining that he needed to send along a copy of *Color* and some early reviews to bolster his chances. His thoughts were turning homeward; "After June I will be a New Yorker once more," he said, having clearly ruled out any plans to attain a doctorate. The elaborate dinner held in May by the Urban League, for which he had made a special trip down, left him feeling like a "prima donna," with all the "handshakes and gushing." It may also have been at this time that an appointment for him as assistant editor at *Opportunity* was first broached. But he told Jackman that that sort of thing "really touches me to the quick . . . I fairly revel in public commendation." Going even further, he added that he was "perhaps the one living poet who will confess that he doesn't write for *his own amusement,* and that what others think of his work can affect him." His sense of social obligations, learned from the religiosity of his father and reinforced by his own specific aesthetic commitments, gathered strength throughout his life. A commending public had noticed him early, and the habit was formed.

No matter how proper Cullen's behavior, he was bound to encounter situations that would test his sense of propriety. One such occurred when he went to Baltimore in the spring of 1926 to give a reading of his poems at the Baltimore City Club, with all of the advance arrangements handled by a Miss Mildred Smith from the speakers' bureau at which

Cullen was listed. Having discovered that Cullen was black, the leading members of the club refused to allow him to appear as scheduled. The incident caused an uproar and attracted the attention of many, most notably H. L. Mencken, the famous Baltimore writer and journalist. Cullen first came to Mencken's notice a few years earlier when he accepted "The Shroud of Color" for publication in the *American Mercury*, even having suggested the title to Cullen. Once he became aware of this discrimination, he decided to make it thoroughly public, and wrote to Cullen: "I had to leave Baltimore immediately after the story of your adventure with the City Club came out and the Baltimore Sun appears to have followed the story very inadequately. Will you please tell me exactly what happened? Had you any notice from the City Club and what was the story they told you? I want to print all the facts in The Evening Sun." Cullen responded in detail:

> I was invited to come to Baltimore to read my poems before the Baltimore City Club on Saturday afternoon April 24. . . . I wrote Rabbi Lazaron telling him I would be in Richmond prior to coming to Baltimore and so could not give him a Baltimore address. He replied that he would be engaged at the Synagogue on April 24 until twelve o'clock, and that I should proceed direct to the Hotel Emerson where he would meet me a little before twelve-thirty. . . . On my arrival at the Hotel Emerson, I asked an official who seemed to be the manager . . . to locate Rabbi Lazaron for me. . . . After having waited for a rather embarrassing ten minutes, I was waited on by the President of the Baltimore City Club and two of the club members, who informed me that when the management of the Hotel Emerson had learned that I was colored, they had refused to allow the City Club to have me read to them. The gentlemen said they had telegraphed Miss Smith asking her to cancel her [*sic*] my engagement, but she did not know where to locate me in Richmond. . . . The three members of the City Club also told me that they had tried other hotels and even a theatre in Baltimore, but apparently there was no place in the city in which a Negro poet might give a reading. The City Club paid the fee agreed on for the meeting.[9]

Because of Mencken's making the facts known, many other newspapers around the eastern part of the country also reported on what happened.

Ironically, Cullen's famous poem, "Incident," about a racial insult, was also set in Baltimore, but written, of course, several years before the denial by the City Club. The denial was likely behind Cullen's subsequent decision to seek a different speakers' bureau, one that would be known as having African American clients.

Other forms of public notice were clearly more pleasurable. New dimensions of his public fame and commendation opened in the field of music. A composer named Emerson Whithorne, well established in the impressionist tradition, had composed a suite using eight of Cullen's poems—the first of several musical settings of his poetry by various composers. Cullen wrote to William Brown to describe the premiere.

> Eight of the poems have been set to music in a rather startling manner by a young New York composer, Emerson Whithorne. The group is called Saturday's Child, and was given its premier in New York on March 13.
> I went down to attend a moment of such grave import to the world, and was quite thrilled by a house at Town Hall which called Poet! Poet! along with cries for the composer. The composer was most generous in allowing me to share his honors. I am still hoping that some day you and I will have a song out.[10]

Before this performance, Whithorne advanced the idea that each time the piece was played the texts of the poems should be included on the printed program. Cullen again enlisted Jackman as a go-between and instructed him to ask Harper's if such an arrangement were acceptable. The answer came back negative. After a number of pleas and approaches, Harper's consented, but with one condition: the poems must clearly be labeled as under the copyright of Harper's. Cullen felt instinctively that the whole idea was a boon to the publicity for the book. Whithorne also wanted to have the exclusive musical rights to the poems lest another composer try to outdo him. The program for the premiere finally included the poems. An especially vivid account of Cullen's reaction to the premiere was contained in a short notice of the concert, by Charles S. Johnson, which he published in *Opportunity*. The piece had quite knocked him out, he told Cullen, and said his first description of the concert was too sentimental and had to be revised. This is how it appeared in print:

When it was whispered that the poet was in the audience there was an immense curiosity. He sat with his father and two friends quietly and with the evident hope of escaping observation. There were demands for his presence on the stage. It was apparently the first knowledge for most of the audience that these lines which they had been following in a rapt delight had been penned by a Negro youth. The applause mounted gallantly as Cullen bowed quickly at the foot of the stage and ran off again to his seat, and it continued at an enthusiastic pitch for several minutes. It was an unexpected and magnificent triumph.[11]

Cullen, a bit later watching for all notices of his work, mused to Jackman that he wondered, "how Paris liked Emerson Whithorne's child," alluding to the European premiere. Throughout the Renaissance and beyond the lyrical quality of Cullen's gift readily lent his work to musical adaptation.[12] Performances of these compositions expanded and refined public appreciation for Cullen, adding to the polished and elite aura of his poetry.

Theatergoing attracted him from the beginning, and he continued attending plays with Jackman and Hughes. He informed Jackman that he was planning a trip to New York during the Easter break and wanted very much to see *Lulu Belle,* which was the latest hit at the Belasco Theater. Written by Charles MacArthur and Edward Shelden, the latter a Harvard graduate from the same class as Alain Locke, the melodrama told a story about a young Negro prostitute in Harlem. Loosely adapted from a series of plays by the German dramatist Frank Wedekind, the character of Lulu became a symbol of modernist sexual angst. The actress who played the title role did so in blackface, and this led to protests by various African American groups. Cullen didn't record his assessment of the play, but he may have been drawn in part to its realism even as he rejected its use of stereotypes. From another direction his attention was consumed by reading *Thunder on the Left,* the recently published novel by Christopher Morley. Asking Jackman if he had read the novel, he barked, "If not do [so] at once." The title referred to the myth that when thunder occurs from the left the gods have an important announcement. As for the novel's plot, it involved a fantasy in which young boys meet their older selves and discover that adulthood is a treacherous and unhappy condition. A year earlier Yolande had told him, "to an extent you're still a boy"—adding, "that is a compliment." For all the precocious talent he exhibited, Cullen—whose tendency to be slightly overweight melded with his pleasant joviality—remained boyish in manner and outlook, a feature often remarked on by his friends.

Other, more public compliments were coming his way. Back in 1923 Locke had written an article about Cullen's poetry, but he was now prepared to give a full-bodied review of *Color*. There had, however, been a brief period of alienation—the first few months of 1925—because Cullen had gone around Locke to request payment from the *Survey Graphic* for his poems that were set to appear in *The New Negro*. The misunderstanding came at a bad time, as Cullen fretted over his first book, and he was eager to mend things. "Should you persist in your determination," he told Locke, "at any rate the break will not be mutual. I still consider myself your friend." Within a matter of several weeks good relations were restored. Locke faced some uncertain days at this time, having been fired from his position at Howard by a vengeful college president. Many people rallied to Locke's aid, and voices like those of DuBois and Franz Boaz were raised on his behalf. Cullen, too, wanted Locke to know what he thought of the situation.

> There is no accounting for the rank ingratitude and stupidity of some
> people, and I am sure most of your friends feel as I do, that all the loss
> is Howard's, and hope as I do that this is a reestablishment of things
> as they ought to be for your good. This world is more of a hell than my
> worst moments have conceived it if there are not open arms for you the
> country through. And I am hoping my hardest that New York City will
> get you. You have done great things, but I think Howard and Washing-
> ton were bushels hiding the absolute splendor of your light.
>
>   Now you can shine!

Eventually Locke was rehired and went on to teach at Howard for almost three more decades. For that long period Locke would remain one of Cullen's strongest backers and most reliable confidants.

For the best placement of his review of *Color*, Locke turned to a friend, Charles S. Johnson, who had featured the philosopher and critic in many recent articles on a wide range of subjects in the magazine sponsored by the National Urban League. Here is the way Locke described the new book in the January 1926 issue of *Opportunity:*

Ladies and gentlemen! A genius! Posterity will laugh at us if we do not proclaim him now. *Color* transcends all the limiting qualifications that might be brought forward if it were merely a work of talent. It is a first book, but it would be treasurable if it were the last; it is a work of extreme youth and youthfulness over which the author later may care to write the apology of "juvenilia," but it has already the integration of a distinctive and matured style. . . . the work of a Negro poet writing for the most part out of the intimate emotional experience of race, but the adjective is for the first time made irrelevant, so thoroughly has he . . . fused it with the universally human moods of life.

Locke's rhetorical flourishes—and there were more to come—try to establish a delicate balance on the issue of whether or not there can be a racial art and what would it look and sound like. This leads him to a paradox, a particular form of rhetorical balance that was an especial favorite of his: Cullen is a Negro poet, but the adjective is unnecessary because the poetry attains a universal dimension. This aesthetic—and by extension, this political—claim is buttressed by the additional notion, complete with rhetorical flourishes, that Cullen's gift is a very hardy plant, one that can survive the crassness and bruises of modern life.

The authentic lyric gift is rare today for another reason than the rarity of poetic genius, and especially so in contemporary American poetry—for the substance of modern life brings a heavy sediment not easy to filter out in the poetic process. Only a few can distill a clear flowing product, Housman, de la Mare, Sara Teasdale, Edna St. Vincent Millay, one or two more perhaps. . . . Cullen . . . has grown in sandier soil and taken up a murkier substance; it has taken a longer taproot to reach down to the deep tradition upon which great English poetry is nourished, and the achievement is notable. More than a personal temperament flowers, a race experience blooms . . . the seeds of a new stock, richly parented by two cultures. It is no disparagement to our earlier Negro poets to say this: men do not choose their time, and time is the gardener.

Cullen was doubtlessly pleased with such an enthusiastic review; he sent Locke a postcard from Wisconsin, where he had gone on a midwestern reading tour, and said, "What a review of *Color*—and what a glorious bit of writing! Bless you for it!" The elevated level of the praise, but also the rhetorical flourishes, implicitly spelled out Cullen's own resolution of the problems of race and art, at least for the moment.

A less formal, but no less resounding, response to *Color* came from a source that may have surprised Cullen, and certainly delighted him: Eric Walrond. A short-story writer and journalist, Walrond knew Cullen as early as 1924. Five years older than Cullen, the two took a car trip together, along with Jackman and another friend, in September of that year. Cullen wrote to Locke about what he described as forwardness in Walrond's attitude that suggests an erotic attraction: "Eric Walrond, Harold Jackman, Wm. Thompson and I recently motored to Boston. The trip was a revelation so far as Eric is concerned. He was most surprisingly sympathetic, and aggressive, but I am afraid he offers no lasting solution; he is too exacting (I almost said abandoned) and there are some concessions I shall never make."[13] Eventually, the two men would be employed at the offices of *Opportunity*, with Walrond serving as the journal's business manager. More than willing to ruffle feathers, he published a very negative review of Fauset's *There Is Confusion*, which brought the protective wrath of several writers onto his head.[14] At the end of 1925 Cullen had asked Walrond to do a review of *The New Negro* for the special issue of *Palms*, but Walrond declined, feeling it inappropriate for him as a contributor to Locke's anthology to pass judgment on it. Almost as soon as *Color* appeared, and while Cullen was still settling in at Harvard, he received a letter from Walrond. He was about to publish ten of his short stories, under the title *Tropic Death* (1926), with Boni and Liveright. Born in British Guyana, he achieved notice and support, especially from Charles S. Johnson, in his chronicling of Caribbean immigrants. In the late 1920s he emigrated to Europe, supported by a Guggenheim Fellowship granted for the same year as Cullen's, and then lingered for a while in Paris, writing about Harlem figures. Later he settled in London, where he married twice and had a family of three daughters. He published little in America beyond *Tropic Death*.

Cullen would often dedicate one of his poems to a close friend. He chose one of the most famous, "Incident," to dedicate to Walrond, and the gesture was deeply appreciated: "I was entirely unprepared for the shock I experienced upon seeing the dedication." Walrond described Cullen's first book as possessing a "regally measured charm . . . which I have yet to find in another Negro poet." The praise mounted, as Walrond continued, "Your words are fraught with a high meaning; there is beauty and magnificence in the sentiment motivating them." He even offered an aesthetic theory, similar to Locke's and very close to Cullen's own. "The ideal which I have secretly held about Negro writing [is]: utilizing material in its very essence virginal the black poet or prose artist should, I think, fuse [it] . . . into drama via the avenue of the classical tradition." He then suggests Fauset has some of this, but her material is "too glaringly that of the school marm," and Jean Toomer relies too much "on the tricks and grimaces of the expressionistic gentry." Briefly characterizing McKay and Hughes, he contrastively says that Cullen is "shy of the obvious," but "without being obscure." He closes the letter, which sparkles with wit and feeling, by happily listing his own stories that are out or about to appear in the *New Age* and *Vanity Fair.*

Cullen also enjoyed seeing his first book reviewed in the April 1926 issue of *Poetry* (Chicago), the preeminent journal of the time as far as the audience for serious verse was concerned. The editor assigned the book to George Dillon, who relished what Cullen had produced. Dillon, just three years younger than Cullen, would a decade later become the editor of *Poetry* and the lover of Millay, while winning a Guggenheim Fellowship and a Pulitzer Prize along the way. This suggests that he was in many ways the voice of the official taste in poetry. Though the review contains some qualifications, its praise is considered and full of positive anticipation: "One feels that he will cultivate his fine talent with intelligence, and reap its full harvest." Commending Cullen for being "most winning when he is most spare and direct," he singles out one complete poem, "The Wise," as "very nearly . . . perfect." The poem represents Cullen at his most late romantic, at least half in love with easeful death, as he admires those who are entombed, ending with these lines:

> Strange, men should flee their company,
> Or think me strange who long to be
> Wrapped in their cool immunity.

The immunity can be seen—and felt—as an analog for aesthetic distance, and Dillon felt Cullen "achieves great intensity with an almost colloquial style." The review goes on to barely raise the issue of race and then immediately puts it aside as "hardly relevant here." Cullen must have felt he had found a sympathetic and discriminating ear and so knew that he could use the traditional tropes and sentiments in a way that would garner him particular praise.

Not all of Cullen's reviews sparkled like the ones by Locke, Walrond, and Dillon. He told Jackman that the first review he saw of it was in the *Harvard Book Shelf*, and "it let me down hard," since the reviewer proclaimed that "he often sacrifices sense to rhyme," his "meter often halts," and "he has a death complex." Still, Herbert Gorman, in the much more widely read *New York Times*, was very impressed. "Mr. Cullen is race conscious and many of his poems are imbued with a somewhat bitter note, but they are all lifted by that indefinable thing we call poetry. There is much that is arresting here, love poems that are sensitive and compelling and faint satire that is unmistakably piercing. Here is a poet to be watched." Mark Van Doren had his rather gnomic say in the *New York Herald Tribune:* "If Mr. Cullen faces any danger it is this—that he shall call facility a virtue rather than the aspect of a virtue." Walter White praised the book in the *Saturday Review of Literature,* then a widely circulated journal, giving Cullen credit for an "inestimably precious faculty of imprisoning in a line of acid brevity and compactness the complete philosophy of an individual, a group, or a race." Babette Deutsch, in the *Nation,* struck a note that would have pleased Cullen, arguing that "the color of his mind is more important than the color of his skin."

Generally positive reviews came in from all over: Canton, Ohio; Salt Lake City; Sacramento; and Boston.[15] It was, however, up to the erratic Wallace Thurman to complicate the picture. Though he didn't review *Color* by itself, he did take notice of Cullen's work by including him in an article in a national magazine.[16] This was "Negro Artists and the Negro," and it was like a late-night bulletin on the Harlem Renaissance, written with the sardonic tone Thurman had mastered. The thoroughgoing tone of mockery anticipated the blanketing satire of *Infants of the Spring,* the roman à clef on which his reputation would largely rest. "Everyone was having a grand time. The millennium was about to dawn. Then the excitement began to die down and Negroes as well as whites began to take stock of that in which they had reveled." He saved his comments on Cullen until the end of the article, which suggested that he placed him relatively high on the emerging list of important African American poets.

Color, a volume of verses by Countée Cullen, was . . . also conventional in theme and manner. True, Mr. Cullen was possessed by a youthful exuberance that occasionally flamed with sensual passion, but for the most part he was the conventional Negro literateur in all respects save that he had more talent than most of his predecessors. . . . And since Mr. Cullen, unlike his contemporary, Mr. Hughes, has not and never will seek the so-called lower elements of Negro life . . . he will probably remain endeared to both bourgeois black America and sentimental white America, more because of this attitude than because of his undisputed talent or his intense spiritual sensitivity.

By mixing issues of class and race, Thurman opened up yet another ground of intermingled values and attitudes that probably did not please Cullen. What would make the case even harder to tolerate is that Thurman had seen fit to compose yet another summary view of the Renaissance, this time for a black readership.[17] Less than a month later there appeared "Nephews of Uncle Remus," where Thurman gave freer rein to his sardonic approach. Cullen again came near the end of the piece, but Thurman was in no mood to balance his assessments. "Mr. Cullen can say things beautifully and impressively, [but] he really has nothing new to say, nor no new way in which to say it. . . . His poetry is not an escape from life in the big sense, but from the narrow world in which he has been caged, and from which he seems to have made no great effort to escape." Thurman does utter some pat phrases about how Cullen "has more talent that any of his contemporaries," but the spirit of the review seems especially unfair since Thurman names no poem nor cites a single line of Cullen's verse. Though many friendships were formed and flourished among writers during the Renaissance, there was also a full platter of negative estimations, less than scrupulously presented.

First Trip to Europe

Cullen somewhat sheepishly decided to skip the graduation exercises at Harvard in June 1926, perhaps because he had already heard about one of his more unexpected pleasures. The reverend had served the Salem Methodist Episcopal church for twenty-five years, and as a gift to mark the occasion, the congregants had purchased two tickets for a trip to the

Holy Land. Mrs. Cullen disliked travel, especially over water, and so the question of who would use the other ticket was soon decided. People had thought at least since the eighteenth century, with its Grand Tour, that the best capstone for serious study was international travel. So quite by happenstance Cullen was offered the rare opportunity for his own grand tour.[18] By the first week in July 1926 he was on board the steamer to Europe. Alain Locke was booked on the same ship, though soon after landing at Le Havre he would go on to Germany, his favorite summer location. First, however, he would offer "indispensable" help to the Cullens when they arrived in Paris. Reporting to Jackman from onboard that "nothing exciting has happened yet," Cullen soon realized that would change. They would enjoy two days in Paris, then go along the Mediterranean—a "marvelous sea, tranquil and beautiful in a way that shys [sic] at description"—to Cairo, on to Beirut, then by car to Palestine for eight to ten days, and so back to Paris by way of Italy, Switzerland, and Germany. Brief stops in Naples, Genoa, Florence, and Rome filled the schedule.

The first stop in Europe produced such excitement that Cullen could not contain himself. As the Reverend Cullen recorded in his diary for July 9, 1926, Cullen joined Locke, Dorothy Peterson, and Arthur Fauset in disembarking from the ship in Le Havre, after paying the steward to let them do it. While the reverend—who had proclaimed the city "the most beautiful port of France"—stayed on board, the party spent the whole day and a good part of the evening seeing what they could in the humming port city. More excitement followed. The next day the travelers arrived in Paris at three in the afternoon, having gone by train from the port to the capital, watching as the "scenery alternated with cities and farms along the way." Cullen went with his father, Locke, and Peterson to enjoy the first bout of sightseeing, taking in the Champs Elysées and the Bois De Boulogne before returning to their hotel. After another two days of visiting all the major monuments, father and son went off to the American Express office and picked up their tickets for Marseille, from whence they departed to Beirut on the fourteenth. The reverend took note of their first sight of the "great blue Mediterranean" and remarked that they "sailed over the place where Jonah was swallowed by the whale."

Cullen wished intensely that Jackman could have traveled with him, saying that he would miss him more and more as he traveled into "strange lands." As for Cairo, where he had a room in Cecil House, he could argue, faint from the heat, that "the best earthly site for hell . . . would be Cairo in the summer." It was a lively city, to be sure, "and in many respects as beautiful" as Paris. His views of the Holy Land diverged markedly from those of the reverend, though they both seemed to relish the camels they rode together. The place where pharaoh's daughter discovered Moses in the bulrushes was pointed out to him, but he confessed that he was always a "little skeptical about the authenticity of such legendary places." His father was, however, "perfectly credulous." The reverend, moved by "poignant associations," planned to bring back "water from Jordan and Nile—even if the customs office will think he's violating the 18th amendment," Cullen impiously joked. For him, they were just "two muddy colored rivers." He was quite impressed, however, with the tomb of Tutankhamen in the Cairo museum.

But it was Paris that won him utterly, starting a passionate attachment that would last for the rest of his life. The city was "all it ought to be and I am completely ravished by it," he wrote to Jackman. It was as much a matter of race as of aesthetic pleasure. He went on, "For the first time in my life I really felt free and uninhibited by my color," a testament repeated by any number of African Americans visiting Europe in the twenties and beyond. It was on the deck of the ship taking him from Paris to Cairo, on Bastille Day, that he had the most emotional reaction, as the band struck up the "Marseillaise." The experience was revelatory: "I thrilled to the French national anthem with a fervor absolutely alien to me when I hear the Star Spangled Banner. Pitiful, but true." But there were other strains on deck, as all on board were "doing jazz," and Cullen was busy learning "the French edition of the *bump*"; he was eager to teach it to Jackman when he returned.

The return visit to Paris on the trip home offered different reactions. By the middle of August, staying at the Hotel Cavour on Rue Lafayette, he had grown a bit homesick for "tan faces and crinkly hair." This reaction was also frequently paralleled by African Americans when they stayed for an extended period in European cities. Added to this was the special phenomenon of encountering prostitutes. Again, his reaction differed sharply from the reverend's, as he made clear to Jackman. "You should see some of the harridans that accost my father and me on the streets. If you were along I know you'd keel over laughing at my dad. He doesn't know what it's all about." Cullen wanted to bring back a copy of the banned *Ulysses*, as a gift for Jackman, but the reverend "forbade it"; in any case, he had run short on money. Not to be completely overshadowed on the score of bonhomie, the reverend added his own little note to Jackman. "I trust you have had a pleasant summer," he remarked, using less than rigorous spelling and punctuation, "with the reds, blonds and brunetts regards to . . . Miss Fassit," the last a reference to Jessie Fauset. Father and son were back in New Jersey by September 7, and the reverend, in need of rest, asked that his parishioners not be told right away of his return. Pleasantville would be welcome home enough and would allow for time to absorb all they had seen and done.

The trip to Europe and the Middle East gratified Cullen in a way that shaped his values and desires for the rest of his life. It made him a devotee of France and most things European. It also bound him in gratitude to the reverend, as shown by the poems he would write about the experience. The additional benefit was obvious, since it made his further trips abroad in the next decade or so just that much easier. Many of these would be undertaken with his father, and with Jackman, and they became irreplaceable parts of Cullen's yearly calendar. In a way comparable to, yet quite distinct from, the generation of white American expatriates, Cullen found in his Eurocentrism a persistent satisfaction. As he proclaimed to Jackman, much of the feeling had to do with escaping the benighted stigma of racism, but it developed as well into an aesthetic enrichment.

Cullen and Hughes

Before Cullen made his first European trip, he was embroiled in a charged discussion with Hughes about the relationship between race and poetry. This was obviously a subject of lifelong concern for both Cullen and Hughes, but it has some detailed consequences as well, when the discussion became a public debate. Early on Cullen and Hughes not only exchanged poems, but Cullen often acted as Hughes's secretary in submitting his poems to different publications. Their critical exchanges began in a very relaxed mode of discussion, generally brief approving comments sufficing to convey the sense of a shared undertaking. Cullen was the more developed of the two in terms of possessing an articulated aesthetic that he could apply to most any verse that came to hand. In May 1924 he responded to one of Hughes poems.

> As you must realize, I was very anxious to receive both your letters and the card you sent me—and especially the poem which I consider, while not the best you have written especially good, and most naturally adapted to music. You have a pronounced gift of singing and painting in your work. I would really give anything to possess your sense of color. I am going to send the poem out immediately. I am also going to send you copies of Opportunity and the Messenger in which poems of yours appeared.

It isn't clear which poem it is that Hughes had sent, though it may have been his "suicide" poem or even the title poem of *The Weary Blues*. Cullen nevertheless recognized what Hughes was doing, and the aesthetic elements of "music" and "color" were desiderata of his own. The problems that Cullen would see in Hughes's work, however, did not have to do with subject or even treatment, so much as audience. That would be one of the complications for both poets when faced with the other man's work.

Faced with the publication of *The Weary Blues*, Cullen chose at first to speak privately of the issues to his mentor, Locke. Six months before Hughes's book appeared, Cullen found out about some of its details from Van Vechten, who had been the major force in publishing it. What Cullen heard disturbed him, and he wanted to see if Locke might not exercise some counterinfluence on Hughes, an active influence that Cullen himself shied away from.

> Carl Van Vechten tells me he is going to get Langston's verse published in book form, presumably by Knopf, and that he hopes of having it out this fall. This is excellent news, and I sincerely hope it goes through. But there is one phase of the matter which is a sore spot to me. Van Vechten, on answer to my query, says the book will be called "The Weary Blues." That is just the title to suit him (Van Vechten), and many other white people who want us to do only Negro things, and those not necessarily of the finest type. To me it seems that Langston will be doing a bad thing in adopting such a title.[19]

Throughout the Renaissance the issue of white readers setting aesthetic limits to black writing ranked very high. Cullen felt strongly that by inducing black writers to present low or sensationalized subjects white publishers and readers would be continuing a form of racial suppression. This could be seen, to some extent, as the negative side of using culture in the service of racial "uplift."

Cullen's stance, however, was not of the standard "uplift" type; he had all along wanted art to be as free as possible of racial categories, whether it was uplifting or not. He knew that black poets would write about racial themes and subjects as they saw fit, reserving for himself the right to deal with any subject in his traditional manner. What bothered him, what created his "sore spot," was any suggestion that a black poet should court the white reader with the promise of the lurid or, conversely, propagandize in a way that was strident. The former would be demeaning, the latter inartistic. He went on appealing to Locke, suggesting a way to deal with the problem. "I feel very keenly about it [the title], but am not in a position to offer him [Hughes] any advice—I acknowledged his call, and he acknowledged my note, but not in a way to invite continued correspondence. He may come to you; if not for advice, at least to tell you of his hopes. If he does, do draw him out, and counsel him." Presumably Cullen had tried to say as precisely as he could what he meant, but perhaps Hughes rejected his advice by defending his aesthetic stance, and Cullen may not have wanted to appear jealous or presumptuous (while possibly being a bit of both.)

His preoccupations would soon recur in the context of what he wrote publicly about Hughes's *The Weary Blues*.[20] First, he pointed to Hughes's strength, calling him "a remarkable poet of the colorful," before looking at the section of jazz poems. Cullen's tone then turned a bit regretful, as he says, "Never having been one to think all subjects and forms proper for poetic consideration, I regard these jazz poems as interlopers in the company of the truly beautiful poems in other sections of the book." Focusing on the jazz poems led Cullen in a specific critical direction. The core of Cullen's judgment can be found in his remarks on what he felt was the way Hughes's jazz poems constituted a form of self-limitation.

Taken as a group his selections in this book seem one-sided to me. They tend to hurl this poet into the gaping pit that lies before all Negro writers, in the confines of which they become racial artists instead of artists plain and simple. There is too much emphasis on strictly Negro themes; and this is probably an added reason for my coldness to the jazz poems— they seem to set a too definite limit upon an already limited field.

Here the rhetoric slips in a number of places: "hurl . . . into the gaping pit" is needlessly melodramatic; "artists plain and simple" would be hard to define and distinguish; and why is the field "already limited"? Cullen was obviously working with a set of aesthetic assumptions that relegated jazz and jazz poems to a lesser order than that of the high romantic lyric. Part of the problem was that some people went on reflexively to assume that because he was cold to jazz poems, he would also be cold to jazz itself, which was manifestly not the case.[21]

After Cullen finished writing the review, he expanded at some length on his feelings in a letter to Jackman. He even enlisted Jackman's discrete help, asking him to take the proofs of Hughes's book to Charles Johnson at the *Opportunity* office to make sure his judgments and opinions were fair. The letter begins defensively, but goes on in other registers. "I never said Langston wrote consciously on Negro themes, although for the life of me I don't see how he could do it unconsciously; methods, I feel, may be unconscious, but one is always conscious of theme-subjects. The charge of jealousy, if it comes, as it well may, is all rubbish."[22] His letters to Jackman some months earlier belie Cullen's claim that any charge of jealousy was "rubbish," but, as was often the case, Cullen had very mixed feelings while his admiration for Hughes, especially as a poet as well as a wanderer, remained firm. As he went on, the problems grew more nettlesome, and even invoking the authority of a leader in the Renaissance did not resolve the matter.

Langston knows I am a sincere admirer of what is fine in his work, and I show that in my review. James Weldon Johnson may be perfectly right about my being more of a racial artist than Langston, and about my being at my best in racial poems. Even so, if that is the truth, I find it bitter and unfortunate truth, and were I criticizing my own work, I should condemn myself from that standpoint. The fact that I am representative of what I censure in Langston is not an adequate come-back, because many of us know what is right without being able to approach it at all.

11. James Weldon Johnson. A man of diverse and imposing talents, he was one of the major leaders of the Harlem Renaissance and a strong supporter of Cullen.

Cullen's argument partly revealed important aspects of his aesthetic commitments and partly expressed a difference of opinion about what white readers felt about poetry by blacks. Admitting he didn't like Hughes's jazz poems, Cullen still insisted that "the one-sided inclusion of so many race poems, be they ever so good, was unfortunate, (as so many white people want Negroes to write only about Negroes)".[23] The aesthetic question—whether there was a purely racial poetry, and what and who could produce it—melded into the other question—whether the readership of poems with racial subjects and themes was as important as their production. Not stopping at this, Cullen brought his dissertation to a close by making yet another claim, which some might regard as the boldest or most wrongheaded of all: "I don't agree . . . that we write about those things with which we are most familiar; and of all persons, of the poet, who is the imaginative creator par-excellence, can that be said least." The English romantic tradition is not the only one to isolate and elevate the vocation of the poet, but in Cullen's mind, as far back as high school, it was the most formidable in doing so.[24]

Hughes soon responded to Cullen's review with a redoubtable essay that has become canonical in African American poetics, "The Negro Artist and the Racial Mountain," which first appeared in the *Nation* on June 23, 1926.[25] Five months earlier, however, he had confronted Cullen about his review of *The Weary Blues* in a much more personal context. In his letter he opened by striking a positive note, telling Cullen, "I like your review for Opportunity and it's provoking enough to make people buy the book just to see what it's all about." But this was in some ways a feint. He rejected Cullen's idea of a "pure art," arguing at the same time that he didn't "see why a Negro artist can't be a pure artist." Both poets wanted to leave the way free for different kinds of poetry and art, yet both needed to reassure themselves and clarify their purposes. This invariably meant invoking some tradition or context to carry the force of the claims. Hughes reached toward a rather surprising context:

> One can write only about Negroes,—even only about one Negro oneself,—and if it is done well enough be a great artist. (I don't mean I am.) But look at the Russians who wrote only about Russians and see what a literature they have. Or the Frenchmen who write largely about Frenchmen. Besides Negroes are more than Negroes,—they're people, and so we aren't writing about freaks when we write about them. Our literature would still be human.

Hughes managed here to be shrewd on several counts, and, as often happens with this sort of argument, it eventually turns to some idea or another about race itself ("Negroes are more than Negroes"). This can be read as replacing one conundrum with another. Cullen's charge against Hughes—that too many poems in *The Weary Blues* were about "Negroes" and this meant looking too solicitously to the titillation of white readers, or ghettoizing black poets, or both—wouldn't stick in the long run. White readership grew more sophisticated in reading black poetry, and the changing mores explored by twentieth-century realism made any threat of titillation from "low" subject matter less a present danger. This allowed Hughes's poetry to escape being judged against the standards of "racial uplift." But in the middle of the 1920s, this sorting out of criticism and the perplexities of the readers' reaction was far from pellucid.[26]

Hughes did not know this twisting argument would turn out the way it did, and so when he came to write "The Negro Artist and the Racial Mountain" he adopted a bold stance that resonated for decades afterward. Though the essay begins by recounting how an unnamed poet—whom most readers knew or assumed to be Cullen—wanted "to be a poet—not a Negro poet," Hughes extended the stance somewhat sophistically. The poet was "meaning subconsciously, 'I would like to be a white poet'; meaning behind that, 'I would like to be white.'" This wasn't in the least true of Cullen, yet he had to accept that when arguments about race and art were mounted the charges and claims became subject to all kinds of distortion. Because Cullen's attitude and commitment on these issues tended to be more complex and nuanced than those of many others, he was vulnerable to such charges as Hughes made, albeit without naming Cullen. By committing himself to an exalted literary tradition, one that claimed universal significance for itself, Cullen might be understood, mistakenly, to want to jettison all notions of race. The Renaissance, however, relied on the values and examples of high art to advance its political and social aims, as Locke and White and James Weldon Johnson had repeatedly insisted. From this point of view, Cullen was merely accepting the interweaving of artistic and social values as a solid foundation for serious "race work."[27]

Hughes joked good-naturedly with Cullen in the January letter. Complaining about how boring it was to give so many readings of his poems, he related how a lady came up to him after one such event and said, "Just keep right on, son, and pretty soon you'll be as famous as Countée Cullen." Hughes turned the screw a bit by saying that he replied, "Surely I hope so!" to kid her along, and so kidding Cullen with the same stroke. Their dialogue about poetry and race had up to this point reflected good feelings and some humor, though the stakes were high in terms of influence and recognition.[28] There were other stakes as well. The way the two poets came to be set up as polar opposites in the field of African American poetry produced, not only a distortion of their friendship, but a failure to see that that tradition was widening throughout the Renaissance and beyond, not least of all as a result of their talents. As happens often with beleaguered and oppressed classes, the dominant group's sense of superiority requires that the minority be seen as an indistinguishable population. Soon, however, if individual distinction begins to occur, and nuance and subtle forms of growth appear, then the myth of superiority begins to crumble.

Caroling Dusk

Even as he was arguing with Hughes about the most pressing issues of African American poetics, Cullen was gaining gravity as the editor of *Caroling Dusk*. The contract to edit and write an introduction to an anthology of African American poets was offered to Cullen because of his already solidly established reputation. In doing the many chores associated with such a project, Cullen was able to impress himself on virtually every one of his African American peers. He conceived of a special approach when he decided to ask each contributor to the anthology to write his or her own brief biography. Such entries, he felt, often became standardized in the hands of the editor and so were uninteresting to the readers. This special feature, however, meant there was extra correspondence, as he often had to write to the poet first for permission (and sometimes to the publisher as well) and then dun each contributor for the account of his or her life and career, occasionally repeatedly. This idea for the "Contributors' Notes" led Cullen to write out one of his rare accounts of his own life. The entire passage is of interest.

> Born in New York City, May 30, 1903, and reared in the conservative atmosphere of a Methodist parsonage, Countée Cullen's chief problem has been that of reconciling a Christian upbringing with a pagan inclination. His life so far has not convinced him that the problem is insoluble. Educated in the elementary and high schools of New York City, with an A.B. degree and a Phi Beta Kappa from New York University, and M.A., from Harvard, arrantly opposed to any form of racial segregation, he finds it

a matter of growing regret that no part of his academic education has been drawn from a racial school.

The modifier "arrantly" rings out here, with its overtones of absolutism, and at the same time the desire for a "racial" school hits against a completely different reality. In a way, this account could be read as an answer to Hughes's charge that Cullen wished to be white. Cullen continued his narrative and its revealing self-portrait.

> As a poet he is a rank conservative, loving the measured line and the skillful rhyme; but not blind to the virtues of those poets who will not be circumscribed; and he is thankful indeed for the knowledge that should he ever desire to go adventuring, the world is rife for paths to choose from. He has said perhaps with a reiteration sickening to some of his friends, that he wishes any merit that may be in his work to flow from it solely as the expression of a poet—with no racial consideration to bolster it up. He is still of the same thought. At present he is employed as assistant editor of *Opportunity, A Journal of Negro Life*. His published works are *Color, The Ballad of the Brown Girl,* and *Copper Sun*.

Consciously or not, here Cullen's mention of the "world rife with paths to choose from" echoes the main point of one of his most famous poems, "I Have a Rendezvous with Life." But the strong optimistic note is joined with the adamant sense that his views are hard-won and fixed: "He is still of the same thought." The possibly "sickening" insistence on his nuanced views probably had done little to clarify them for many of his friends. However, the echoes of Locke's aesthetic, and those of others, namely, that one's art cannot—or should not—be severely circumscribed by one's racial identity was the main motive behind the anthology itself.

In his preface to the gathering of almost forty contemporary poets he made discriminations about the racial impact and resonance of certain contributors, but he argued that he "called this collection an anthology of Negro poets rather than an anthology of Negro verse." This redescription, so to speak, has echoed in comments on Cullen's aesthetic ever since. His arguments about the issue are somewhat cryptic, but they introduce contexts that are not generally considered. For example, he maintained that "Negro poetry, it seems to me, in the sense that we speak of Russian, French, or Chinese poetry must emanate from some country other than this in some language other than our own." This would argue that the poems in *Caroling Dusk* are African American, as written in English in America. Cullen's view could extend to the argument that Negro poetry should rightly, then, come from Africa; it would be defined by the fact that its authors are of a race that African Americans share in part. However, African American poets have a distinct culture, distinct, that is, from the culture of strictly African peoples. In this, he may echo Locke's views that race as a category applies to culture much more illuminatingly than to essential identity.[29] Cullen goes on defensively to say, "As heretical as it may sound, there is the probability that Negro [i.e., African American] poets, dependent as they are on the English language, may have more to gain from the rich background of English and American poetry than from any nebulous atavistic yearnings toward an African inheritance." Such a "probability" lies alongside another suggestion, this one drawn from the famous remarks by W. E. B. DuBois about a double consciousness; as Cullen puts it, "the double obligation of being both Negro and American is not so unified as we are often led to believe." As racial consciousness can be double, so, too, can aesthetic aims, combining a sense of group and individual experiences even while aspiring to universal applicability. The central arguments that Cullen advanced about race and art exist in several different texts, but the foreword to *Caroling Dusk* captures as well as any other the balanced tensions of views that he never entirely abandoned nor thoroughly simplified.

There were innovations in *Caroling Dusk* that speak to Cullen's skills as an editor. Using the poets' own thumbnail biographies was one of them. Another was the use of unknown poets to broaden the base of what counted as "Negro" poetry. It was through a submission that originated from Hughes that Cullen came to use some poems of a then little known poet, Gladys May Casely-Hayford, four of whose poems were included in the anthology. She was a member of the Fanti tribe and a native of the Gold Coast in Africa, she lived for a while in England, and Hughes knew her by her pen name, Aquah Laulah.[30] In accepting the submission of the poems from Hughes, Cullen wrote that, "I think it is very fine of you to get these poems for us as they [are?] of decided merit, and I should enjoy seeing some more work of a person of such decided talent. When you get her address I will be very glad if you will send it to me in order that I may write her a personal note of appreciation." In her biographical note for the anthology, she wrote: "I argued that the first thing to do, was to imbue our own people with the idea of their own beauty. . . . I studied the beautiful points of Negro physique, texture of skin, beauty of hair, soft sweetness of eyes, harm of curves, so that none should think it a shame to be black, but rather a glorious adventure." The sensuality of her poems, especially "Rainy Season Love Song," would have appealed to the Cullen who wrote "Heritage."[31]

The advantages attached to the making of *Caroling Dusk* gave Cullen moments of pleasure: practice in handling the language of polite compliment, for example, but also a chance to establish the beginnings of a friendship. Claude McKay's poetry impressed Cullen, but the first two attempts to reach him to ask for contributions failed, as the Jamaican-born writer was constantly traveling. A third letter from Cullen caught up to McKay and secured his cooperation even while it praised the older poet's skills. Meanwhile, McKay had expressed less than enthusiasm for Cullen's poetry, writing to James Weldon Johnson that he wasn't at all taken with the poems he had seen so far. But another of Cullen's contemporaries, also destined to become an important poet, wrote back to the initial request with good humor and sharp wit: Sterling Brown. At the time Brown was not yet teaching at Howard University, where he would become an important influence and mentor to many. In this instance Cullen wrote to say he had read aloud one of the poems from Brown's *God's Trombones* at his father's church. For his part, Brown expressed himself characteristically.

> As I said before, I had planned sending some to you as poetry editor of the magazine [*Opportunity*]. But bread has had to come even before the wine of poesy (or to be honest, the homebrew of jingling, in my case) and the little annoyances, and big jobs of teaching have kept me from doing so.—I am lucky however this year. Almost at the same time with your letter came a lad from St. Louis who types fairly well and cheaply and above all can hold his tongue. I am giving him some of my best?— O what father can pick out from a flock of children—his best?—to type for you. Maybe it will seem that I am submerging you with manuscript.

I'm not. But I can't select.—(Surely this is no malady peculiar to me.) I am sending about a score. You have assured me that these will be well cared for.[32]

Such brio confirmed Cullen's sense that when a talented poet speaks about his own work something in the tone becomes unique, as it does here with Brown's special whimsy.

Not all the responses could have made Cullen smile. Many came from people whom he hadn't meant to solicit specifically and were in response to an announcement in *Opportunity* requesting contributions to the anthology. Cullen at the time was the de facto poetry editor of *Opportunity*, and so some of the contributors to the anthology had come to his attention by submitting individual poems to the magazine. The editorial activity also kept Cullen busy, supplying polite rejection or acceptance as the cases warranted. Added to these were other suppliants, people who had heard Cullen read his poems publicly, were genuinely appreciative, and wanted to show it through emulation, of a sort. Yet another group of correspondents—one that didn't shrink for years—was comprised of people who had bought a copy of *Color*, or in some cases wanted to but couldn't afford it, and were seeking Cullen's autograph for their copies. Rex Littleboy, a wealthy and sophisticated English friend from his recent Harvard days, wrote Cullen to ask for an autograph for his copy, while at the same time deploring the practice that only made autograph hunters seek to capitalize on the signed volume's increased monetary value.

Opportunity

Cullen's position as an assistant editor at *Opportunity* lasted but two years, yet it put him near the center of African American letters during the time he held the position.[33] He worked under a most understanding and supportive supervisor in Charles S. Johnson, a University of Chicago trained sociologist who had a keen sense of aesthetics and culture. Years later Johnson would eulogize his young office mate by describing him as "a restful, stimulating, whimsical and gay person, who was hard working as a helper, and able to fit comfortably into small, homey quarters as they had to do when working together" at the magazine.[34] However cramped his quarters, his desk seemed to overflow.[35] He was also given his own column, called "The Dark Tower" after one of his poems. An editorial that appeared a few months before he joined the magazine lamented that many submissions had levels of artistic skill that were not always as high as the editors wished: "The encouragement that they [the new writers] are receiving from established writers is a gracious and valuable aid. . . . But this does not mean that simply because they are Negroes they can sing spirituals or write stories and verse or even dance *instinctively*" (italics in original). Complaints like this had originated with black critics, some of whom, like Benjamin Brawley, heaped scorn on the now generally praised work of Hughes. As often as the disagreements revolved around matters of artistic talent and skill, the question of "uplift" continued to circulate as well. Cullen himself, in the March 1928 issue of *Opportunity*, editorialized in his column:

> Whether they relish the situation or not, Negroes should be concerned with making good impressions. They cannot do this by throwing wide every door of the racial entourage, to the wholesale gaze of the world at large. Decency demands that some things be kept secret; diplomacy demands it; the world loses its respect for violators of this code. . . . Let art portray things as they are, no matter who is hurt, is a blind bit of philosophy.[36]

The professionalized side of being a writer now descended on Cullen and took him away from the atmosphere of the high school and its literary awakenings. Now there was the "wholesale gaze of the world at large" that needed to be measured. Often of two minds on questions of art, he felt that speaking and writing for an ever-larger public brought with it a weight of experience, and also carried the danger of empty exhibitionism, to use a term his mentor Locke favored.

Still he retained some marks of youthful innocence. A reporter at the *Pittsburg Courier* remarked on his "chubby baby face lit up by sparkling eyes and a disarming smile."[37] Added to his correspondence duties were Cullen's various travels, most confined to the eastern half of the nation, to read his poems at various venues. These ranged from Greenwich Village writers' groups to women's religious committees to colleges and other educational institutions. The latter were sometimes at the request of his fraternity brothers in Alpha Phi Alpha. Cullen used a book-

ing agent at a speaker's bureau to arrange these visits. He made two demands: that he not be asked to give a formal lecture and that his fees
always cover the travel expenses.

Cullen's growth as a professional writer began just months after he
left Harvard. But the seeds of his stature as a writer had been planted
some time earlier when his poetry brought him national notice. Equally
important was the respect he had garnered from the senior leaders of
the Renaissance. These men—chiefly Charles S. Johnson, James Weldon
Johnson, and W. E. B. DuBois—controlled the access to print and the
prizes, as well as the prize-granting mechanisms, that are crucial to neophyte writers. Cullen probably impressed the men as much by his po-
liteness and polish as by his poetic abilities. Still it remained true that
it was his poetry that opened the doors. Even as he had begun his first
semester after NYU, Charles S. Johnson was making his path considerably freer and most tempting. Near the end of 1925 he wrote to Cullen,
who was busy at Harvard, to discuss whether or not it was advantageous
or desirable to make Cullen one of the judges for the *Opportunity* awards:

> On the matter of judgeship, I have been torn between two very strong
> desires; one of them that you should assume your natural position as
> perhaps the most brilliant of our poets in the role of judge, and the
> other that you should add one more brand to the accumulated fire of
> your success while you are at Harvard this year. You could, of course,
> with grace and ease, step off with the Pushkin prize. As I think it over,
> this is the more logical, inasmuch as we have asked persons like Frost
> and Braithwaite who give the impression of "out-in-the worldness." My
> sections are not yet closed of course. It has been necessary to suspend
> the work on the judges almost a month, while other threads are picked
> up. The scale can be tipped either way, but there has been a loathness
> lurking somewhere on my part to entice you into being an old man.[38]

This expresses such confidence in Cullen's maturity that it virtually fore-
tells Cullen's future as an editor at *Opportunity*. Johnson combines professional solicitude with genuine personal warmth in a way that is remarkable, even considering the then-rising arc of Cullen's star.

Through his friendship with Charles S. Johnson, Cullen was indeed
appointed associate editor at *Opportunity*. Johnson was a sociologist

12. Charles S. Johnson. Sociologist, editor, and eventually college president at Fisk University, he employed Cullen as his associate editor in the office of *Opportunity.*

who had been trained by Robert Park at the University of Chicago. Park's expertise, which influenced all of American sociology, was in the field of urban studies, and he passed this commitment along to Johnson. Starting in the early 1920s, Johnson intended to use his position in the Urban League to make its official publication, *Opportunity,* into an important exploration of life in the cities of America and at the same time to track the cultural progress of African Americans.[39] His aesthetic tastes were highly developed, and he was greatly impressed by Cullen's talent. He reported to Cullen in 1925 that he had recently heard Robert Frost remark, "Cullen's certainly a find. I have been much struck with his work." Johnson agreed with this assessment to the point that he used copies of *Color* as Christmas presents for his friends and associates. Attending the first performance of Emerson Whithorne's setting of Cullen's poems, he was deeply moved, and he continued to support Cullen's poetry for many years. In 1929 he left the editorship of *Opportunity* and took a teaching position at Fisk University in Nashville, where he would later unsuccessfully attempt to entice Cullen to come as a professor. In all, he was one of the chief benefactors of Cullen's career.

"The Dark Tower"

In late 1926 Cullen published one of his first prose essays in *Opportunity*. It would be followed over the next two years by fifteen more, all of them appearing under the title "The Dark Tower."[40] The title, taken from one of his poems, was made famous beyond the precincts of poetry when A'Lelia Walker borrowed it for the name of her salon, which opened in October 1927.[41] Walker had started the salon, for which she charged admission and sold drinks, as an extension of her mother's very successful line of hair products marketed exclusively for African American women. The salon was designed specifically for the younger artists, as Walker wrote to her business manager: "I let it be known that it is opened for the New Negro writers and the younger group such as Countée Cullen and a number of others in the same field." In the main room of the salon Cullen's poem was painted on the wall, just opposite Hughes's "The Weary Blues."[42] The popularity of the salon only attested to the following that Cullen had developed as a result of his stylish prose and especially his racial consciousness.

The tradition of the feuilleton served as the model for Cullen's column. This tradition—of brisk and witty commentary on cultural matters—was an important one in European newspapers, especially those in capital cities. American newspapers, however, less often adopted such a model, and yet *Opportunity* and its readers found something both entertaining and valuable in this brief but well packed form. Part of Cullen's success (in keeping with the generic lineaments of the form) was his ability to shift tones, from the heavily ethical and political to the light and breezy. This involved a measure of wordplay, but even more important was a certain playfulness in the elevated diction and syntax, where the writer is skirting the borders of a camp sensibility. Most of the columns mixed their subjects, as in July 1927, for example, where Cullen discussed a book on South African apartheid and then went on to offer a summer reading list, complete with recommendations for books to take to the beach. In November 1927, however, the entire column was devoted to recently staged plays, most with black casts, and Cullen was able to offer a nuanced critique of acting skills, musical accomplishments, and script efficiencies and inefficiencies. All the while he maintained a liveliness in his own language, as he does speaking about the new production of *Porgy*: "To the belligerent role of Maria (and in Cat Fish Row they don't wait until you drop a hat to fight; you merely have to twiddle it in your fingers) Georgette Harvey brings a fine voice and a vehement piece of character acting."

The first of the "Dark Tower" columns was in many ways typical, if such a protean form can be typified. Cullen signaled the timeliness of the column by echoing Edna Ferber's recent call to playgoers to help a play, *White Wings*, stay alive and extend its run. Then he lamented the closing of two other plays that he considered worthy, especially as they starred the likes of Rose McClendon and Paul Robeson, both great stars. From these recommendations, he swerved to quote a poem by one of his mentors, Witter Bynner, called "Black Lucifer." It ends with the insouciant lines, "where would you rather be on parade— / In heaven or in Harlem?" but this only after suggesting Lucifer frequented the fabled neighborhood. There followed a quip about the man who showed "the high water mark in race consciousness" when he asked a librarian if there was a copy available of *Negro Heaven*. That this dig at Van Vechten's novel and its scandalizing title followed the passage on a Harlemite Lucifer may not have been totally innocent.

Then, shifting to a serious note, Cullen recounted the dismissal, by the administrators of the University of North Carolina, of two editors from the *Carolina Magazine* for publishing a story "in which the principal characters were a white girl and a mulatto." Since the theme of miscegenation always fascinated Cullen, to use a mulatto as a marker of an unacceptable character in fiction was more than demeaning. Cullen took a moment to reveal the higher hypocrisy involved in the administrators' action, by further pointing out that the most recent issue of the journal had a story by Eric Walrond and "a pronunciamento asking for contributions from people of all races, colors, creeds, and political leanings." The *Carolina Magazine* became a somewhat unexpected outlet for African American writing, and it even later featured a special issue on the "Negro Poets Today." So Cullen's criticism was not without a special focus.

Turning the problem of racial identity through one more aspect, Cullen went on to discuss how DuBose Heyward's race was a mystery to people who assumed that a white author could not deal artistically with black characters, as Heyward had done in *Porgy*, to Cullen's high approval. Quipping that DuBose might be admitted to "gratuitous and unwilling adoption into the Negro race," Cullen again jabbed comically at Van Vechten's being "taken into the fold," though "more to his amusement than to his alarm, if any word of his initiation has come to him." The column ends by treating books that merited special attention. Cullen lists those most requested at the Harlem library (a feature that became a staple in subsequent columns) and adds a paean to the novelist Elizabeth Madox Roberts for *The Time of Man,* her first novel, without mentioning her race. Then he discusses the Braithwaite anthology of the year's best poems and singles out the Negro poets included, praising the editor, saying "we may all be pardoned a bit of selfish pride in this nationally recognized work of one of ours." Race—and moreover the boundaries between the races— weaves throughout all the items, but only in some is it the main focus.

Cullen often joined the subjects of race and aesthetics, and so he frequently noticed when the subject of miscegenation or the question of racial uplift was the focus for a poet or playwright. In March 1927 he wrote about *Stigma*, a four-character play that dealt with the failed love affair of a Negro woman who rejects the white father of her child, not for any racial reason but because she finds him "a clay-footed god." Donald Duff, who coauthored the play, was a good friend of Cullen and Jackman and acted the part of the man. It was Doralyne Spence, however, playing the woman, who won Cullen's highest praise.[43] Cullen then added a brief passage praising *Fine Clothes to the Jew*, Hughes's second book of poetry. Mentioning with a pun that he "fingered the fine-wrought texture" of the poems with "admiration and some pardonable envy," Cullen may have been making up for his earlier negative judgment about parts of *The Weary Blues*. Racial identity and poetry figured again in Cullen's correction of his previous column where he had incorrectly identified Chaliss Silvay, whose work was included in Braithwaite's anthology, as an African American poet. Cullen excused this mistake, saying that it was caused in part by Silvay's having published in Negro journals and having had his efforts encouraged by Charles S. Johnson. He then, however, went to the trouble of listing all the national journals and newspapers where Silvay's poems had appeared, so as to remove any suggestion that he had been easily granted a place in Braithwaite's annual anthology. Meanwhile, Cullen recorded the number of reserve requests at the library for *Nigger Heaven*, which were twice that of the second most requested novel.

Drawing on his own deep feelings about issues, Cullen quoted from other contemporary writers and did so sometimes at length. In April 1927 he cited a long quotation from an essay by Devere Allen,[44] on "The New White Man," which had appeared in the March issue of *World Tomorrow*. At first, Allen acidly described the white man as having "allowed himself to be sold by his desire for dominance into a spiritual slavery." But this harsh assessment was mollified, allowing Cullen to take up Allen's meliorist suggestion that the "new white man will break the bonds of superstition," and this induced Cullen to offer his own prediction: "Let us hope that the new Negro and the new white man will soon be able to clasp congratulatory hands at the summit." Cullen then turned to poetry, discussing Louis Untermeyer's *The Forms of Poetry*, with its focus on traditional poetic forms and techniques. This led to the occasion to mention Amy Spingarn's new book of poems, which were quite polite and regular in their formal qualities. Undeterred by her standing in the community as the wife of one of the founders of the NAACP, he remarked on her "too complacent, too yielding" attraction to weak rhymes and argued (with a hint of self-criticism) that "we realize . . . when it wills there is no greater despot than rhyme." Two months later Cullen again addressed the issues of race and art, first by quoting an article by Frank Luther Mott on the Harlem poets, which turned prescriptive: "a writer has the privilege of writing about anything that interests him, but he ought to be interested in the things which, luckily, he stands possessed of here and now." Cullen demurred, insisting instead, "Only at his dictum that an author *ought*, by virtue of birth or any other circumstance, be interested solely in any *particular* thing do we utter protest." Continuing along this modest antinomian line, Cullen invokes a quixotic image when he adds, "The mind of man has always ridden a capricious wandering nag, that will just not stay reined into a beaten path." Neither the rules of art nor the boundaries of the races were improved by excessive rigidity.

"The Ballad of a Brown Girl"

Cullen profited from his position at *Opportunity* in another sense as well. In 1927 Johnson decided to bring out Cullen's "The Ballad of a Brown Girl" in a special edition limited to five hundred copies. Harper and Brothers were the official publishers, but *Opportunity* subvented the book, which was only eleven pages long. It contained elaborate paper with bordered pages and an illustration by Charles Cullen, no relation to the poet. Cullen decided to dedicate the poem to Witter Bynner, clearly in return for the support the older poet had given him. Bynner, though pleased by the dedication, felt the poem should have been included in *Color;* Cullen, indeed, might have meant to keep it back for inclusion in *Copper Sun.* By standing alone, however, the book's traditional structure as a medieval ballad was highlighted. While Cullen would occasionally revert to chivalric images and vocabulary in later years, this ballad was his last use of such an anachronistic form. On the other hand, like "The Shroud of Color," and "The Dark Christ," which would be published three years later, the ballad dealt with issues of race. Cullen eventually found out that, as far as the original legend of the poem went, the "brown" of the ballad was not a reference to the girl's skin color but to that of her hair. Given Cullen's use of race as a recurrent subject in his poetry, however, for many readers the ballad was clearly about racial difference.[45]

The history of the poem's composition, which begins five year before its publication, may well complicate its interpretation. Cullen first mentioned the poem in a letter to William Brown, dated November 12, 1922, telling his schoolmate "My latest endeavor is a ballad, quite a gruesome affair with no less than three murders in it. It is founded on an old song which every colored Kentuckian knows." The poem even at this point was too long for Cullen to transcribe, but he hoped to show it to Brown when they met over the coming holidays. During the fall 1922 term, Cullen typed the poem up and submitted it to his English 30 class at NYU, where it came back with marginal notes and suggestions. On February 1, 1923, Cullen sent this typed and annotated version to Brown, telling him insouciantly that he could keep it, "since it is not in long hand it hasn't the slightest value."[46] He confessed to Brown that he had deliberately kept the "character" of the brown girl cryptic, despite Brown's suggestion that it needed further development. But the description of the brown girl shows heavy revision on Cullen's part and suggests that he had a different sense of the girl's character.

The main change Cullen made in the poem comes in the irregular six-line stanza describing the brown girl, which begins with "Her hair was black as sin is black / And ringed about with fire." In the printed version this description not only breaks the form of the traditional ballad quatrain, it presents the girl as siren-like, invoking sin and seduction. Cullen appears to have originally written two regular quatrains of description. But he heavily reworked the first quatrain, discarded two lines, and melded the remainder with the following four lines to create the irregular six-line stanza. In his hand, he had written this:

> Her hair was black as sin was black,
> But she was pure as Christ
> And her heart [?] all grace and good
> Kept chaste [?] and tranquil tryst.

This creates a very strained discordance between the girl's character and her physical appearance. Furthermore, conferring a salvational role on the brown girl opens the poem to an even more implausible religious reading, so Cullen abandoned this possibility and kept the ballad soundly secular. In a sense he was following Brown's advice.

The plot is simple. A lord is loved by two women; one, "Fair London," is white, and the other is "the dark Brown Girl." He consults his mother as to which he should choose for his bride. The mother, who "loved the clink of gold," says the brown girl is the better choice, but mentions as well that she brings with her a valuable dowry, consisting of gold, silver, and land. The wedding is arranged and completed when suddenly the fair girl arrives, uninvited and unannounced. She insults the brown girl, and the lord fails to answer or reject the insult. Enraged, the brown girl draws a dagger and kills the fair one, whereupon the lord suddenly reacts by choking the brown girl with her own "rippling" hair. Cursing and disowning his mother because of her greed—"No mother of mine, for gold's the god / Before whose feet you fall"—the lord goes mad and kills himself. In "a grave dug deep and wide," the lord is buried with the fair girl by his side and the brown by his feet. In his madness the lord sings what at a simple level can be taken as the moral of the story:

> "Oh lovers never barter love
> For gold or fertile lands.
> For love is meat and love is drink,
> And love heeds love's commands."

As with most ballads, the reliance on a simple plot, frequently implicit motivations, and sudden narrative turns, invites a psychological interpretation. Cullen's poem can easily be read as a symbolic rejection of social approval in favor of idealized love or a covert admission of a divided attitude toward commercial success. Whether autobiographical or not, the poem expertly fulfills the requirements of the ballad genre.

Copper Sun

In August 1927, as his second volume of poems appeared, Cullen saw his name in the headline of a review in the *New York Times*. But the content of the headline continued to foreground the issue of race. Being called "a Poet First And a Negro Afterward" reduced to a crude slogan the troubled and nuanced sense that Cullen had lived with for some years. Such reductiveness would later solidify and determine the contours of his reputation. Meanwhile, however, the *Times* review of *Copper Sun* contained considerable praise. Herbert Gorman, who had earlier reviewed *Color,* testified to what would please any young poet, saying, "it is encouraging to observe" that *Copper Sun* "reveals a profounder depth than *Color.*"[47] Gorman was also perceptive about a central feeling in Cullen's poetry when he pointed to the "primitive naiveté [that] underlies his work, yet, curiously enough, the surface values are sophisticated." The review went on to discuss the problem of race (and nationality) and poetic talent, claiming that while Hughes was nearly always a "negro [sic] poet," Cullen transcended his race, escaping the "*cul-de-sac*" that cuts the poet off from the "universal gestures."

As glowing as some of Gorman's phrases are, other reviewers slipped into condescension, especially when the impulse to counsel and support a young poet blended with an unconscious racist undercurrent. For example, Harry Alan Potamkin thought he clearly saw the lessons Cullen needed to learn. "Mr. Cullen has capitalized the fact of race without paying for such capitalization by the exploitation of the material and essence of race. Once race becomes to him more than capital and its poetic form more than the statement of its fact, he will create, upon what are undoubtedly unusual gifts, poems of import."[48] Potamkin may have been alluding to the opening section in *Copper Sun* that Cullen labeled "Color." What the reviewer meant by referring to the poet's "capitalization" and what exactly constitutes the "essence" of race are harder questions to settle. Both more positive and more direct was a note Cullen received from one of his favorite poets, Edwin Arlington Robinson, who said that the new book "has given me a great deal of pleasure and satisfaction. There is something in your work that makes it entirely your own. You may remember that your first book made a similar impression on me."[49]

The division of the contents of *Copper Sun* into various labeled sections was a format Cullen would later use in *The Black Christ and Other Poems*. That later volume ended with a section called "Color," whereas *Copper Sun* opened with one. This was followed by four sections: "The Deep in Love" (a punning title referring to the people who were lovers and to the dark and often hidden state of intense emotion); "At Cambridge" (dedicated to Robert Hillyer and including more love poems, most composed while at Harvard); "Varia" (a catch-all category, also repeated in *The Black Christ*); and "Juvenilia" (containing some lyrics written back at DeWitt Clinton). The volume as a whole continued to seek intense states of love, which were often shadowed by death and loss. "What ever I have loved has wounded me," begins one of the "Juvenilia" lyrics. Yet this poem is titled, "A Poem Once Significant, Now Happily Not," indicating Cullen's awareness that his youthful effusions were often driven more by a love of poetry than by a direct claim on experience. Many of the poems in *Copper Sun* contribute to Cullen's spiritual and emotional autobiography, and they are less flavored with the schoolbook techniques and rhymes of the earlier poetry, though they retain their commitment to high lyricism and a vocabulary of transcendence.

The book opens with a poem dedicated to Charles S. Johnson, "From the Dark Tower," and this title, since it was used to name his column in the pages of *Opportunity*, became one that was especially associated with Cullen's name. It was also used to introduce the poetry section of the single issue of *FIRE!!*, which appeared in 1926. This radical journal foundered chiefly because of its lack of funds, but its content was also challenging. Not only did it use Cullen's poem as a way of introducing its poetry section, that section included a poem about lynching by Helen Johnson and one by Lewis Alexander about a very insouciant prostitute, who sported the ironic nickname of "Little Cinderella."[50] Cullen's poem, placed at the head of the section that included other poems with anti-racist challenges, contained a polished surface and subsequently was not mentioned as often as protest poems by McKay and Hughes. The content of the poem, however, demonstrated that Cullen was politically and socially conscious of the direct depredations caused by racism.

The chief symbol of the dark tower added to the poem's symbolic thrust and made it usable in other contexts, especially for African Americans who prized their racial culture and its lofty aims. Cullen's Italian style sonnet contains a cry, isolate but elevated, against racial oppression, though it is at once sharp in its testimony ("We were not made eternally to weep") and muffled in its reaction ("in the dark we hide the heart that bleeds"). Indeed, the poem's sestet enunciates a tempered melancholy. The connotations throughout, however, form a medley of attitudes that can ring different tones, and there is even more than a hint of occluded vengeance in the opening: "We shall not always plant while others reap." Cullen charges this agricultural metaphor with a bitter sense of the failures of distributive justice in America, and the shifts in tone lend a dramatic urgency to the poem that resembles but is distinguished from more direct protest. Other lyrics, such as "Confession" and "Uncle Jim," address the theme of racial suppression with a similar tone. The section called "Color" contains a total of seven poems, out of fifty-eight in the book, yet by opening with these poems Cullen was ensuring that the subject of race remained, if not central, certainly of great importance to his poetry.

Much of the rest of the volume is dedicated, in one way or another, to the idea and ideals of romantic love, in all its transcendence and tortuous intensity, whether fulfilled or unrequited. The largest portion of lyrics deal with love and its loss, though some poems, like "A Song of Sour Grapes," express feelings that derive from frustrated or even twisted love.

Beyond all cavil or complaint,
Love's ways are double-dyed;
Beneath the surplice of a saint
The cloven hooves are spied.

A number of poems treat the question of Cullen's religious faith; "The Litany of the Dark People" and "At the Wailing Wall in Jerusalem" demonstrate that his attitude toward the reverend's piety had become part of his own aspirations, or at least what his troubled conscience would call a "credible inheritance of grace." In the "Varia" section, Cullen also celebrated his first overseas trip by composing a poem for his father and three others about his trip to Jerusalem, as well as two poems written at the graves of Shelley and Keats in Rome. Individual poems were dedicated to various friends, including John Trounstine from Harvard; Emerson Whithorne, who had set his poems to music; and Sydonia Byrd, with whom he had a brief flirtation while in Cambridge. Three other poems, heavily marked by the vocabulary and imagery of courtly love, about the vicissitudes of love were dedicated to women, including "One Day We Played a Game" (to Yolande),[51] "Pity the Deep in Love" (to Fiona Braithwaite), and "Sonnet to a Scornful Lady" (to Ruth Marie Thomas.)

The poem to Sydonia, "Advice to a Beauty," contains a warning against the solipsism that results when a person is blessed, and cursed, with extreme beauty ("Sweet bird, beware the Fowler, Pride; / . . . . / The prey is caged and walled about / With no way in and no way out"). A different sort of warning, this one directed in part against religious hypocrisy and moralizing, animates a song about the ambiguities when appearance and value are disjointed. Cullen dedicated "More Than a Fool's Song" to Edward Perry, the dancer and Broadway actor, who was likely on sexually intimate terms with him as early as 1927 and so would appreciate the ending:

The world's a curious riddle thrown
Water-wise from heaven's cup;
The souls we think are hurtling down
Perhaps are climbing up.[52]

The metric of up and down as measures of spiritual worth suffers at the very least a possible, ironic reversal. This sort of wry, or even caustic, sense of Cullen's personal characterology and ethos was overlooked by many of his readers, and it would increasingly assume a larger place in the development of his poetry, from *Color* to *Copper Sun* and on to *The Black Christ*. Still, *Copper Sun* is replete with evidence of Cullen's complex and nuanced feelings about a range of subjects, and as a volume on its own it is full of rich things, even while being a worthy successor to the laudable *Color*.

Jackman, himself an inveterate gossip, felt that African American poets were ill served by the overvaluing of the new for its own sake and that literature might be better served by a loyal and discriminating audience. His test case was Cullen, of course, and he wrote to McKay in the fall of 1927, venting his frustration at the way talent and ambition often mingled in complicating ways, and irregular support from the community did little to make things easier.

> I find that among so many Negroes who have "arrived" they are reluctant about pushing the fellow who is striving. They seem to say to themselves let him get there by himself. A very selfish attitude but when the obscure "arrives" they flock to him. It's a great world! I have been able to notice this particularly in Countée's case because I knew him when he wasn't one of the best-known younger poets of the country. We often spoke about it and still do.[53]

Jackman countered these rather bitter remarks by praising the recent appearance of *Copper Sun* and telling McKay that he thought that the book showed a "more mature grasp and insight" than the first book and that the love poems were especially "superb." Jackman was not necessarily in the majority in this reaction, however, as Cullen's earlier readership did not always follow his development with the same sort of enthusiasm they showed earlier. All too soon, Cullen would no longer be one of the "best-known younger poets," and the nature of his fame began to alter.

Cullen's schoolboy experiences had tempered him when it came to meeting deadlines and answering requests, disciplined skills that came fully into play during his editorship at *Opportunity*. But his correspondence at this time began to reflect other pressures. Yolande often pointed out that his letters were infrequent and short, and this was not only the concern of a fiancée. The travel to public readings, which he could not whole-heartedly enjoy, and his continued duties in the reverend's house and church added to the daily scheduling. Often he referred to the inability to find time to work on his poetry, having become more of a public figure than he guessed would have been possible while at DeWitt Clinton. Responding to a birthday card from William Brown, Cullen allowed himself a brief session of self-pity.

> Life goes on for me in a very desultory sort of way. My job is pleasant, but there are many chores that are not conducive to a healthy muse. Yet poets must work, since we cannot speak with any effect to the accompaniment of a growling belly. What millionaire would make himself immortal? Let him endow the poets of the land!—My new book, *Copper Sun,* comes out in the fall, but it is all work done over a year ago, nothing recent. But I must not complain.[54]

The appearances of "The Ballad of a Brown Girl," *Caroling Dusk,* and *Copper Sun* certainly added to his reputation, and though he was not yet twenty-five years old, as seems inevitable after a poet's second book appears, the aura of young genius would soon lose some of its intensity. More and more he complained of how months went by without any visitations from his muse. One large-scale respite, however, would come in the form of a fellowship, providing him free time to return to those assiduous habits that led him to many past prizes. Just three months into 1928 he would receive word that, with the backing of, among others, his soon-to-be father-in-law, W. E. B. DuBois, he had won a Guggenheim Fellowship. With a reliable if limited amount of monetary support he would be free to pursue different projects, and he would also be on his own, in terms of where he might take up his new residence. He had very little difficulty deciding where to spend the months of leisure granted to him.

4

Europe and the Widening Circle, 1928–1930

In an undated entry in an exercise book Cullen defined a place he returned to often with never a trace of boredom or routine:

> It was only a thing of the heart. . . . In Paris I used to build my castles in the air. Again, when I graduated, we were all filled with dreams and hopes, and each had slightly different ones. But our different hopes were all linked by a hope which bound us together: we all wanted to go to Paris.

A second passage in the same book compared New York, the place Cullen sometimes referred to as his hometown, to Paris. Paris was "a peerless city" where the words "Liberty, equality and fraternity are not only words," since they expressed the spirit of which the capital is made, "where one has fun according to one's liking, a sympathetic and tolerant world, in sum, a true civilization." Such sentiments were hardly unique to Cullen, but few if any held them more sincerely. One of the last poems he wrote, called "La Belle, La Douce, La Grand" and published posthumously, celebrated his second home country. By the middle of 1928 Cullen was sailing to France, where he would spend a year on a Guggenheim Fellowship in Paris, followed by another without a grant—and so began a series of twelve straight blissful summers visiting the City of Light. His wedding in April 1928, however, would fail to bring anything like bliss, and within eighteen months he would be divorced. He would counterbalance that loss by joining forces with a community of African American artists. Most significant of all, perhaps, was his decision—partly conscious, partly determined by circumstances—to move beyond lyric poetry to other forms of literary expression.

After graduation from Harvard and his trip to Europe and the Holy Land in 1926, Cullen had returned to Harlem to take up a job as assistant editor at *Opportunity*. But travel overseas would become something close to an addiction. The feeling of liberation from racial prejudice that he had felt while sailing in the Mediterranean was shared by many, though not all, black expatriates. He applied for the Guggenheim Fellowship trusting it would fund a year abroad. Notice arrived of his selection in March. His friend Eric Walrond was also awarded the same honor, and also, somewhat ironically, Allen Tate, the Southern poet who would be known for his anti-integrationist views and agrarian thought in *I'll Take My Stand* (1930). Meanwhile, there was his wedding to plan and poetry readings to give, some faraway in the Midwest. *Caroling Dusk* appeared to positive reviews, and it had every chance of becoming an anthology that could shape taste and the sense of a tradition. His public figure was increasingly held up as a model, and his reputation for kindness and probity remained secure.

In April of 1928, however, Cullen received an unexpected communication that very likely frightened him. It was from a George Greene, who claimed that he had worked with Mr. Henry Porter at the "Murry [sic] Hill Theatre." He was now out of work and was hoping that somehow Cullen could give him a job. This abrupt intrusion was probably a result of the wide newspaper coverage of the imminent wedding with Yolande. Here a hidden cost of fame and public notice suddenly needed to be paid. It wouldn't do, of course, to have his status as an orphan brought up for widespread notice and comments. Mr. Greene, however, might have had some light to shed on Cullen's early years, assuming he wanted such enlightenment. In any case, Cullen answered a month later, rather coldly, telling Greene that he was unable to help him.[1]

The relatively brief period—from April 1928 to December 1929—of the marriage and divorce of Yolande and Cullen began as a social triumph and ended in pain, confusion, and scandalized whispers. The courtship itself, which had begun in cheerful friendship as early as the summer of 1923, proceeded with a number of tense moments, though often the couple clearly enjoyed the attractions and affections they shared with one another. Cullen's poetry served to bring them closer, as did Yolande's cultural and artistic aspirations. She had denied another suitor, a musician, while Cullen flirted inconclusively with Fiona Braithwaite. But once the couple decided to become engaged, the pressure from the parents—and the African American community at large—began to gather force. Dozens of letters, from writers, fellow students, and leaders and spokespeople of the community, all mentioned the upcoming nuptials in their letters to Cullen at this time, more often than not alerted by the announcement in one newspaper or another. Once the marriage had broken down irrevocably, and so soon, the whispers started. Many remarked on Cullen's sailing off to France in the company of Jackman, usually without mentioning that the reverend was with them. The gossip also depicted this voyage as taking place in lieu of a honeymoon, ignoring the couple's brief stay in Philadelphia immediately after their wedding. Overlooked, too, was the fact that Yolande followed Cullen to Paris fairly soon after he sailed. The conclusions the gossip led to nevertheless seemed obvious. Jackman and Cullen, whatever the stage of intimacy at which their relationship stood, must have heard or guessed at the rumors, but they acted as if there were no troubles or complications to face. Yolande apparently did the same. So the wagging tongues had it their way: Jackman went with Cullen on his honeymoon, in place of his wife. But the details offer a more nuanced picture.

Cullen and Yolande had become officially engaged at the beginning of 1927. If they hoped their new state would smooth out difficulties in their relationship, they were soon disappointed. The bouts of jealousy and misunderstanding on both sides seemed to intensify. Yolande grew somewhat wary from an early stage, saying, "Something tells me that being *merely* your wife will be a lonely job when you get busy." She was duly proud of Cullen's reputation, to be sure, telling him how her students were asking for all sort of news about him, especially during Negro History Week. And he dedicated *Copper Sun* to her, writing "To the Not Impossible One." She called the book's title "a lovely name—it's been ringing in my ears ever since I've read it. You know I'll be more than proud of the dedication." But by March things became muddled, and months later both referred in their letters to a serious disagreement. Yolande spoke of going through "the depths of hell" and tried to reassure him that her mental state was not due to the presence of another suitor. Recriminations and fits of jealousy, however, run through the correspondence for much of 1927.[2]

Despite all that, they settled on announcing the plans in June, with an April wedding to follow the next year. Cullen was now installed in his office at *Opportunity*, where the prize dinners continued to be held annually, and Yolande, busy with her students in Baltimore, missed coming up for them. She spent some time in the summer at a camp in Quebec, learning French and taking drawing lessons prescribed for her by her father, and so their time together was further limited. Some incident in Quebec, not specified by either of them, caused Cullen distress, and though Yolande said it was done only to tease him, he gave her an ultimatum, to somehow or other make amends or break off the engagement. She was remorseful, telling him "I pray that someday you will come to believe in me again," and she further apologized for "being too stubborn and bad-tempered and in saying foolish smart things." Her next letter complained that he wanted "to put his wife on a little pedestal." Near the end of October she got a letter from him, which she answered by protesting that she had not broken the engagement, he had, and at the same time she said she deserved it. She fell ill later in the fall while back teaching and suggested, perhaps playfully, that it was a "ruse" to get him to visit her in Baltimore. But she mentioned she would bring his ring back when she came home in November for the holiday.

By the end of 1927 a little mending had taken place, and things went forward with a somewhat more harmonious tone. Yolande was "praying" for Cullen's Guggenheim application to be successful. There was talk of a honeymoon to California, and concerted effort went into shopping for new furniture. Yolande wanted her father to arrange for notices in the major newspapers, the *Age, Amsterdam News,* and *"The Afro,"* the latter of which earned Yolande's scorn for releasing the notice too soon. For a while the honeymoon plans focused on Great Barrington, where her father raised her and where she had not visited in a few years. The bride-to-be especially wanted Langston to be an usher, and all her sorority sisters—the "Moles," as they were nicknamed—would be part of her cohort of sixteen bridesmaids. As winter turned to early spring the fastidious arrangements were made, even as Yolande was busy teaching in Baltimore and Cullen was working assiduously at his editorial desk at *Opportunity.*

Apparently from the first all agreed that the nuptials would be on a grand scale, and it easily became the largest of any African American wedding ceremony in New York City that year.[3] The father of the bride was consulted on all the details, such as the time of day when the ceremony would take place. DuBois worried over whether the hour of the ceremony would be confusing as to which way to dress, in formal afternoon or evening attire. He also felt they had to hire an auditorium for the reception afterward. "Otherwise, the difficulty of separating the sheep from the goats would be quite insurmountable," he told his soon-to-be son-in-law. He chose Madame Walker's Studios, from 4 until 8 p.m. As it turned out three thousand people attended the church service, yet only three hundred were invited to the reception. DuBois and Cullen lunched together a number of times to coordinate the many arrangements. Cullen, meanwhile, was able at the end of March to send DuBois a thank you note for his support in seeking the Guggenheim.

In addition to Yolande's sixteen bridesmaids, Cullen invited a number of friends to serve as ushers. He asked William Brown, his old friend from DeWitt Clinton, who would have to come over from Cornell where he was studying math and science, having put aside his more aesthetic pursuits. Several months earlier Cullen had been very moved to receive birthday wishes from Brown, to whom he hadn't written in a few years. Touched by Brown's faithful friendship, and nostalgic about their days as schoolboys, Cullen had responded in a letter in June of 1927, before the final plans for the wedding had been set. But even though the early plans for a Christmas wedding in December of 1927 would be changed, Cullen had already planned on including Brown in the ceremony.

Christmas week of this year I am to marry, and I have so little accomplished and so much upon my heart to do. And yet marriage seems the most natural thing, in spite of the attempts of various friends toward dissuasion. There will be a church ceremony, Guillaume, performed by my father, a wedding march and ushers and a long aisle to traverse to the altar. Nothing would please me more than to have as one of my ushers yourself, whose friendship of all I have is that of longest standing. Do you think you could do it, would you be willing? We have not decided on the exact date as yet but it will be during Christmas week.[4]

The "dissuasion" of friends remained without details, though they might have included Jackman or Bontemps, or both. Obviously driven—or led—along toward marriage by the pressure of social convention, Cullen was evidently not settled in his own mind as to what it all would mean. He allowed himself a bit of wistfulness, closing the letter with his blend of hope and sorrow, and at least a touch of guilt: "How have the days used you? How have they used your dreams? That is most important. If the dreams remain all will be well. So there's some small chance I may grasp at and hope to hear from you soon—not meting out to me that same silence of which I am so truly repentant? Be your own magnanimous self and write to me soon." In any event, Brown did attend and served as an usher. It would be one of their last meetings.

Jackman, of course, and Hughes were also asked to serve as ushers and gladly consented. They were joined by Arna Bontemps, James Weldon Johnson, and Ferdinand Q. Morton, the civil service commissioner for the city. Rodriques signed on to be the official photographer, and DuBois later declared that his results were "very excellent." The Reverend George Frazier Miller, Yolande's pastor, performed the service, but the Reverend Cullen was invited to assist. Members of the Salem Church also joined in, working on the food and lavish decorations. Attendees included Locke; Charles S. Johnson, Cullen's boss and avid supporter; and Mary Ovington, who two decades earlier had joined with DuBois in creating the NAACP. Newspaper coverage was extensive. Many accounts mentioned that Cullen was the recent recipient of a Guggenheim, and of course they all identified DuBois as the editor of *Crisis*. The *New York City News* reported that thirteen patrolmen and two sergeants were detailed to keep the crowds in order.[5]

The couple's only honeymoon was a brief stay in Philadelphia, little more than a weekend. DuBois wrote them on the twelfth of April to ask them to stop by when they returned. Signs of deep stress, however, began to appear almost immediately. Just days after the wedding Yolande had gone back to Baltimore to resume her teaching duties. A panic had seized her, yet she was anxious to tell Cullen it wasn't because she didn't love him, or that she didn't want to be married to him, but it was just "a terrified feeling."[6] She lamented that she would "never belong at home anymore—I felt disowned—shut out." This reaction, which Yolande called an "unnecessary hysterical terror," might have intensified because her parents had recently been forced to move to a new residence in Harlem as a result of a fire the previous November that burned the first floor of their house. But with her "nerves stretched to the breaking point," she admitted it was "a horrid beginning," but she would make it up to him.

By early May Yolande knew that Cullen was preparing to go to France on his Guggenheim without her. Their economic circumstances dictated that she stay employed at her school. They had both been strapped for money; in May he had had to pay for her train ticket from Baltimore to New York. She remained blithe in her letters and planned to see him off when he sailed in July, accompanied by his father and Jackman. The reverend was taking the usual summer trip, but for health reasons he needed Cullen to accompany him; this meant he would pay part of Cullen's expenses, a compelling circumstance, considering that his funds were limited. Better accommodations were being sought for Yolande. This arrangement was explained when Cullen wrote to her father in May, saying "Yolande . . . felt . . . she would not be able to have herself in readiness before late July or early August [and] has consented that I leave the end of June and to follow me herself the first of August."[7] As it turned out, both departures were delayed by several weeks. Her first letter to him in France, sent from the summer camp where she continued her studies in French and her drawing lessons, cheerfully wished that he would "give my love to Harold & a whole lot to yourself and remember me to your father. Be good—I know your [sic] having a good time."

Yolande traveled to Paris in the early fall. Not long after her arrival, in late October, while Cullen was in Geneva visiting friends, she became quite ill and spent several days in the American Hospital in Paris, the first two of them in quite distressing circumstances. "Before the 48 hours were up," she wrote him, "I was nearly dead from starvation." Cullen had written her a letter that cheered her, and she managed a wry moment: "I haven't wept—much!!" Assailed, however, with an infection that swelled her bladder and filled it with "pus," as she clinically described it, she reported that the doctors would have to wait for the bladder to subside before they could examine her further. Not only scared to death about the impending procedure, she was distressed to see the hospital bill was already over 360 francs, a forbiddingly large sum. However stressful the weeks just after the wedding were, the first months in Paris would be much more so.

Jackman, meanwhile, sailed back home to America at the end of the summer and began to supply Cullen with gossip-filled letters about Harlem's round of rent parties, plays, and literary comings-and-goings. Jackman included in these letters, secondhand accounts of which have long created interest among students of the Renaissance, several reflections on Cullen's marriage and his, Jackman's, sense of Yolande's shortcomings. Emotional estrangement, and occasional bitter arguments, marked the months in late 1928 and early 1929. At the end of November 1928 Jackman expressed his skepticism about the marriage. "I can see that you two aren't going to 'hit' it no matter how many tears are shed and promises made. You might as well make up your mind to get a divorce over there, especially now that you expect to remain over another year." Cullen reported on his domestic situation, telling Jackman details that set him off. "But I would have cussed her out! . . . When I hear of anything like that it makes me so damn mad I could knock her down." Friendship more than rallied him to Cullen's side, it exacerbated his sense of the situation. "You're too nice for her, but I think one day you'll give way to your feelings—you'll break loose—it will eventually reach that stage." Two months after New Year's, having heard the plans for an imminent divorce, Jackman could exult, "So the inevitable has come about!" He hadn't thought it would be so soon, and he warned Cullen not to let Yolande use her "crocodile tears" to get him back. By May Jackman saw reports about the coming divorce in the *Afro-American,* telling Cullen, "They are certainly featuring your troubles."

Cullen, perhaps to escape the crumbling matrimonial situation, went to London in April of 1929, and Yolande wrote him from Paris. Though she begins in a very casual way, she ends by bringing up their predicament. "In regard to our reconciliation—Do as you like. I was perfectly willing to try again and still am. I believe that if both of us tried sincerely we could succeed but if you'd rather not—well suit yourself. In the meantime—good luck to you and a good time. Write when you can. Cheerio!! As ever Yolande." Tension was beginning to show all too visibly through her usual bravado; in May she wrote again, this time complaining of her chronic ills, saying she was sick "as usual" and suffering from indigestion and hives. This was offered in part to excuse her from her failure to "get to the lawyer," since the marriage was already at or beyond the breaking point. Still, the insouciant note was sounded; "see you in the funny papers," she said in signing off.

Meanwhile, though Yolande's father knew the marriage had begun to deteriorate before the end of 1928, he remained in the dark about just how badly things were turning out. His first intervention, so to speak, occurred in September of that year, six months after the wedding and apparently just weeks after Yolande arrived in Paris. DuBois tried stoically to take the news that the honeymoon was failing and the situation in Paris wasn't improving; a separation was probably already being contemplated. He wrote to Cullen feelingly, but trying to put all of it into a broad context, and with a level of objective detachment that was his forte, and for which some would fault him.[8]

Addressing Cullen as "Dear Countée" he took a judicial and paternal tone:

> I am more grieved and overcome than I can say. I had never dreamed of this. I knew Yolande was spoiled and often silly but if I had not thought she respected and loved you I would not [have] thought of marriage. I knew your honeymoon was trying and I thought it due to weariness & excitement.
>
> I still think the main trouble is physical and psychological. When a girl has been trained to continence & then suddenly loosed, the universe tumbles. Yolande does not know what she wants or loves or hopes for.

DuBois lacked sympathy for his daughter, even as he tried to be reasonable, asking Cullen, "If perhaps you could just bear with her & try again perhaps all would yet do well." The special agony of a heartbroken parent faced with a grown child in pain comes through as he qualifies his own desires: "I have no right to ask this—you have already acted the forbearing gentleman and yet remember that the inexperienced girl—despite her years—does not really know what she is doing." But of course by this time Yolande knew a great deal.

As the news from Paris got no better, DuBois apparently proceeded with the assumption that the problem was a failure to consummate the marriage and that the difficulty was Yolande's timidity or possible frigidity. A month later, DuBois, faced with the threat of an eventual divorce, said it would be "tragic to beget a child," and he explained the need to use contraception. He would also contribute financially to help Yolande and her mother, who would sail to France in February or so, and maintain a residence apart from Cullen. He again wrote Cullen, at length, drawing on his own experience and advising him to not be sexually demanding of Yolande. Pointing out that women do not enjoy marital relations as fully as men do, he spoke frankly: "That then which gives her husband pleasure may be exquisite torture physically and mental humiliation for her." DuBois at this time apparently had no hint that Cullen's homosexuality was the issue.

It is unlikely that Cullen had yet confessed his homosexual orientation even to Yolande. The fall went along with the couple managing to have a social life, visiting artists and other members of the expatriate community. An especially notable trip was a visit with Henry Ossawa Tanner at Étaples, his country home in Normandy. Tanner had achieved his fame, and now, near the end of his life, his stature as a great African American artist was well beyond dispute. Before the spring came, and after Yolande's mother joined her, Yolande's hospital stay and her recurring illnesses had worn her down. DuBois had hoped somehow to "keep down unkind gossip and enable the break to come after a decent interval." He earnestly advised his son-in-law to keep working hard at his writing, acknowledging Cullen's standing as the community's preeminent poet: "I hope to hear that this terrible thing will not stop *your work*. Your career has been very dear to me from the beginning & I had dreamed fine things from the marriage. But life at best is grim & paradoxical. . . . Work on steadily & regularly & *work* out your salvation and triumph." The exhortation was unavailing, and the couple agreed on a separation by early spring; reconciliation never gained any momentum, and by the early summer of 1929 nearly everyone knew that divorce was inevitable.

On May 23 Yolande gathered her nerve and wrote to her father, explaining the cause of the irrevocable break. She hated to do it, but his suspicions needed to be answered. Once she began writing, the details and the emotions came out furiously. "Shortly after our attempt at reconciliation Countée told me something about himself that just finished things. Other people told me too but I thought and hoped they were lying. If he had not told me *himself* that it was true I would not have believed it but since he did I knew that essentially I'd have to leave him." Having managed to say this much, she went on to declare that a bad situation had even worse elements for her.

> I never loved him but I had an enormous amount of respect for him. Having lost that—and having an added feeling of horror at the abnormality of it I could not "make it." I knew something was wrong physically, but being very ignorant and inexperienced I couldn't be sure what. When he confessed things he'd always known that he was abnormal sexually *as far as other men were concerned* then many things became clear.

Any chance that Yolande might be able to overcome her sense of outrage was already gone, and she went on to her other emotions. "At first I felt terribly angry—I felt he'd no right to marry any woman knowing this. Now I feel only sorry for him and all I want is not to have to be anywhere near him." The thought of his being near her filled her with "horror & disgust," recalling she had heard gossip, but "never known it before about anyone." So far she had kept the worst from her mother, who "doesn't like Countée much," and Yolande didn't want to worry her. Faced with the revelations, Yolande retrospectively rewrote the terms of her relationship with Cullen, trying to make sense of it for her father at least, if not for herself.

Yolande made plans to sail home at the end of July, escorted by her mother, but she was reluctantly forced to ask Cullen for forty dollars to cover the deposit for her reservation; in fact, he also contributed to the mother's ticket as well. By November she was back teaching in Baltimore. Here the news took on a different, but no less futile tone. "Hello Boy friend—the dead will rise won't they? Here I am just when you thought I'd disappeared for good," she chirped at the start. Then came the latest, seemingly inevitable, bad luck, taking shape as she gave her account of a perilous car wreck. Traveling by automobile back to New York from Baltimore, with one of her former students at the wheel, the car ran out of control at ninety miles an hour, launched over a sixteen foot ditch and turned over three times. Luckily, incredibly, there were no serious injuries. The letter ended on a plaintive note: "my father is very agitated because I don't hear anything about the divorce." Yolande had forgotten the lawyer's name, and so she closed by asking Cullen to send it to her. This may have been her main reason for writing to Cullen, but she did manage to send him a few more letters—combining a very chipper tone with relatively little news or gossip—in the years following.

Jackman had urged Cullen to arrange for a divorce before he returned to America, thinking it would be better to make a clean break. But he also cautioned that the French authorities were becoming less willing to grant divorces to foreign visitors. The papers on the divorce, dated July 5, 1929, were nevertheless prepared by French authorities, and the divorce was granted on December 19. In their punctilious way the papers begin by establishing that Cullen had set up a household in Paris, "pour permettre à Monsieur CULLEN d'etudier l'art poetique et lyrique francais, Monsieur CULLEN, sans aucun motif a abandonné sa femme." Obviously Cullen was willing to accept the charge of abandonment in order to facilitate the process. The papers concluded: "Monsieur CULLEN répondit qu'il ne voulait plus vivre avec sa femme et que sa decision était irrévocable."[9] Yolande maintained a friendly tone in the face of the irrevocable, and since Cullen's letters to her at this point are not available, his reaction is not known. Occasionally he sent her checks and even saw to it that she received a copy of *The Black Christ*. If there were any recriminations, they weren't recorded in the correspondence.

DuBois, before the marriage was over, had responded with advice and throughout managed to maintain a friendly relation with Cullen. In fact, some of his most pointed advice was addressed to the husband rather than the wife, since obviously he could talk to Yolande face to face, while Cullen remained in Paris. DuBois had told him back in September, "You have my sympathy & love my dear boy." That affection may have grown a bit more formal over the ensuing months and years, but it didn't vanish. DuBois, even after the news of the separation had reached him, conceived of a plan where Cullen would write short essays for *Crisis* about his travels, and Yolande would illustrate them. Even though he could

13. W. E. B. DuBois, for a short while Cullen's father-in-law, and the leading African American intellectual of his time. Photograph by Carl Van Vechten.

offer only a "pittance" in payment, DuBois pursued the idea enthusiastically, probably hoping the joint effort would have some healing power. Months later Cullen was in the embarrassing position of having to ask DuBois for payment on a different account. He had advanced Yolande and her mother seventy-five dollars to buy their steamship tickets back to New York, and to this he added the cost of the divorce, "four thousand francs ($160)." DuBois, meanwhile, was struggling with financial exigency, as the *Crisis* accounts were depleted and the worrisome effects of the Depression increased. Telling Cullen that the wedding had cost $1,500 and he was nearly insolvent, he asked for forbearance, eventually settling the debt in 1930. However, the two men never faltered in their respect and courtesy toward each other.

The Black Christ

Whatever the amount of energy his failed marriage and divorce drained from Cullen, he continued with his poetry and even expanded his sense of his writerly vocation. Though a novel and a libretto had been mentioned as projects he was working on during the Guggenheim period of 1928–29, neither appeared. The opera libretto was to be based on a novel by Grace B. Still, the wife of William Grant Still, the famous composer. Called "Rashana," the narrative would be "a Romantic opera in three acts," according to the synopsis Grace supplied to Cullen.[10] Set in an imaginary African country, the melodramatic plot revolves around a beautiful native woman who is taken off to America by a "white financier," who wants to save her from a vengeful chieftain. She eventually returns to Africa, only to be freed as the "heathen" chieftain dies of his own uncontrolled rage. No records survive to indicate why the project was apparently abandoned. It would not be Cullen's last attempt at writing for the stage.

Unfazed by this false start, Cullen gathered two dozen of his poems and added one of his longest—and most challenging—narratives, "The Black Christ," to make up his third volume of poems, published in 1929. Using the narrative poem as the title poem of the book signaled in some way what Cullen wanted to do poetically. This period, and the next year which he spent in France, 1929–30, formed a watershed for Cullen as a lyric poet. Critics often remarked on his falling off in terms of productivity, but his outlook changed, his ambition shifted, and his work went in different directions. On either side of this change stood two defining series of events—the failure of his marriage at the start of his Guggenheim year and his need to find a steady job after his sojourn was completed.

The Black Christ, and Other Poems is the most difficult of all of Cullen's books to interpret comprehensively. The lyric poems develop recurrent subjects, largely revolving around departure, unrequited love, and death.

Some of them, such as "Nothing Endures," open up new currents of feeling, or at least new tonalities that shift the register considerably.

> Nothing endures,
> Not even love,
> Though the warm heart purrs
> Of the length thereof.
>
> Though beauty wax,
> Yet shall it wane
> Time lays a tax
> On the subtlest brain.
>
> Let the blood riot,
> Give it its will;
> It shall grow quiet.
> It shall grow still.
>
> Nirvana gapes
> For all things given;
> Nothing escapes,
> Love not even.

This can easily be read as another poem about the transience of all things, but a closer look and hearing finds in the two-beat lines a mix of bitterness and insouciance, as if Cullen is speaking from a redoubt of considerable strength and distance, yet is just nearing the edge of tolerable despair. The absolutist moments—such as "nothing endures"—are followed by an even more clipped claim. The syntactic inversion of the final line shifts the tone from curt dismissal to an undercurrent of terminal regret. The poet introduces a wealth of emotions, while trying to negotiate the line between excess and honesty.[11]

The temptation persists to read several of the poems, thick with the feelings of loss and despair, as allegorical reactions to his marriage and divorce. In fact some of them refer at least glancingly to a suicidal impulse that goes back to the "Requiescam" of *Color*. Adding to a gloomy mood are some poems that understand or at least present the pains associated with love as not only inevitable, but as a stoic badge of lyric attainment. Here is one example, "Minutely Hurt," more or less typical in its attitudes, at least considering its sense of in extremis.

> Since I was minutely hurt,
> Giant griefs and woes
> Only find me staunchly girt
> Against all other blows.
>
> Once an atom cracks the heart
> All is done and said;
> Poison, steel, and fiery dart
> May then be buffeted.

The bizarre use of "minutely" as a modifier in this context has just the right sense of unique disorientation, as if the speaker's pain were not only his alone but proves oddly satisfying. The bravado of the closing lines approaches a sort of heroic masochism that follows logically from the absolutism of the experience: "All is done and said." Cullen may have felt his own lyric impulse had reached a sort of limit. Lines from other poems in the book underscore this sensation: "My hands grow quarrelsome with bitterness" ("Mood"); "Poor foolish heart that needs a grave / To prove to it that it is dead" ("The Foolish Heart"). The two political poems in the book, "Not Sacco and Vanzetti" and "Black Majesty," are built on recrimination and hauteur, respectively, rather than on any model of political idealism. All told, the sweet singing of the first two books is nearly completely absent from this volume.

But it is the title poem that most stands out. With different terms, but with some of the same daring, "The Black Christ" serves as a counterpart to "The Shroud of Color." Both are verse narratives, but the earlier poem is largely a work of fantasy while the latter is realistic. At least in parts, that is, since the crucial event in "The Black Christ" is not only spiritually otherworldly but deeply ambiguous.[12] The settings and characters, however, could come from a short story in the naturalistic tradition. Complicating the poem yet further, the opening thirty-eight lines or so read like an invocation to the muse, as Cullen clearly signals that he intends to work at the highest levels of poetic inspiration. The poem, "Hopefully dedicated to White America," confronts the facts and evil of racism more directly than any other writing Cullen published. He obviously decided to reach into the storehouse of homiletic Christian symbols and axioms in order to speak resoundingly of the experience of all African Americans. At the same time, the ethos of the South provided the milieu of the poem since Cullen was determined to ensure the relevance of the moral point of the story. It was a daring gamble, since the black church had developed a long and complex traditional rhetoric, but not one that was easily adapted for either lyric or narrative poetry by a contemporary writer.

Cullen uses a four-beat line, with rhyming couplets, though there are some triple rhymes here and there. There is considerable runover in the lines, which adds somewhat to the naturalness of the diction but also occasionally makes the verse run too swiftly and yet unevenly. The plot is simple but stark. Two sons and a mother are living on an impoverished farm in the otherwise unspecified South. The younger, unnamed son serves as the speaker of the poem. He is passive and reflective, even brooding, in contrast to his hot tempered and unbelieving brother, Jim, whose harshness and angry atheism the mother's sweet patience has failed to soften. The failure of belief on Jim's part threatens to engulf the speaker. When Jim indulges in a seemingly innocent flirtation with a white woman, he is set upon by a single white man whom he kills with the branch of a tree, and he then escapes back to the farm. But shortly a lynch mob appears at the homestead. The younger brother tries to conceal Jim in a closet, swearing to the mob that his brother isn't in the house, but they are relentless and eventually drag Jim out to be lynched. Rather than fight or flee, in a moment of spiritual transformation Jim suddenly surrenders.

> The air above him shaped a crown
> Of light, or so it seemed to me,
> And sweeter than the melody
> Of leaves in rain, and far more sad,
> His voice descended on the mad,
> Blood-sniffing crowd that sought his life,
> A voice where grief cut like a knife:
> "I am he whom you seek, he whom
> You will not spare his daily doom."

The archaic and Christlike language does nothing to still the mob, who indeed complete the "daily doom," which the speaker describes in detail. But then the metaphoric and spiritual high moment comes when the speaker and his mother discover that—somehow, inexplicably—though they have seen Jim hang, he returns alive. The speaker describes the transfiguration-like moment.

> Out of my deep-ploughed agony,
> I turned to see a door swing free;
> The very door he once came through
> To death, now framed for us anew
> His vital self, his and no other's
> Live body of the dead, my brother's.

His return occurs even as the speaker is taunting his mother with God's seeming failure to save Jim, a taunt the mother quietly answers. Cullen seriously challenges the suspension of disbelief as he creates the impression that somehow both figures—the Jim who hides until dragged out to be hanged and the one who returns from being hanged—are both Christ. The double substitution, so to speak, of Christ for the passive and the resurrected victim recapitulates the Christian message of hope, sacrifice, and redemption. The message, however, deviates from received opinion and offers an unorthodox belief, with not only racial inflections but elements of the prayerful and the defiant. Never again, and never at such length, would Cullen bring together the elements of his race and his religion. The results of this effort are complex and offer little by way of completely clear thoughts about his theological or racial commitments.[13]

Because of the way "The Black Christ" uses the intersection of race and religion, it remains hard to place it in Cullen's canon. Doubtlessly, he knew that. In one frame of reference, it is the high-water mark of his confrontation with the Christian religion, refracted as it was for him, not only through the reverend's sermons, but by his, Cullen's, personal doubts and yearnings. The poem in its claim of transfiguration draws as well on the prophetic tradition of African American theology. Added to this vortex of feelings is the fact that Cullen's marriage was irretrievably broken down by the time the book of poems came out. The other poems in the book, of course, reflect the many attitudes and emotions he was dealing with during the second year of his stay in Paris. Poetically speaking, he was trying to come to terms with modern society and the role poetry might play in it. Drawing as he did on the high romantic tradition, he saw some of this conflict in terms of the limited—perhaps terminal—fate of poetry itself. This took the form of a questioning of poetry's underlying myths. Could the poetic vocation flourish, or even survive, in a total secular, urbanized mass society? Though he never recorded his opinion on this subject at length, the opening poem in *The Black Christ, and Other Poems* recorded some of his feelings about it.

The book is dedicated to three of his friends: Harold (Jackman), Edward (Perry), and Roberta.[14] The opening poem is entitled "To the Three for Whom the Book," and it is singular in the way it reveals Cullen's self-awareness at the time, especially in regard to his poetic vocation. Beginning by invoking the myth of the Garden of Eden, Cullen moves on to a host of classical figures whose employment in the world of the arts was for centuries central and crucial: "Dragon and griffin / And basilisk," as well as Medusa and Theseus. But this is no idle catalog. Cullen's main concern is the loss of spirit, in general figured as the loss of youth. Entering his late twenties, Cullen was looking back fondly to the days of the "League of Youth Address" and the feelings of artistic confidence he felt at DeWitt Clinton and New York University.

> Body slim and taut,
> How they go down
> 'Neath the juggernaut!
> Youth of the world,
> Like scythèd wheat
> How they are hurled
> At the clay god's feet.

Cullen's represents his deepest concern, however, and the antidote to it, by the models of his three friends.

> But you three rare
> Friends whom I love
>
> . . . .
>
> A book to you three

Who have not bent
The idolatrous knee,
Nor worship lent
To modern rites,
Knowing full well
How a just god smites
The infidel;
Three to whom Pan
Is no mere myth,
But a singing Man
To be reckoned with . . .

In the context of the age this reads as an attack on the mercenary, market driven ethos of the later 1920s (the book would appear just before
the crash of the market that sparked the Depression). In the context of
Cullen's own life and his poetic vocation, it reads more like a recommit-
ment to traditional poetry and to the acceptance of a pagan imagination (note the uncapitalized deity), deriving its force in aesthetic terms.
Though the poem's versification is not always regular, it works with a
two-beat line, echoing a lapidary tradition often devoted to axiomatic
utterances.[15] The poem not only celebrates an affinity group, it draws a
magic circle around friends bravely dedicated to higher things, spiritual
companions without any authorized or ecclesiastical protection. This
sort of artistic group reoccurs throughout modernist culture, sometimes
taking an antimodernist turn, as it does here.[16]

More than one poem in *The Black Christ* expressed not only soulful
regret but also extreme bitterness. The praise of his friends serves as a
strong counterforce against the bitterness, but only to a certain point.
Poems from *The Black Christ* such as "Little Sonnet to Little Friends,"
"To an Unknown Poet," "There Must Be Words," and "The Proud Heart"
generally work by turning over in the speaker's mind some ennobling or
praised virtue, only to recount how such elevated thoughts uncover the
shortcomings of all human aspiration. "The Proud Heart" ends by saying this: "But being proud still strikes its hours in pain; / The dead man
lives, and none perceives him slain." Lyric emotion is by definition eva-
nescent and gestural, but a collection of lyrics can establish a tenacious
net of associations in which the resonances of some poems are heard

as overtones in others. One of the poems that echoes at length is "Self-Criticism," and in it Cullen appears to question whether or not his own lyric talents might not be extinguished. After asking at the start,

> Shall I go all my bright days singing
> (A little pallid, a trifle wan)
> The failing note . . . ?

the poet wonders if he shall "never feel" enough inspiration to produce his gloomy vision that "only fools trust Providence." Yet he finds an even darker resolution and ends with a yet harsher evaluation:

> Than this better the reed never turned flute,
> Better than this no song,
> Better a stony silence, better a mute
> Mouth, and a cloven tongue.

To the poetic nemesis of silence, Cullen adds the weight of falsehood, as the "cloven" tongue suggests the speech, if not of a devil then that of a sophist or false prophet. If read as a capstone poem for the volume, then Cullen was facing the point in his spiritual autobiography where lyric poetry alone would not suffice.

Responses to *The Black Christ* were mixed, hardly surprising considering the tones and ideas it expressed. Cullen must have known that he had gone into a completely different area of his sensibility and the lyric tradition. His friend and fellow poet Merrill Root, whose poems Cullen had reviewed back in *Opportunity* a year earlier, wrote an appreciation of the book in a Quaker publication of limited circulation, the *Friends Intelligencer,* dated "Ninth Month, 1930." It contains the sort of critical evaluation that echoed perhaps too strongly the language of the jacket blurb: "Countée Cullen's poems are rich, burning, magnificent; he has in his very blood tropic suns with their bronze and gold, the smouldering [sic] blue of southern skies, rivers flashing and burnished like pythons of color." For Root, "critics in this minor decade of an inferior century" cannot "understand or do justice to *The Black Christ*." Such a review in such a journal would have pleased Cullen, but it did not add to his stature, and the volume contains many poems that have received little or no critical attention or commentary. The mantle of the "boy poet" was already a bit out of date, and it was hardly a fitting garment for the poet who had written this book.

To make matters worse, Cullen received a letter at the end of November 1929 from one of his first strong champions that would deflate the heartiest writer. Witter Bynner was now living in Santa Fe, having many notables, including D. H. Lawrence, Ansel Adams, and a number of Hollywood stars as friends, or soon to be so. His role as a mentor in Cullen's career derived, of course, from the fact that Cullen's prize poems were honored in a contest named after Bynner. It might have struck Cullen that he was a better poet than Bynner, but he might have felt compelled to pay the older man honor for reasons of age and experience. Much of Bynner's standing in Cullen's eyes derived not only from Bynner's close friendship with Millay, but his knowledge of the tradition she melodramatically represented and Cullen passionately admired. They also knew each other socially in the mid-1920s, as both were frequent guests of Van Vechten. Bynner, for his part and to his credit, treated Cullen as a peer in most instances, and Cullen was able to critique Bynner's poems sent to him in draft form.[17] But Bynner had the authority, and he was intent on using it, in part by mixing a certain flattery with a stringent sense of insisting on excellence in the demanding scope of the lyric poem. It was back in June 1924 that Cullen had sent Bynner the full manuscript of his potential first book, for review and stern critique.

> Your manuscript has been a long time with me, and I a long time with it, for the reason that your intention of making an immediate book of it has greatly perplexed me. After reading and re-reading it, I find only about 25 poems which seem to me good enough to be contained in a volume as good as we now have a right to expect from you.[18]

Cullen, perhaps out of anxiety, had sent Bynner a large number of poems, perhaps more than a hundred. Though Bynner at first suggested using only twenty-five (though he was willing to expand the count as time went by before publication), the volume would eventually appear with almost seventy-five poems. Clearly, Cullen could deal with Bynner's standards and strictures. But the older poet went into detail, naming the poems to keep, to revise, and to reject. He ended with this advice:

Your title, by the way, seems not very good. There is no reason why you should not use for the volume one of your own excellent titles like The Brown Boy, or To a Brown Girl. In these judgments you will see that I have usually found the poems in which you touch on your race much surer poetry than those which reflect your course at college. You, like other poets, are happier in expression when life, rather than literature is the well-spring.

In some sense this was the criticism that would be lodged at Cullen in the years to follow, yet he knew that both his approach to his "race" as well as his "course at college" had been hard-won. It was striking the bal-

14. Witter Bynner, poet, who sponsored the poetry contests that brought Cullen considerable fame.

ance between these two sources of material and inspiration, or at least the attempt to do so, that defined him as a lyric poet. Cullen took Bynner's advice to heart, though he not only looked beyond it, but managed to maintain the role of the ephebe, the neophyte for several years after the appearance of *Color*.

Bynner, faced with the newer work, felt he had a duty to further instruct the winner of the prize named after him, and so he read *The Black Christ* and then sat down at his typewriter.

> Alas, as your friend, I cannot report to you the same sort of satisfaction this time I have had from your other books. . . . I find you this time writing a book which almost anyone might have written. Temporarily something has happened to you. You have fallen into other people's language, you have lapsed from your own swift simplicities. This, of course, may not be the judgment of others of your friends and critics; but it is mine, and no matter how you may dislike me for expressing it, I have no choice . . . the piety of the book oppresses me. There is an element of eloquent smugness in it which does not in the least sound like you. Snap out of it, dear fellow. Come back to your keen, clear-seeing straightness. . . . Stop being a nice, fanciful boy, and be the man you were headed towards being. . . . Don't let yourself be crucified on a Guggenheim cross, if that's what it is, and forgive me for my bluntness. I can't help it.

The bluntness would be hard to forgive, or even appreciate, if Cullen considered the views Bynner advanced in this instance little more than wrongheaded and subjective. Cullen, however, may have felt a fair paraphrase of the letter would say simply, "Keep writing like me."[19] Somewhat surprisingly, Cullen mustered his best manners and took on again the role of the student. He replied to Bynner, "Far from being offended by your letter I love you the more for it. I am keenly distressed that the book pleased you so little, but I would not have had you withhold your true sentiments regarding it. I'll try to do better next time, but I really did try my darndest this time." But there were reasons for him not to restrict himself to the emotional register that Bynner was urging, and Cullen had weighed them seriously. He had set himself an especially arduous goal, of remaining traditional even while he extended the limits of his own sensibility.

There was another point of similarity between the volumes of *Color* and *Copper Sun*. This was the use of illustrations by Charles Cullen, a white graphic artist, not related to Countée at all, but whose work many in the Renaissance knew well.[20] Charles S. Johnson brought a wider public attention to Charles Cullen's drawings, using them in an eclectic volume called *Ebony and Topaz*, and it was probably through Johnson that Cullen came to meet the artist. The Johnson collection also used illustrations by Bruce Nugent, whose homoerotic work bore a close relationship to Cullen's, and both illustrators contributed to *Opportunity*. The editorial point of view in *Ebony and Topaz* praised the idea of racial mixing, or hybridity, and the illustrations had a decidedly erotic cast. Often featuring nudes of both sexes, Charles Cullen's use of a languid line in an art nouveau tradition and sharp black-and-white contrasts made available through the printing process gave his work a charged sexual and racial atmosphere. Later magazine illustrations in commercial outlets were less erotic, but he also supplied illustrations for an edition of Walt Whitman's *Leaves of Grass*. In *Copper Sun* the final illustration depicts a black mother and son gazing devoutly up at a heavenly Christ, posed in the background with a simple cross. The frontispiece conveys much more drama: a bare and numinous black body has been lynched from a tree limb, while many rays of light shoot up toward a detailed Christ, who hangs crucified and suspended in the sky. Six other illustrations—Charles Cullen referred to them as "decorations"—illustrate specific moments in "The Black Christ." The other ten illustrations, some of which are more like colophons, are often less directly tied to the text. But the ambiguity of the illustrations aptly echo the longings of the poems.

Even as Cullen was indulging in the social whirl of Paris, complete with frequent trips to concerts and the theater, and tea and parties with a host of American and French artists, Jackman was keeping him posted on the various whirls in Harlem. Shortly after returning to Harlem from Paris in the late fall of 1928, Jackman found steady but meagerly paid work as an instructor at the Berlitz School, teaching French. He was attending plays and concerts as frequently as Cullen, if not even more so. His first letter cited plays by Shaw, Ibsen, and Shakespeare, as well as a concert by Roland Hayes, the renowned African American tenor. A week later he observed that at some recent parties there were now more

15. The always well-dressed Harold Jackman. His letters to Cullen are models of cultural gossip. Photograph by Carl Van Vechten.

people in attendance that he didn't know than those he did. But the pace of Jackman's socializing seemed designed to right that balance any day.

His aesthetic opinions and cultural tastes often overlapped with those of Cullen. But there were discrepancies, too. Hale Woodruff painted a striking portrait of Cullen in Paris, complete with bow tie and classical statuary, in reproduction, of course, on the table next to the sitter. Somehow the portrait did not please Jackman, though Cullen went to some pains to ship it back to America where Jackman kept it for him.

Jackman also expressed a distinct dislike for sound movies, much prefer-
ring the stylized artistry of the silent versions, perhaps because it was
closer to the gestural traditions of the stage. For a Christmas present
Cullen sent Jackman an elegant silver cigarette case, but the recipient
had trouble using it with American brands that were so fat the lid didn't
close properly. But all was not swank and soigné. Jackman's stepfather
was very ill with stomach cancer, and he passed away months later.

Though the men were exceptionally close friends, Jackman for a
time had kept at least one secret from Cullen. He had met Anne, a white
woman, and had fathered a baby with her. Diana, the child, was delivered after an extended labor and while Jackman was back in Harlem.[21]
After he told Cullen of the situation at the end of January 1929, he asked
Cullen to go and see how mother and child were doing. (Anne's deliv-
ery apparently took place in Paris.) Jackman was especially interested
in whether or not his daughter looked white or black. Months later he
would arrange for her and her mother to come to America, where they
took up residence with Jackman at 444 Manhattan Avenue. At Jackman's funeral, so rumors had it, Anne appeared and startled the mourn-
ers, but little has ever been documented about her or her relationship
with Jackman in America.[22]

Jackman continued his running commentary on Renaissance writers.
Wallace Thurman's novel—*Infants of the Spring,* with its heavily satirized
versions of a number of Renaissance notables—was "By no means . . .
the Negro novel." On the other hand, Jessie Fauset's *Plum Bun* was declared "lousy, absolutely terrible. . . . It is bad, bad, bad." Jackman liked
Cullen's new poem, "The Black Christ," but he had had to read it twice,
calling it a "seething piece of work." (Later, at the end of the year, he
would express his disapproval of the drawings by Charles Cullen in the
published volume.) He wanted to know how Cullen's work on the libretto was going, probably a reference to the opera he had undertaken
with Grace Still. Then, rather abruptly, he suggested that Cullen consider
writing children's poems, an idea that would rest almost ten years in ger-
mination. It could be that the effervescent Jackman found the poetry of
The Black Christ too bleak to adorn the lifestyle of an aesthete. He also
ran into Hughes backstage at a Marian Anderson concert, dressed in a
tuxedo and aiding an elderly woman, "at least an octogenarian"—probably Charlotte Osgood Mason, Hughes's wealthy white patron.

All the while he supplied Cullen with gossip he was also receiving letters himself from several writers in a network of correspondence. Claude McKay had written Wallace Thurman, who then relayed the news to Jackman, that he, McKay, felt Cullen "has learned to play that kind of politics already. I hope his poetry will not have to pay the debt." This referred to what McKay felt was Cullen's hypocritical praise of the poetry of James Weldon Johnson, whose influential book of poems, *God's Trombones*, had recently appeared and was reviewed by Cullen in the *Bookman*. Jackman enjoyed an introduction to Richmond Barthé, arranged by Locke, who was taking his "godfather" position seriously, convinced that Negroes had not used their opportunities to the best advantage. Jackman always kept the keen edge of his satirical eyes well honed. Describing Jesse Fauset's new husband as an insurance company assistant manager, he quipped that Jessie insisted on being called "Mrs. Harris" and that she always referred to her spouse as "Herbie." During a party celebrating Fauset's *Plum Bun*, "Pappa [*sic*] Du Bois said a few fitting remarks." While there, Jackman had to fend off the gossipmongering of someone named Bob Douglas, who was pumping him for news of Cullen and Yolande. Another party seemed markedly more lively; this was the farewell gathering for the cast of *Porgy*, and both Jack Johnson, the heavyweight champion, and Bojangles, the legendary dancer, were in attendance.

By the spring of 1929 Jackman had made plans to spend the coming summer months in Paris, where he would stay with Anne. But several pleasures intervened before he left Harlem. He met Bessie Smith; he heard Stravinsky's "Les Noces," his dance cantata that some consider Bronislava Nijinska's choreographic masterpiece; and he was introduced to Princess Violette Murat at a party at the Dark Tower salon.[23] Jackman recorded an anecdote that shows he was a skilled raconteur. Some of Hughes's contributions to a book were thought to have been plagiarized, and Jackman was interviewed by the grievant's high-priced lawyer, in order that he might explain Hughes's lyrics. The sight of the very proper gentlemanly lawyer quizzing him about the precise meanings of terms like "jelly roll" and "shake that thing" left Jackman in stitches. There appeared in the spring two of Jackman's artistic efforts: he had a bit part as a camel driver in a Lord Dunsany play called *Tents of the Arabs*, and he published a small review of a play for the *Tatler* under the pseudonym "Basil Winter," his great-grandfather's name.[24] He also further indulged his theatrical leanings when he directed Georgia Douglas Johnson's one-act play, *Plumes*. Then on July 5 he gladly sailed for France.

After the end of the summer and his return to Harlem, where his wife and daughter joined him, Jackman continued to advise Cullen on emotional and personal matters. He referred to Edward—Edward Perry, the dancer who was intimate with Cullen—warning Cullen that he should not confide in him about his birth parents.[25] Apparently, the relation between Cullen and Perry was under strain. Cullen had obviously already shared things about his childhood with Jackman, who was himself reserved when it came to facets of his personal life. That Jackman would consider Cullen willing to share such confidences with Perry means that Perry and Cullen had been intimate for some time. Jackman also urged Cullen to break loose from the reverend; "your father's eyes are not yours," he counseled. The *Amsterdam News* had reported on the divorce, referring to Yolande as "Miss Y. DuBois." Cullen at this time was enrolled in French courses at the Sorbonne, perhaps already contemplating becoming a teacher of French, or getting a PhD in it, as he had once told Yolande. Previously he had asked Jackman to enquire about the New York City Public School System's requirements for a teacher's license. The French diet, meanwhile, was catching up with him, that and the strain of the divorce; he shared with Jackman the fact that he had dental problems, hives, and stomach complaints.

In the spring of 1930 Cullen made plans to visit the Riviera. Jackman had several months earlier heard his doctor advise him to cut back on the socializing, but he was also resting up for the coming crossing, where he would rendezvous with Cullen in Paris. At this point their correspondence breaks off and doesn't resume until 1944, since the two men were together often as they shared some of Cullen's twelve straight sojourns in Europe and of course communicated frequently in person and by phone when Cullen returned to Harlem after the summer of 1930. He had extended his Guggenheim for an extra year, so from the fall of 1928 until the late summer of 1930, he had resided in Paris. For some of that time he settled at 4, rue du Parc de Montsouris, a charming little street that ran alongside the park. A lovely and extensive green space, the Parc Montsouris itself was located in the southeastern part of the city, in the fourteenth arrondissement. A number of artists from the School of Paris, such as Alberto Giacometti, had studios not faraway, and relatively few tourists ventured into that part of the city. Sometime later Cullen moved to a more centrally located Left Bank room on the rue de l'Ecole de Médecine, to which he returned a number of times in the following summers.

The period that Cullen spent in Paris during his Guggenheim Fellowship and afterward coincided with the adventures of fabled expatriate groups, some of whom included American writers who were already famous and were growing more so, like Ernest Hemingway and Gertrude Stein. In addition to these writers, there were many people involved in the arts and the cultural ferment that embraced African American music, avant-garde magazines, and bohemian nightlife. The crash of the American stock market in October 1929 at first fueled the frenzy, but eventually it caused many expatriates to return to the United States. Only occasionally, however, did an African American artist join a group of white writers. One exception was Claude McKay, who was friendly with some of the people associated with Robert McAlmon, and of course renowned singers and dancers like Bricktop and Josephine Baker had many white fans. But Cullen appears to have been restricted to his fellow African Americans, with a few notable exceptions. An evening at the dazzling Bal Colonial Martinique, for example, would include mingling with natives of Martinique but also African Americans and white Frenchmen. Edward Perry, in a newspaper column about the changing fashions in dance steps, titled "Beguine Is Shimmy Plus Mess Around," described the patrons, the music, and the atmosphere in terms of something like total stimulation, yet he was able to testify that the moves of the French dance were softer than those of its two components.[26]

The experience of being an expatriate and an artist satisfied Cullen in deeply important ways, though he did not automatically achieve the social freedoms that awaited the white artists when they returned to America.[27] Throughout the nearly continuous thirty months Cullen resided in the city he came to know almost all of the community of African American artists, many of whom he visited frequently and all of whom he seemed to admire. Many visitors to Paris sought out one or another of the expatriate communities, and the many African Americans who took up residence there were generous and supportive with each other, forming their version of such an enclave. Obviously, the favorable exchange rate between the dollar and the franc supplied sufficient encouragement to those like Cullen and Walrond who had won American fellowships. Not every aspect was perfect. Hughes, for one, had struck a negative note back in 1924, when he was short of funds and working long hours at night in menial jobs in Montmartre. Complaining of the lack of hot water and the mercenary attitude of the Parisians, he shouted to Cullen, "Kid, stay in Harlem!" adding that Parisians didn't like Americans "*of any color.*"[28] Another skeptical but keen-eyed visitor left a telling retrospective description; this was from the redoubt of Claude McKay's 1937 autobiography, *A Long Way from Home.*

> The cream of Harlem was in Paris. There was the full cast of *Blackbirds* . . . just as fascinating a group off the stage as they were extraordinary on the stage. The *Porgy* actors had come over from London. There was an army of school teachers and nurses. There were Negro communists going to and returning from Russia. There were Negro students from London and Scotland and Berlin and the French universities. There were presidents and professors of the best Negro colleges. And there were painters and writers and poets, of whom the most outstanding was Countée Cullen.[29]

This unqualified praise of Cullen might well have surprised the poet, since the often dyspeptic McKay used his autobiography to settle several scores, most notoriously one with Alain Locke ("a perfect symbol of the Aframerican [*sic*] rococo," as he put it). Off and on McKay had felt uneasy in Harlem and with his own role in the Renaissance, mainly because he sensed his Jamaican origin was held against him, but he was generally content in Paris. Perhaps it was Cullen's unalloyed pleasure in Parisian things that McKay took note of, and it helped soften his views, which were often mercurial. In any case, Cullen's years in Paris at the end of the 1920s were only additive elements in his reputation. To the extent that he thoroughly enjoyed Paris, so equally did the African American community there welcome him into the midst of their cultural pursuits and personal pleasures.

The list of names in the plastic arts that he came to know, or know better, reads like a who's who of African American sculpture and painting.[30] There was first of all Henry Ossawa Tanner, by then aged but still a beacon of international fame and prestige. A recent winner of a Rosenthal Fellowship, Augusta Savage, the doyenne of African American sculpture, came to know Cullen well. So, too, did Hale Woodruff, who had met Cullen a few years earlier. Woodruff was often impecunious but striving to perfect and broaden his painting, and he made a point of meeting Tanner when he first came to Paris and briefly studied with him in his studio. Cullen also met the sculptor Nancy Elizabeth Prophet, in part at the urging of DuBois. She had arrived in Paris in 1922 and stayed for a decade. Palmer Hayden was also there, spending five years studying at the Ecole des Beaux-Arts. A decade younger than Woodruff, he had won one of the Harmon prizes given to painters while working as a janitor in the basement of the foundation. Among the authors in this veritable colony whom Cullen knew, or came to know, were René Maran, whose Goncourt Prize novel *Batouala* endeared him to many African American writers, and Eric Walrond—Cullen's fellow worker at *Opportunity* and also the winner of a Guggenheim, who arrived in Paris just months before Cullen.

Some of the members of Cullen's circle in Paris were friends of his before the Guggenheim Fellowship began. Hale Woodruff was perhaps the most important of these. One of the more highly celebrated African American painters in the twentieth century, Woodruff was born in Cairo, Illinois, but soon moved to Indianapolis, where his study of art intensified. In 1927 Cullen met him there when he had gone to give a poetry reading at the local YMCA. Eventually, he was able to spend time in Paris during Cullen's stay there, and his work began to gain support from the Harmon Foundation and other patrons around this time. Later he studied mural painting with Diego Rivera in Mexico, and his three-part mural depicting the Amistad rebellion (1938) still graces the library at Talledega University. Woodruff had also befriended Locke, who would include the work of many of his students in his important book, *The Negro in Art*, as Woodruff, through teaching at Atlanta University, and eventually New York University, was formatively influential for many painters throughout the forties and fifties.[31] He and Cullen were close from the beginning. He sent Cullen a painting or drawing the year they first met, saying: "The picture is merely a slight token of my deep appreciation for the regard in which you seem to hold me. All my pictures are like children to me. Being the father of so many I can hardly take care of them all, so I have only appointed you guardian of one of the youngsters." Arriving in Paris several months before Cullen, he was on good terms with his fellow painter Palmer Hayden. Woodruff was decidedly under the sway of Henry Ossawa Tanner, who had expatriated to France some years earlier. Woodruff tried to arrange a meeting with Tanner, only to discover that the older artist (he was nearing his seventieth birthday) was at his retreat on the Normandy coast. Undeterred, Woodruff traveled to see the master and spent time with him in his studio. In a sense this meeting formed one of the main force fields in the Paris circle of African American writers and painters during the late 1920s and early 1930s.[32]

Woodruff possessed an experimental streak, or at least a curiosity about the new styles of painting that had come to the fore in Paris after the waves of impressionism had begun to recede. Spending many hours in museums and at various exhibitions, Woodruff was largely self-taught, in part because he couldn't afford tuition at the art schools. His friend Hayden chose not to share Woodruff's taste and stayed at work in more traditional styles. But Woodruff combined a personal modesty with his talent and his willingness to struggle along with little money. Locke made him loans, and Cullen purchased the portrait he did of him. Woodruff maintained himself on precarious terms, writing tourist observations for his hometown newspaper, the *Indianapolis Star,* and continuing to beseech the Harmon Foundation for advice and support. During this time he was beset with contradictory impulses: the people at the Harmon Foundation urged him to use European styles along lines that would satisfy white patrons and at the same time asked him to work more on Negro subjects, advice that Locke seconded. Cullen shared this tension, driven as he was by his love of the high European style and yet bound to his attachments to his race. For both writers and visual artists the Renaissance meant, among other things, facing the problematic question of just what sort of audience should be addressed.

Augusta Savage, who became perhaps the most famous African American sculptor of her time, met Cullen when she spent two years in Paris, beginning in 1929. She was already known for her artistic skills, despite the fact that her parents' religion, which felt that the making of "graven images" was sinful, had at first hampered her growth. Eventually, after winning local prizes, she arrived in New York City in 1921 with less that five dollars in her pocket. By 1923 she had won a fellowship for summer study from the French government, but it was retracted when racist fellow students objected. Still, she possessed the shine of a Harlem luminary, as she helped inspire the group that published *FIRE!!*, and her work was exhibited by the Harmon Foundation. Despite economic hardship, she made her way to Paris with the help of a fellowship from the Julius Rosenwald Fund, and there she was able to exhibit her work and travel more widely throughout Europe. Cullen not only fantasized about starting a salon with her, Dorothy West, and others, but he commissioned a set of bronze bookends from her. She came home to New York City in 1932 and became active in establishing and promoting community art groups, such as the Harlem Artists' Guild and the Harlem Community Art Center, where she served as the first director. A commissioned work, *The Harp,* inspired by James Weldon Johnson's "Lift Every Voice and Sing," graced the entrance of the Contemporary Arts Building at the New York World's Fair in 1939. She ended her days teaching art classes in upstate New York.[33]

Cullen's love affair with Paris began, of course, on his first trip there in 1926. During that visit he saw Josephine Baker and commemorated the experience in his "Dark Tower" column for February 1927.[34] "She was like Cinderella touched with the magic wand," he wrote, "only this Cinderella balked at clothes." All of Paris was "in a state of violent hysteria over her," and Cullen described how women went sunbathing just to emulate her skin tones. From then on, each subsequent visit provided him occasions to praise the city. In one of the three columns he wrote for the *Crisis,* keeping to the arrangement he had made with DuBois, he discussed French manners, contrasting them favorably with those of his native land. Still, the manners of mass-market tourism had already developed. In the first of the *Crisis* columns he described observing an encounter that dealt with language. An American lady tried to convey her needs to a French train conductor by shouting ever louder in his ear. Cullen then observed: "When this novel method of teaching a foreign language in one lesson failed, she remarked with real feeling and disgust, 'Why I thought everybody over here spoke two languages.' The conductor surely spoke French and it is not past belief that he may have been well versed in Chinese. But to the Lords of the Earth two languages mean your own and English." The column went on to tell of a missed meeting with Claude McKay, as Cullen and Jackman sailed for Algiers before McKay could join them. On board both of them wore berets and were mistaken for Egyptians. Later they went to a beach in Algeria where there were only people of color, most of them poor Arabs who couldn't afford the more elite resorts. Cullen took an auto tour of the northwest coast of France, which allowed him to visit with Henry Ossawa Tanner at Étaples, where the master painter duly impressed him, as he watched him "cut and mix salad at his table, seasoning it with the meticulousness of the conscientious artist." He quoted the line from the Robert Browning poem about memorable meetings with artistic geniuses: "And did you once see Shelley plain?" The city of Paris and the whole of France, and parts of Europe, were responding eagerly to the New Negro: "always and everywhere a keen interest in the Negro, in many instances a livelier knowledge of what he is doing than is found in his own purlieus." Clearly, Cullen fit in remarkably well, and the expatriate experience thoroughly delighted him.

Keeping a semblance of balance, he recounted in the November 1929 *Crisis* a visit with Claire Goll, a multilingual novelist who also translated Maran's *Batouala* into German. She herself had recently finished her own novel, a story of miscegenation between a white European woman and a black African prince. Cullen's fascination with this topic went back at least as far as his high school days, when he mentioned to William Brown the plot of a projected novel he never managed to write. As for Madame Goll's treatment of the topic, the story turns melodramatic and concludes with infidelity and murder. Cullen's reaction to Madame Goll tells something about how he might have handled the topic, complete with hesitant ellipses. "I have no personal brief for inter-marriage, but I do await eagerly the advent of that pioneer who will in the face of . . . it is true, not millions, but surely several . . . successful interracial marriages forget his formula and write one such story in which the ending will be happy and probable." Going on to spell out his objections to the "formula," Cullen says that in his opinion such marriages are likely to end for any number of reasons other than that of the interracial basis, and it is too easy "to cast all blame in that direction." It isn't easy to determine what drives Cullen's demur in this case, whether it is an aesthetic offense involving probability and formulaic plots or simply the persistence of racist superstition. But the encounter with Goll demonstrated that issues of race and art would persist even abroad.

Cullen fitfully kept diaries for his years in Paris and recorded many of the cultural events he attended.[35] In November 1928 he heard the Jubilee Singers at the Theatre Champs-Elysées, where they merited six encores, and saw *Rigoletto* at the Trocadero. He enjoyed an introduction to the English poet Richard Aldington and "his first wife." Cullen must have been misled, however, as Aldington was still married to Hilda Doolittle (H.D.), since their divorce was not made final until 1938, though the two had not been together for almost a decade. Aldington was probably in the company of Brigit Patmore, with whom he lived in Paris at this time. Cullen visited the Rodin Museum with Woodruff, and the two also went to see *Napoleon,* the extraordinary film classic by Abel Gance. He also coolly added an entry for December 13, probably 1929, which read: "Yolande and I separated. Tea in the afternoon with Henry O. Tanner. The Irving Underhills there, with Miss Profit [*sic*], a sculptor."[36]

Prophet, who would go on to win much praise in America and France and teach art at Atlanta College with Hale Woodruff, at this time was barely surviving the poverty and loneliness she experienced in Paris. Coming from a wholly unsupportive family, and separated from an unhelpful husband, she arrived in Paris in 1925, strong willed but with little more than three hundred dollars. Her studio and living arrangements were especially meager, but she eventually enjoyed financial support from the Harmon Foundation and from private patronage, derived in part from DuBois's effort to secure her assistance. She came to know, not only Tanner, but also Augusta Savage, who spent her Paris days equally impoverished. In the later 1920s she went back and forth between Harlem and Paris, finding ways to exhibit her carved and sculpted busts and statues, made in realistic idioms and out of traditional material, though many unfortunately survive only through photographs.

In the summer of 1929, Cullen came to know Prophet better, and he interviewed her for a feature article that would appear in *Opportunity* a year later, in July 1930. Cullen was struck by her mixed heritage and described her in haptic terms: as she walked across her studio, he saw her as "revealing her Indian ancestry in her straight, unbending gait; unleashing her Negro blood in a warm smile." In July Cullen hosted a party for Prophet, to honor her for her exhibition mounted by the Société des Artistes Français. The event was significant enough that it was covered by J. A. Rogers, the famous historian and columnist, who was working on pieces about the African American colony in Paris for the

Baltimore Afro-American.[37] Prophet wrote Cullen shortly after the party, her letter filled with criticism about writers and artists who forced their work rather than discovering something new and urgent to write about or paint. She was fairly sweeping in her critique but held up a positive criterion as well: "It seems to me that the Negro has something more than petty grievances and prejudices or light pleasure to express. I do believe that underneath there is something more vital. In deed in your poetry one senses this. . . . When the negro [sic] had not education he sang the spirituals. Now that he has it, it should only facilitate the expression. There should be the same sincerity and ardour." She concluded by opining, "it seems hard to believe that the race has gone so far that an individual could become content." Within months she returned to the United States and enjoyed something like a triumphant reception, as one of her sculptures won the Otto Kahn Prize, and she went to parties with Jackman and Owen Dodson, the writer and Howard professor. Still, she missed Paris, telling Cullen, "I long to be there in the solitude of my own study, I do not like being famous." Her commitment to her art remained imposingly ascetic. Cullen imagined that one of her statues could "exemplify the unfathomed laugh of her race at a world it does not understand and which can never understand it." She and Cullen shared many affinities, not least those concerned with the issues of race and art.

One of the chief sources of pleasure that Cullen enjoyed in Paris during his years there—and in subsequent summer visits—was the friendship of Stephen and Sophie Victor Greene.[38] This couple possessed considerable wealth and their Parisian social life was the stuff of dazzlement. They partied frequently, often enjoying the company of Augusta Savage and Hale Woodruff, among others. Travel played a large part in their entertainments as well, for they went with Woodruff to Cagnes-sur-Mer, on the French Riviera, and on other occasions spent time in Morocco and Seville, from where they sent Cullen a postcard describing the "bull fights and music and dancing, hand clapping and pale golden sherry." They encouraged Cullen in his writing, and Steve, as Cullen addressed him, wanted to make sure that the poet stuck to his plan to visit Abyssinia (perhaps in connection with the opera he was to work on with Grace Still), though apparently this fell through. Playfulness marked many aspects of the friendship, as Steve often signed his postcards and letters with the paw prints of the Greene cats, Monique, Unique, and

16. Sophie Victor Green, one of Cullen's friends in Paris, in a portrait taken by Man Ray. The inscription reads "To the most adorable person in the world Countée."

Siki. Steve also bragged about how he had learned the Lindberg hop from Augusta, and he routinely sent Cullen recipes to recall his Paris taste for onion soup and *crème au chocolat*.

Sophie seemed especially enamored of Cullen, inscribing the photograph that Man Ray took of her, "To the most adorable person in the world, Countée." Ray, of course, was one of the century's most praised art photographers and moved in surrealist circles, but evidently Cullen did not meet anyone in the white avant-garde. Sophie loved to gossip, and she once regaled Cullen with an anecdote about Claude McKay. McKay was visiting in Fez at the same time the French president was in town. Somehow the authorities feared that McKay, known then for his radical political beliefs, would cause trouble, so they conspired to have someone send McKay a letter that drew him out of town. A Moroccan guide that she had hired related all this to Sophie, so there may have been considerable exaggeration involved in the transmission. Six months later she offered Cullen a place to stay should he return to Paris in the summer of 1931. In the same letter with this offer she described a night of heavy drinking and carousing, all of which culminated in Eric Walrond being stuck with the tab. Walrond forlornly offered to leave his watch or a personal check as a partial payment, but the café owner was unimpressed. The police arrived and took control, with Walrond spending the night in jail. The next day, back at the café, Walrond spotted Jackman walking by and breathlessly filled him in on the episode. Jackman coolly remarked, "I didn't know anything new could happen to you." Walrond, with a clipped response, said he didn't think it was funny.

The Greenes were involved in the film world, mainly as technicians rather than producers or directors. But their abilities led them at one point to become involved in a project with Isaak Kitrosser. Along with Berenice Abbott, also a close friend of Sophie, Kitrosser worked among the art photographers in Paris at the time; this also accounts for Sophie having her portrait photograph taken by Man Ray. Kitrosser's project, however, involved portraying New York City in a way that would mimic "what an intelligent European would see in his first 24 hours . . . if he went everywhere and kept his eyes open." The plan involved Kitrosser's round trip to New York to do the filming and then returning to Paris, where Steve and Sophie would edit the work. Like many other projects at the time, this apparently faltered, and Sophie never alluded to it again. A few years later the Greenes returned to America, living for a while with Steve's mother in Philadelphia. They maintained their friendship with Cullen, writing to him from Argentina, where Steve worked for a film company, and later from Washington, DC. In 1945 Cullen invited them to come and visit in his then-new house in Tuckahoe, some of the money for which came from a loan the Greenes made to him. As a couple, Steve and Sophie might easily suggest comparison, to some degree at least, with Scott and Zelda Fitzgerald, minus the melodrama but reflecting the lifestyle. In any case, for Cullen they conveyed the spirit of Paris between the wars, and they helped intensify his commitment to a place he was always reluctant to leave.[39]

More distant from the routine events of Parisian life, however, were the idealized aesthetic values that led many African American artists and writers to look beyond the everyday to larger sources of cultural energy and authority. Cullen was enthusiastic about Paris, not only because of its daily pleasures, but because it put him in touch with a community of artists striving to go beyond the narrow confines of Jim Crow and the remaining feelings about white supremacy that were rife in American society. Cullen went to the vital center of his love for Paris and for France in his sonnet "To France," included in the volume he published in 1935. The imagery was at once pagan, medieval, and mystical. The sestet intensifies the background of deprivation and denial that acutely offsets the final note of purest desire.

> As he whose eyes are gouged craves light to see,
> And he whose limbs are broken strength to run,
> So have I sought in you that alchemy
> That knits my bones and turns me to the sun;
> And found across a continent of foam
> What was denied my hungry heart at home.

Realizing that he could not expatriate himself permanently doubtlessly saddened Cullen, even as he knew that the reverend, along with countless other ties of duty and love, would keep him bound to Harlem. In a sense Paris became the site of deep desire, and Harlem remained the place of responsibility. Ahead lay financial stress, creative frustration, and professional limitations. Before the 1930s were half over Cullen would have written virtually all of his lyric poetry, but his life as an American writer still had some horizons yet to be measured.

5

Remakings, 1930–1935

The years that followed the Depression in America were even harder for many black authors than they were for white ones. Though Cullen's steady employment as a teacher in the New York Public School System, beginning in 1934, would keep him far from penury, he was unable to generate the royalties he hoped for a few years earlier. This larger social and historical context contributed—in imprecise but unignorable ways—to Cullen's feelings that he should try to redefine himself as a writer. His commitment to lyric poetry lasted throughout his life. But the drive and promise he showed in that uniquely absorbing field tended to fade after 1930. In significant ways, he remade himself as a writer. Always attracted to the theater—especially considering that it was an enthusiasm he shared with his closest friends—it was as a playwright that he spent most of his compositional energies. Though unable in the short run to obtain a producer for the plays he wrote, he never gave up hope that these dramatic efforts would eventually be staged. There were several formats that he wrangled with—a translation of a Greek classical tragedy; an opera libretto; the adaptation of two different novels about African American life into dramatic form (his own and one by Arna Bontemps); a one-act play that used political agitation; and a radio serial. The Depression did not transform Cullen into a sociopolitical activist, but it did bring forward his long-held beliefs about racial justice. Doing so, the period of economic collapse and travail also forced him to readdress the issues of art and racial identity that had impelled him for many years.

The community of African American writers that had formed various friendships among themselves in the Renaissance saw those friendships either draw back or intensify in the decade of the 1930s. In the early part of the decade Cullen's friendship with Dorothy West deepened, and it offered important consolation to both writers. West was born in 1907, in Boston, into one of the wealthiest African American families there; her father had been industrious and highly successful as a merchant, though he began life as an emancipated slave. She attended elite schools, including Girls' Latin, one of Boston's most prestigious. Like Cullen, she was an exceptional student and displayed literary aspirations from her very early years. Her short story won second place in the *Opportunity* contest for fiction in 1926 (Zora Neale Hurston shared the prize with her), and she probably met Cullen around this time. After traveling to New York City, and Harlem, to accept the *Opportunity* award, she was dazzled by the city and decided to stay. Few if any were more enthusiastic than she about the sense of innovation and expansion offered by the Renaissance. Taking an apartment in Harlem with Helene Johnson, whom she referred to as her cousin, the two women began to socialize with all the Renaissance writers, while living on very modest means. She and Cullen especially took to dancing, gin, and all-night parties, sharing confidences and literary ambitions. She often arranged for the farewell party that marked Cullen's departure for Paris each June or July. Working for several years on her first novel, *The Living Is Easy* (1948), she saw it appear to strong notices but weak sales. Surviving the late 1930 and early 1940s by securing support as a WPA writer, she eventually retired to Oak Bluff, on Cape Cod. She continued writing until her death in 1998, generally hailed as the oldest surviving member of the Harlem Renaissance.

West's affection for Cullen was deep and lively, extending for two decades; she often discussed affairs of the heart with him (she also later reminisced that she had proposed marriage to Hughes), and concern for their writing projects occupied much of their interchanges. At one point, in an undated letter, she voiced uncertainty about how close she and Cullen might be able to grow. Her affection comes through, though, as she tells him, "I do love you, Countée. Do go on loving me. You aren't a rock or an anchor, but sometimes be a shoulder." Eager to have him write her once a week from Paris (a schedule he never approached), she probed a bit, perhaps not knowing of his sexual orientation, and said, "I don't think you've got another girl. But I daresay you've got another hobby." In another letter, also undated, she bluntly questioned Cullen about her sense of propriety: "do you disapprove of people trying to re-form others?" In the same passage she refers cryptically to Bruce Nugent, whose rather dissolute behavior earned him considerable notice during the Renaissance. West then added (whether referring to Nugent or Cullen is not completely clear): "I did want our lives to mean something together and, of course, to me that meant a baby." With a mix of naïveté, genuine talent, bravery, and a generous heart, she was able to form a friendship with the normally reserved Cullen that was seldom matched by other writers.[1]

Cullen's sexual orientation, combined with the regretful situation after his wedding, likely conditioned his response to West. But she seems not to have addressed the situation between them in simple terms. As he did with Yolande, Cullen treated West with more than gentlemanly solicitude, and the time they spent apart allowed them both to work out a certain sort of fantasy. At one point, in yet another undated letter, West hinted strongly that they had made some sort of tentative arrangement; but she also rehearsed the negative examples of the marriages of two other couples they both knew well. "Of course I'll wait two years if you want me to. It was simply that I thought it was while life seemed so much fun that we should be enjoying it together. (Yet watching Aaron and Alta [Douglas], and Rudolph and Jane [Fisher], and Aaron and Rudolph not being attentive, one thinks perhaps marriage is a dull business for the woman.) Ugly thought! I've dismissed it."[2] Here a feminist sense of fairness jangled against a proper Bostonian sense of how women should serve in their social roles. Perhaps overriding any sense of conflicted feelings, however, West continued to display her resilient romantic yearning. "I wish I could dismiss you," she tells Cullen, "but I can't. I believe in your talent. I don't want you to rest on your laurels of twenty-one. That

17. Dorothy West, circa 1925. Recently arrived in New York City, West was able to live in her own apartment in midtown Manhattan.

beautiful performance! There are so many attainable stars. Fetch me a handful." Some of the recurrent pathos in their relationship came from the fact that, at times at least, West believed more in Cullen than he believed in himself.

In October 1929, while Cullen was in Paris, he asked her if they could still hope to set up a "utopian household," in effect a sort of literary salon, which would include many with whom they both shared friendships. Cullen proposed including both Augusta Savage and Eric Walrond as part of the group, but he quickly added that he had to hold that suggestion in "abeyance," since Cullen and West were to be "the guiding spirits of the venture," and West had not yet had a chance to meet Savage. Meanwhile, Cullen settled for pleading with West to come and let him show her Paris. Several months later he was back in Pleasantville and hoping to have a chance to read West's work in manuscript. By this time Cullen had started work on his novel and was "having a damn wretched time" with it. He had also described his plans for writing plays, hoping that he could earn a reasonable living in the theater. Arrangements for a party were being formulated, and Cullen wanted to give it a special format: "But let's draw the color line for once, and invite *no whites*. Make it a pure nigger party. We can get off better like that!" In literary matters Cullen was occasionally reluctant to display for white amusement the more raucous entertainment of all-night parties, but he never hesitated to enjoy it firsthand.

Cullen, in this particular instance, wanted to make sure West invited Jackman, Edward Perry, and Arna Bontemps. Perry had performed in *Porgy,* the dramatization of the Dubose Heyward novel (this was prior to the famous Gershwin opera), and stayed with the troupe that traveled to London in 1928. West herself took a small part in the production but was not with the troupe in London. Perry and Cullen, according to some accounts, were lovers, but if West knew this—or knew anything about Cullen's sexual orientation—she never mentioned it in her correspondence with him.[3] The summer months of 1931 saw Cullen back in Paris, recovering from a bout of seasickness and thanking West for serving as hostess at the good-bye party. He lamented that he left America before he and Arna could get any positive news from producers about their play. It was the start of a tiring and decade-long attempt to write and have produced the two men's version of Bontemps's first novel, *God Sends Sunday.* Novel writing was also the order of the day, and Cullen continued to wrestle with his first novel, *One Way to Heaven,* telling West he was "hoping and praying everyday to have something definite decided" about the conclusion to the narrative. But there was the most enjoyable company of Augusta Savage, one of Cullen's "prime delights," to serve as compensation, even though she was facing the probable forced return to America due to lack of funds. Later that year—on September 26—back in Harlem, he had seen *Fast and Furious,* the latest theatrical effort by Hurston, but found it "trivial" and "unworthy of her talent." Meanwhile, his and Arna's play went begging, though he kept telling himself that "some enterprising producer will arrive and find a gold mine in little Augie," referring to the play's central character.

However, some progress was possible, and he could finally exclaim, "The leaky old novel was just finished this afternoon. I don't think I shall ever do another one. The torture was too exquisite." On the other hand, Cullen expressed his darker mood when he included in the letter to West his sonnet "I have not loved you in the noblest way." After opening the octave with this line, Cullen begins the sestet, "The noblest way is fraught with too much pain." The poem concludes, with pained but stoic indirection, that his heart is too easily wounded:

> My mother never dipped me in the Styx.
> And who would find me weak and vulnerable
> Need never aim an arrow at my heel.

This poem, like others from this time, can obviously be read as referring to his broken marriage, but might just as easily apply to other relations of the period. In any case, the typical poem from this period mixed affection and pain, inextricably.[4]

Cullen made use of his friend from Harvard, John Trounstine, to try and help West publish her novel. He had enjoyed reading the manuscript, but felt the ending was weak, as it seemed "too much of a slow down." But "the conversation is so good, and much of the straight writing is quite biblical," he added, meaning to keep her believing in her ultimate success. Then in 1932 West used her adventurous spirit to the full and signed on for a trip to Russia on the S.S. *Bremen.* She joined a party of about twenty-five actors and technicians, headed by Hughes and Louise Thompson, all engaged in producing a movie there, *Black and White,* which would explore the contrast between race relations in America and Russia. Various difficulties stymied the enterprise, and it was scrapped in part because of opposition from anticommunist officials.[5] Her letters to Cullen, the first of which was "infectiously happy," impressed and delighted him. "I wish I could be in Moscow with you. None of the anti-Soviet tales have frightened me, and although I have no communistic tendencies, I have a keen desire to see the place." He lamented that it was only the pressure of his family ties that kept him from applying for a place in the "contingent." At the same time he continued urging her to visit him, instructing her that it "would be a spiritual catastrophe to come to Europe twice and not see Paris." But, in the wake of the film project's failure, West elected to travel throughout Europe, while Hughes went further east and spent the next two years exploring the Soviet republics.

Though Cullen had sailed back to the States after the summer, he made it a point in November to send West the addresses of his Parisian friends. Chief among these was Sophie Victor Greene and her husband Stephen, Cullen's close companions while he was in Paris. He was glad West was "not going to pass Paris by," as it was "the loveliest, most humane spot in all the world." Though he claimed there was little to report from Harlem as far as the theater went, he did speak of West's friend Edna Thomas, who worked with her in *Porgy* and was currently acting a modest part in *Ol' Man Satan*, in which she "looked her own beautiful self." However, the play ran only three weeks. This called to mind Cullen's own frustrated efforts in dramatic writing, as he had still found no luck in a producer for what he and Bontemps were calling *Lil' Augie*, and he had also completed two acts of the theatrical adaptation of his novel. Financial pressures continued to weigh: "I am making no money; but then I am not alone; so I don't complain too loudly." Though he said he talked with God about the matter, God didn't seem ready to help; Cullen used a dash of blasphemy when he quipped, "Poor spirit; I suppose there is a run on His bank too."

In the early spring of 1933 Cullen arrived at a very low point. He felt bad that he was unable to cable to West, still abroad in Europe, the extra money he had promised her. But he was nearly broke and dependent on the reverend's largesse to carry him through. Fewer and fewer lectures meant even this meager supplement was drying up. "I cannot fool myself into believing that I am worse off than ever so many people, but I am so much worse off than I have ever been before." Still involved in the "dreary sickening attempt to get [his] plays on," even though many plays were failing weekly, he was left "very much without hope." He went on gloomily:

> Added to this I am getting more and more neurotic as the days go by; I haven't written a line of poetry in months, and I begin to wonder if

I ever will. I have ideas for all sorts of things, poems, plays, a novel, a child's story, part of an autobiography, but nothing gets beyond the plan stage. . . . And I do wish you were here. It would be sort of stabilizing to be able to go down to sixty-sixth street and get things off my mind.

Despite this despair, he rallied himself to tell West that she should thoroughly enjoy her European travels: "nothing New York can offer [is] as valuable and as soul-filling as the things you are seeing and doing now." The best of the rewards of travel fostered an aesthetic fulfillment. "So far removed from bad gin, the color question, number[s] playing, even spirituals; so near the things a lover of beauty can take to his heart and hold there in an eternal embrace."

West's father passed away while she was overseas, and her mother had grown frail (both of which likely prompted her return in the early summer of 1933), and Cullen himself was still mourning for Mrs. Cullen, who had passed away in October of 1932, succumbing to "severe infection and pneumonia," and having suffered from other maladies as well.[6] He had written "Tribute (To My Mother)" to mark the "heavy loss," but it was one of his most dark and cryptic poems, in which he describes himself as someone "least noble of a churlish race, / Least kind of those by nature rough and crude."[7] Only through the image of his mother's face is he able to gain the least sense of worth and redemption. After returning to America, West decided to settle near Roxbury, Massachusetts, where she could comfort her mother. She had missed seeing Cullen on her way through New York, and he was curious to know how she had fared in faraway places: "I want to see if Russia has done anything for your smile." Meanwhile, Cullen had taken and passed the test that would qualify him for teaching French in the public schools, though there were no positions available at the time. Often in the past he expressed his reluctance to teach, anxious that it would interfere with his literary work; nevertheless, an appointment would solve many of his problems.

Throughout the middle years of the 1930s Cullen and West carried on their correspondence with barings of the heart and repeated attempts to bolster one another's spirit and ambition. Each had discovered a lodestar of sorts, Paris for Cullen and Russia for West. She told Cullen that her "mind matured in Moscow. I have a deep richness in me." Hoping to cheer him, she insisted, "you with your young heart will never be more than nineteen, so what does it matter about a grey beard." But moments of self-doubt were not easy to dismiss. She confessed that she didn't attend a single lecture in Russia, she didn't read "one socialist work," and no one there thought she was serious enough. Complaints about the lack of audiences for black literature and theater burst out. "And you know if you invited a half-dozen ofays, every darky in Harlem would contribute a dollar. Oh, my poor race!" she moaned. The absence of resources at times seemed to determine all things. Speaking with tones of sentimental consolation, she told Cullen: "For you to be without plenty is to be without peace . . . yes it is over two years since we felt our future—that future based on a complete understanding, respect, and gentle love—was together." After her return from Moscow she found herself in Massachusetts longing for his companionship. "I sit here alone and am not alone. You will never leave me in spirit again. We said nothing in actual words to this end. Yet I was aware of it our last evening. And that is when I began to know this peace." Hoping fiercely that he will write poems in Paris, she pleads, "Feel thru me. Be glad of the good earth. Let your heart trust. And you will find a poem tripping off your tongue as easy as easy." In all likelihood, Cullen must have hoped rather desperately that she was right.

For her part, West decided to move ahead with plans for heightening her sense of herself as a professional writer. A plucky decision, given the economics of the time, but one West took up eagerly.[8] She began by approaching various black newspapers to add a full-dress literary section that would include not only book reviews but creative contributions as well. "Let us try to recapture the spirit of '26!" she trumpeted. Calling on Cullen's experience at *Opportunity,* she enlisted him as a reviewer, and he also sent her a few poems to use as well. But her efforts achieved very little. Undeterred, she then switched her attention to inaugurating a new literary journal, which she called *Challenge.* The title could refer to many things, not least the fact that the capital she had available for the project totaled but forty dollars. Cullen contributed to two issues, sending along two sonnets in the inaugural issue and a poem, "Magnets," for the second. Though not as aggressive as *FIRE!!, Challenge* contained remarkable things, including two pieces on "Black Paris" by Eslanda Robeson, the wife of the great singer, and "Comments" by Van Vechten, as well as fiction and other essays. Coedited with Jackman, the venture foundered, running for only six issues over the next four years, with decreasing frequency; submissions were so slow to come in and often of such low quality that West decided, right before its demise, to make it a quarterly. Less than two years later she tried again. This was named *New Challenge,* and it included in its solitary issue work by Richard Wright, who served as coeditor; Ralph Ellison's first published work; and Alain Locke's review of McKay's autobiography, *A Long Way from Home.* When she sent Cullen a copy of the new publication, she said, "This magazine is the most unselfish thing I have ever done." After the first few issues of *Challenge* appeared, West moved back to New York City for a while, taking an apartment on Manhattan Avenue next door to Harold Jackman, and then on Sixty-Sixth Street, where she clearly intended the journal to extend and enrich the spirit and the productivity of the Renaissance. By the late 1930s she had returned to Oak Bluffs, Massachusetts, on Martha's Vineyard, where she lived for the remainder of her life.

One Way to Heaven

As early as 1922 Cullen sent Brown a sketch of the plot of a novel he thought about writing, but he put it aside, as he said, until he could ballast it with more life experience. In 1925, during his first semester at Harvard, Cullen wrote to Jackman about the growing interest in the African American novel, alluding to the desire of several writers to gather up the enthusiasm for the Renaissance into a successful work of fiction. The time seemed right, and the audience seemed eager. However, Cullen wasn't yet party to the striving in that arena. Then, by 1930 he had made up his mind and began to spend great amounts of time and energy on writing his novel, as he explained to West and others. *One Way to Heaven* was published in 1932, the same year Wallace Thurman's *Infants of the Spring* appeared and preceding George Schuyler's *Black No More* by several months. Satire apparently had become the order of the day, signaling among other things the weakened status of the literature of racial uplift.[9] Again Cullen faced the questions about presenting unedifying material about members of his race to a white readership. Now he seemed ready, even eager, to depict several aspects of African American society, and even used the novel as the instrument to reveal what he thought of such issues as white supremacy—for example, he took a thorough delight in skewering the "Nordicism" of Lothorp Stoddard. There were decent, immoral, comic, serious, plainspoken, and high-minded characters: his entire social milieu drew Cullen's attention. Though focused on Harlem, the novel's canvas was broad and varied.

One of the first responses Cullen received about his novel came from Charles Johnson when the book had not yet been completed, and it offers a remarkable set of observations, which Johnson, with his characteristic modesty, described as being "two or three things which might prove more or less useful." In fact, they said much more than usual about "the Negro novel." On May 18, Johnson wrote:

> In the first place I was struck with the fact that of all the novels written about Negro life this is perhaps the first that seems to carry a real internal interest. For the most part we have been writing from the inside for outsiders who must view this group according to the grosser conventional patterns. You have managed to achieve a treatment which reveals some of the possibilities of the field for finer and more intimate exploitation. Most of the reading of novels of Negro, on the part of those Negroes who read, is, as you know, not as much with the expectation of sheer entertainment and social exhilaration as to see what the race writers are doing. So far, then, we may consider this a distinct step. I can imagine that if general interest in Negro life proceeds pari passu [goes hand in hand] with Negro literary development, the reading public will find this type of thing just as interesting as the Negroes.

Again the question of the readership arises in connection with literary work by an African American, though here the issue is nuanced. Johnson goes into detail, saying to Cullen that, "you have done I think a very daring thing, paradoxical as it may seem, in making a black girl actually charming, and you have done it rather well." He then gives Cullen one of his higher compliments. "It has been unfortunate that the patterns adopted both by the general public and the Negro public have demanded of writers that they produce a snicker every time a black girl comes into the picture. I looked closely for an overdrawing of this as one tends to lean backwards in overcoming a popular stereotype, but I do not think this appears." Johnson then goes on to offer more advice, all of it along the lines of adjusting details and making characters both more focused and deep. Cullen was able to make some adjustments in his novel, but then it eventually had to stand on its own.

Cullen opened his story with a striking set piece, a scene in which Sam Lucas, a wandering trickster, arrives at a New Year's Eve church service in Harlem. There he fakes his conversion—as he has done may times along his way up from Texas—by throwing away his deck of cards and straight razor on the altar, to the satisfaction of the preacher and the astonishment of the congregation. The beginning paragraphs depict Lucas as a parody of the pilgrim, allegorizing the Great Migration, and they ironically reverse the stereotypical story of the enchainment of good country people in the flesh pits of the metropolis.[10] Nearly everything that follows in the novel is satirical, sometimes in broad strokes, sometimes in almost tender ways. That Cullen used his mother's family name for that of the main male character in the novel suggests he wanted to deal with deep feelings, but in estranged situations. As Reverend Johnson astutely points out, referring to Sam's shape-shifting ability to fake his conversion: "I am not sure that you are not the most despicable man I've ever come across; I'm not sure that you aren't a genius in your way, and I'm far from being certain that you aren't an unwilling instrument in the hands of Heaven. . . . There are some things which we cannot understand." These disjunctions, between different forms of desire and self-presentation, sharply etch the loner, full of amoral conniving, against the social matrix or urbanity and piety. That is largely what supplies the material for the novel.[11]

After the opening chapter, Cullen introduces Mattie Johnson and her aunt, Mandy. Mattie is converted through watching, unknowingly, Sam's pretense at discovering his salvation. The two women make up a peculiar household, as Mandy is both a pious churchgoer and a believer in superstitious folklore. Mattie, beautiful and blameless, falls in love with Sam right away. Her station in life is determined by her being a maid in the service of Constancia Brandon, a high society woman who resides in splendor and runs a salon, called the Booklovers' Club, generally intimidating everyone with her learning and regal vocabulary. Soirées at her house provide Cullen plenty of opportunity for his satirical impulses and allow him to depict the African American elite. She also imperiously demands that Mattie and Sam have their wedding in her house, an event she arranges in a matter of hours. Guests include Walter Derwent, a barely disguised version of Carl Van Vechten, and a brief glimpse of Lawrence Harper, a poet who strongly resembles Langston Hughes. In addition to his dedication of the novel to Jackman, Cullen added an epigraph: "Some of the characters in this book are fictitious." This led many to look for models for each and every character. One obvious link was between Constancia and A'Lelia Walker, the famous patroness and supporter of Cullen. But who, for example, was the Duchess of Uganda based on? Could it have been Princess Violette Murat, a famous lesbian who visited Harlem and whose Parisian exploits had been reported to Cullen in one of Jackman's gossipy letters? But a roman à clef is not what Cullen was really after.

The high society scenes, built around Constancia's relentless hauteur, use satire, while the domestic plot, involving Sam's infidelity to Mattie, employs sentimentality. The high point of the former is the appearance of a professor who is an egregious white supremacist, modeled on Lothorp Stoddard, who delivers a lecture, at Constancia's invitation, on the subject of "The Negro's Threat to Civilization." Her invitation originates only in her desire to see if her guests can sit still while Stoddard spews his bigotry, and the evening turns out rather anticlimactically. More stinging are the satirical thrusts directed at two of Constancia's friends, one being the Duchess of Uganda, who of course has never been to Africa; both are even more voracious seekers after high culture than their hostess. Devout supporters of the "Back-to-Africa" movement, the two ladies are easy targets, and Cullen takes his time making sure that their pretensions are fully displayed.

When Cullen turns to the domestic plot, after finishing with Constancia's evening with the professor, he seems relieved. The novel moves to its conclusion with the last four chapters devoted to Mattie's marriage to Sam, which dissolves according to familiar melodramatic expectations. One of the pivots between the two plots at this point is marked by a long artful excursus that begins chapter 11, describing the arrival of spring in Harlem and conveying Cullen's love for his home territory.

> And like children playing a game, Harlem ran in and out, sloughing over-coats today, loitering on street corners, sowing in laughter and rich talk the rumors of spring, tomorrow shivering back into yesterday's discarded mantle, grumbling at the indecent insistence of winter. But grad-

ually the cold subsided, day by day lost ground, as Harlem, in Harlem's way, rushed out to meet the spring.

The earlier parts of the novel take place during the cold winter, introduced by the New Year's "watch hour" ceremony, and it may seem as if Cullen is setting up a strong thematic rendering of a rebirth for the final third of the book. However, there is a twist, as Sam, "besieged by restlessness," finds the spring far from joyous. "Anything that savors of duty and routine becomes torture," serves as an apothegm that forecasts the infidelity that follows. Sam's conniving and untrustworthy character, hidden by a pleasing physical appearance, though marked by the loss of his left arm (severed when he fell from a train he had been hitching a ride on), holds the central focus of the story.

Cullen takes the occasion to thematize the seasonal changes by contrasting the way Constancia's neighborhood greets the changing weather with what happens in Mattie's. As a set piece, the writing reads well—though more detailed than his use of nature in his poems, it demonstrates Cullen's imaginative feel for the natural world—and clearly it is meant to draw the two plots together. Readers of the novel have often commented on the disjunction between the two plots, with some praising its unique attempt to show Harlem at the high and low ends of the social scale, while others argue that it leaves the novel without a firm structure. Thematically, however, the overarching shape of the novel builds on a sense that all the tricks we can—or are forced to—play on others and ourselves must face an unveiling, even an irony that confounds deceit and honesty. Describing the denouement where Sam indulges in one more, large-scale deception, which in fact contains a different moral charge, Cullen presents his exit line: "All his life he had played tricks. . . . Now one more trick was left him, the sweetest, kindest trick of all."

Cullen skillfully uses the deck of playing cards and the straight razor that serve as Sam's props for his theatrical conversion scene. First, the preacher recovers them from the floor where Sam throws them, and he ponders how they could be seen as instruments of God's will. But the Reverend Johnson, an itinerant singing preacher, recognizes Sam from an earlier false conversion in a church in Memphis and realizes that they are mere props. Mattie, however, asks for them from Reverend Johnson, holding on to them and considering them as talismans of her good luck and spiritual salvation as occasioned by Sam's "conversion." Aunt Mandy sees them and suspects Sam's character, but she herself has a deck of cards, which she uses in her fortune telling. Later the razor plays a near-gruesome role in a scene where Sam flies into a rage at Mattie. Eventually they end up under Mattie's pillow as a mystic charm, put there by her in response to a medium's advice on how to bring the unfaithful Sam back home. All in all, their artistic function suggests something like a stage prop, and there are other elements in the novel that strongly echo stage conventions. Cullen's later efforts to turn the novel into a stage play retrospectively explain part of its construction.

Reviews of the novel in the popular press were generally positive, though the sales of the book disappointed Cullen. The *Boston Evening Transcript* called it an "extremely able piece of fiction." The *Chicago Evening Post* said, somewhat condescendingly, that it was "one of those rare instances when a poet tries his hand at light fiction—and succeeds." The *Minneapolis Journal* claimed that Cullen had "the daring which makes him write with vividness." The *New York Times Book Review* ran a reproduction of the Winold Reiss portrait of Cullen, and they asked Elizabeth Brown to review the book, and, attentive to its various virtues, she pointed out that "the picture is sometimes amusing, sometimes very moving, and at all times interesting." She ended by saying that it was an "excellent and highly readable book that should not be missed."[12] Rudolph Fisher, himself a noted Renaissance novelist, writing in the *New York Herald Tribune,* delivered the most intelligent review. He began by speaking to a recurrent concern: "The danger of falling below expectation is especially great in the case of the poet who turns novelist. Mr. Cullen, whose poetry is admired by so many, and whose danger is therefore the greatest, has nevertheless challenged fate successfully. His first novel goes over." For the lovers and Aunt Mandy, Cullen "has given them a beauty which his predecessors have been reluctant to dwell upon—a black beauty." So good is Cullen at showing how the beauty of these three characters comes from within that "it should never again be necessary for anyone to insist that fine souls are really white inside." As heartening as such praise must have been, the book languished in terms of sales and influence.

Cullen's approach relied in part on his sense of the nineteenth-century novel, but he also clearly wanted a broad canvas in order to represent African American society in all its variety. The use of the double plot thus becomes the novel's most imposing structural device, but this produced varying reactions, many of them negative, or at least qualified.[13] Speaking of the double plot, Fisher described it positively and accurately as presenting a pastel and a cartoon in the same frame, and he argued that the cartoon exaggerations of the satire are much less important than the pastel tones of Sam and Mattie's love. But the negative assessment was represented by the February 19, 1932, *New York Sun* review, in which Robert Cantwell focused on it, though with a touch of condescension: "One feels that a superb short novel has been sacrificed to convention or that Mr. Cullen has been unwilling to regard Sam and Mattie as important enough to justify devoting all his novel to them." Alan Shucard, writing many years later, echoes the complaint: the novel "suffers the consequences of having two plots that touch each other only tangentially and are never adequately reconciled by incident or theme."[14] This omits the way the theme of deception operates in both plots and also overlooks the way the deck of cards and razor act as shifting and multivalent symbols.

Of course, Cullen had no clear and immediately available model for how to write an African American novel that was fully modern and racially accurate and resonant. Richard Wright's *Native Son* and Ralph Ellison's *Invisible Man* were, respectively, eight and twenty years in the future. But at least one critic saw that *One Way to Heaven* was a step forward in presenting African American life with corrective humor and honest feelings, beyond stereotypes and crude caricature. Locke, writing in his annual review of books by African Americans, said that the book was "path breaking . . . as to theme," though by casting Sam's struggles as external rather than psychological, the story "just barely misses distinction." This balanced criticism, typical of Locke's approach to aesthetic matters, nevertheless included finding fault in the double plot. At the same time he clearly appreciated the ambition evident in Cullen's attempt to "weld a low life and a high society theme into the same story."[15] If Cullen's account of his labors in his correspondence with West is any guide, he paid in full for the completion of the novel, and he apparently never contemplated writing another.

In November of 1931 Cullen had been in London and there met up with his friend from Harvard, John Trounstine, hoping to get his assistance in publishing the novel. Trounstine regretfully reported that most English editors felt there was no audience for an account of Harlem life. Cullen might have had a premonition about the limits to his readership. Still, once the novel was in the world it might attract some attention. A year after it appeared, Jean Stor, a composer who had written music for a poem, "The Swart Maid," by Paul Laurence Dunbar, wrote Cullen with an offer to turn the book into an opera. But nothing came of this. These efforts were taking place as Cullen's financial condition was growing unstable. After he took his position at Frederick Douglass Junior High, he apparently put the novel and the script, behind him. He would, however, go on to consider other projects for the stage.

The Medea and Some Poems

Three years after his novel appeared, Cullen published one more book of poems, which would be the last to appear in his lifetime, and it included a translation of a Greek tragedy that occupied most of the book's pages. As for the poems in the book, they were various in form and theme. Out of the eighteen poems included in *The Medea and Some Poems,* two were translations from Baudelaire, and eleven were sonnets. Though these were not the last poems Cullen wrote, together they resound with a valedictory tone. Some of them are driven by a suppressed anger, most notably "Scottsboro, Too Is Worth Its Song," perhaps Cullen's fiercest political poem. In it he chides his fellow poets for failing to response to the injustice faced by the young black men falsely accused of rape and facing harsh penalties driven by racist viciousness.

> Here in epitome
> Is all disgrace
> And epic wrong.

Inside the political call for justice lies another charge, one that says that the lack of a "song" of protest is lamentably a poetic failure.

Yet the failure of poetry to come forth, to mark the emotional moment with distinctive song, is a theme in some of the sonnets as well. The selection of poems begins with a haunted lyric lament, "After a Visit," that turns to affirmation, as Cullen recognizes the Irish poets he was visiting worship their muse in a way that he can seldom emulate.

Even as the poem ends with a promise of sleep to ease the torment the poet faces, the emotion is stark and punishing:

> And shame of my apostasy was like a coal
> That reached my tongue and heart and far off frigid soul,
> Melting myself into myself, making me weep
> Regeneration's burning tears, preluding sleep.

The imagery, rife with religious feeling, echoes the coal that burned the biblical prophet's lips, as well as the sense of apostasy and the spiritual degradation of the frozen heart. The most stunning phrase, however, when Cullen speaks of "Melting myself into myself" makes it clear that as religious as much as of his feelings were, it is poetry's ability to define the self that has sustained him. Such a heavy price is to be paid though, when inspiration is tardy or absent altogether. The price of losing the poetic soul and thereby one's truest self seemed at times the price Cullen was facing.[16]

This sense of a threat to one's self is operating in almost all of the eleven sonnets in *Medea*. In the three quatrains of "Only the Polished Skeleton," though not a sonnet, this despair is most clearly marked as the bones are pictured as being "Of flesh relieved and pauperized." But the bones are grimmer than the poet's heart and mind, the subjects, respectively, of the two preceding quatrains, which merely engage in and accept the inevitability of deceit and fraud. The skeleton goes further. With grimmest irony it finds comfort of a sort: it "Can rest at ease and think upon / The worth of all it so despised." If the worth of what was despised turns out beyond the grave to be greater than the skeleton realized, the irony stings implacably. One can only hope for the best, that what was hated, deserved it. It is not only rhyming "pauperized" with "despised" that suggests that this may be Cullen's darkest poem.

The gathering of sonnets in *Medea* was never considered as a group by any commentator during Cullen's lifetime, and the poems may have been overshadowed by appearing in the volume with his translation of the Greek tragedy. The decision to present them in this format suggests a certain fatigue on Cullen's part, as the years of the Guggenheim and the pleasures of Paris were fading into the need to find a job that would provide a steady income. Looked at through a more melodramatic perspective, Cullen may have realized that his poetic gifts were nearly spent. Indeed, after *Medea* appeared he would only write six more poems before his death a decade later. "After the Visit" stands like a claim to further poetic accomplishment and an acknowledgment of its unlikelihood. The sonnets, operating in the nimbus of that ambiguity, are self-consciously striving to use poetry to unravel the mysteries of love and desire, romance and eroticism. Their entanglements form at once the subject matter of the poems and the music of their melancholy.

Though death figures in these late poems, as it did often in some of the earlier ones (as critics have often observed), here it is little more than a stop to consciousness, a limit to the self-awareness that threatens to culminate only in silence. The real subject of most of the poems is love, though it takes on many shapes and circumstances. One poem depicts a devout monk, who "Writhes piteously on [his] unyielding bed." Another poem's victim, struck "divinely mad" with love, "may only stare, / And out of silence weave an iron oath." In some of the sonnets love is less imposing than desire; in others it is more. One sonnet, of the former camp, begins almost cheerily: "Some for a little while do love, and some for long." But by the time the end arrives, love hardly endures at all: instead it "is a rare and tantalizing fruit / Our hands reach for, but nothing absolute." Where the opening tone in one poem may be cheery, in another it can start by being harshly self-critical: "I have not loved you in the noblest way." This accusation turns slightly toward self-justification, but of a stern sort: "Loved have I much, but I have not been blind." He goes on to complain that, having never been dipped in the Styx and so rendered free from harm, anyone who "would find me weak and vulnerable" need not aim at his heel; he is subject to harm at every point, but especially his heart.

Still, Cullen kept the ability to imagine that love could take on transcendent forms. In "To One Not There," the sonnet dedicated to Dorothy West, he reverts to the chivalric imagery he once used for poems dedicated to Yolande. He mingles his love of France with his deep affection for the writer with whom he shared considerable longing.

> Your voice is in these Gallic accents light,
> And sweeter is the Rhenish wine I sip
> Because this glass (a lesser Grail) is bright
> Illumined by the memory of your lip.

The sense of chivalry continues in a sonnet about poetry's ability to render justice to romance, even as it must know its instruments are weak: the speaker imagines a previous poet, trying to find some comfort in the "anguish" of his love. The sestet reads:

> And then he too, as I, will turn to look
> Upon his instrument of discontent,
> Thinking himself a Perseus, and fit to brook
> Her columned throat and every blandishment;
> And looking know what brittle arms we wield,
> Whose pencil is our sword, whose page our shield.

The use of puns here invites a reading in which the "instrument of discontent" is at once the loved one and the poem that attempts to capture her, or more precisely, as the octave hoped, to reach a state of "disdain" so as to escape that "throbbing wound, his brain." By mentioning Perseus Cullen tries to heroicize the love poet, though he ultimately admits to possessing no more than "brittle" defenses. Taken all together, the poems in his last volume show Cullen as a fully mature and tough-minded—albeit wounded—poet of love's many guises.

Medea

It was, of course, the inclusion of his translation of the Greek tragedy that not only gave Cullen's book its main title, but dominated that book by its length and gravity. Cullen took the honor of being the first African American to translate a Greek tragedy, though by most measures the accomplishment garnered little notice and less praise. He left almost nothing behind by way of letters or notes that indicate how and why he chose this particular drama to turn into English. A persistent wish to enter into the theater had been a part of his aesthetic life for some time, and this manifested itself in his efforts on first dramatizing *God Sends Sunday*, Arna Bontemps's novel, and then turning it into a Broadway musical. These efforts were in the future, however, when *Medea* appeared. So blank is the record on the translating efforts that there is no firm date as to when Cullen began it. Most likely he began after the two years in Paris and clearly sometime before the play's publication. This would suggest sometime in 1933 or 1934. If this is accurate, it means he initiated an arduous writing project when he was burdened economically and searching for gainful employment. But he may well have been involved in an intense reading of classical literature. The volume that included the play also had at least three poems that contained allusions to Greek myths: Medusa, Perseus, and the Euminedes.[17] Cullen had started studying Greek at least as early as his freshman year at NYU and was able to tell his friend Brown that he had gotten a B in his first semester. However, it remains unclear just how much Greek Cullen knew or if he resorted to a "pony." Though his knowledge of Latin was considerable, apparently he had not made frequent use of it since his days at DeWitt Clinton. In any case, he faced a play that contained furious emotions and gruesome acts, and he did so directly, without blinking.[18]

Whatever drew Cullen to Euripides's play, he obviously wanted to render it into spoken English, a clear sign that he could imagine it being staged successfully. He hoped to have Rose McClendon star in the title role. McClendon was the most famous black actress of her generation. After studying at the American Academy of Dramatic Arts, she went on to become one of the founders of the Negro People's Theatre, where both her acting and directing skills drew audiences in large numbers. She played a key role in Hughes's *Mulatto,* which ran for 375 performances. But in yet another of the misfortunes that hampered Cullen's authorial plans, McClendon passed away in 1936 at the age of fifty-two, just as Cullen's *Medea* was being readied for the stage. Plans for the production had advanced to the point that Carl Van Vechten took pictures of the actress in the costume she would have worn as the tragic heroine. Eventually, Cullen's version was performed at Atlanta University, in 1940, with Dorothy Ateca in the title role. Cullen was unable to attend, but his friend Owen Dodson arranged to send him pictures of the production.[19]

The language of Greek tragedy presents considerable difficulties, as the translator must choose how to render the exalted and ritualized language of the ancient dramatic form without becoming stilted or bombastic. Cullen was not opposed to translating rhymed originals into English rhyme. He was able to use rhyme when he translated two of Baudelaire's sonnets, which he included in *The Medea and Some Poems.* While in Paris he had even practiced his skill at translating by rendering his own poems into French. But these were modern lyric poems; the aesthetic challenges

18. The Atlanta University production of Cullen's translation of *Medea,* 1940.

when faced with an ancient Greek classic were not limited only to the question of rhyming or not. Nevertheless, Cullen's lifelong use of rhyme likely suggested a possible choice that needed to be considered.

Gilbert Murray was one of the most renowned translators of *Medea* who preceded Cullen, and Murray chose to use rhymed verse to raise the level of the rhetoric. Near the opening of the play an "Attendant" tells of how he heard about King Creon's plan to banish Medea and her sons, and Murray renders it like this:

> I heard an old man talking, where he sate
> At draughts in the sun, beside the fountain gate,
> And never thought of me, there standing still
> Beside him. And he said, 'Twas Creon's will.
> Being lord of all this land, that she be sent,
> And with her two sons, to banishment.
> Maybe 'tis all false. For myself, I know
> No further, and I would it were not so.[20]

Even though Cullen once told an interviewer that he would never resort to free verse, he decided that Murray's metrical rhyming could not serve as a model. Having elected not to use verse at all, Cullen may have looked toward the other end of the lexical and rhetorical spectrum, to the use of poeticized prose. Here is an example of that sort of translation, from E. P. Coleridge:

> I heard one say, pretending not to listen as I approached the place where our greybeards sit playing draughts near Pirene's sacred spring, that Creon, the ruler of this land, is bent on driving these children and their mother from the boundaries of Corinth; but I know not whether the news is to be relied upon, and would fain it were not.[21]

The drawbacks here are obviously equal to those of Murray. Cullen decided to try something different, a language that he felt was in between the two alternatives. In his version the speaker of this passage is called a tutor, and he proceeds more directly:

> I was down by the fountain where the old men sit in the sun playing dice. I heard a man say they were going to send them away, Medea and the children, away from Corinth. Perhaps it isn't true, just fountain talk and public gossip.

Cullen has dropped the reference to the sacred spring, avoided the stilted diction of words like *fain*, and simplified the sentence structure. What the language conveys is the essential situation, unadorned with allusive references or stylized gestures. If one would fault Cullen for failing to achieve a sense of exaltation or grandeur in his language, it should at the same time be admitted that what he arrived at allowed for a clear narrative energy in the speakers' accounts and expressions.

One of the consequences of his choice is that certain scenes in the play—most notably, when a witness relates the death agony of Creon's daughter, the result of Medea's necromantic use of poisoned garments—startle with their brutality. Overall the effects of the play in Cullen's version are grounded less in ritualized or exalted actions, and more in the simple passion of Medea, for whom no quarter is asked or given. Seen in the context of some of the poems Cullen added to the volume with the tragedy, an exchange between Medea and Jason offers grim echoes. This takes place after Medea's monstrous filicide:

Jason: My sons, from what a devil's womb you come!

Medea: Oh, my babies, you know it was your father's fault that you are dead.

Jason: Not mine! I am free of their blood. I never touched them!

Medea: Not with your hands, but with insults to me, and with your new marriage bed.

Jason: The truth at last! Because you still hankered after me they had to die.

Medea: I loved you, Jason.

Jason: You lusted for me!

Medea: Look at your sons, Jason, you little dead sons. Why do you turn away? Does it hurt you so?

Jason: Not dead! Not dead! I cannot believe you have done this thing.
The gods will reward you well for this, Medea.

The estranging conflict between love and desire continues even after Jason claims Medea is ruled by the latter, not the former. She resorts to low taunts, driven by her anger, and he (sarcastically) calls on a higher power to provide justice.

Cullen's translation might be read more fairly as an adaptation, since there is much in the original Greek that is omitted. Almost all the typical Greek passages and expressions that convey an elaborate supernatural, or at least preternatural, realm—such as epithets, the names of gods, references to other mythic tales and places—by being absent tend to focus the play more on the destructive, even pathological, strife between Jason and Medea. Her magical powers are understated, as are his heroic attributes. By using some rhymes in the passages of the Chorus, for one thing, Cullen heightens the play above the level of naturalism, but it reads on the page, at least, as a story of domestic destructiveness. Many of the moral axioms formulated by Medea, in part to justify her inhuman qualities, are not included. Still, others that are—such as "charity begins at home," and "I am my own worst enemy," both spoken by Creon—retain some of the moral issues in the play, but with less of an air of cosmic or superhuman authority. This change in the moral tenor of the play invites a biographical reading, and it is perhaps tempting to see Medea as an alienated rebel, as a version of Cullen himself—cut off as he was in Paris during the last days of his marriage, away from home, suffering ostracism and recriminations, and locked in a fierce and destructive marital dispute. However, certain things remain stressed—not least the role of kingship and royal houses, as well as the gruesome descriptions of the magical killing of Creon's daughter—that defy any one-to-one allegorical interpretation that would make Cullen's own psychology the focus.

Then there is the matter of the prologue and the epilogue. These are dramatic pieces that Cullen wrote to precede and follow, respectively, the tragedy *Medea*. He entitled the two pieces "Byword for Evil." The prologue is rather short and introduces Jason and Medea while they are still in Colchis, where his capturing of the Golden Fleece will take place. We also see Medea's younger brother, who will later be slain by Medea and tossed overboard as she and Jason flee to Corinth. The action allows the audience to see Jason and Medea before their enmity tears their relationship apart. Dramatically rich in tragic irony, they recall other Greek tragedies that open with speakers who aren't yet aware of their fates the way the spectators are. The epilogue is considerably longer and details how Medea manages to become involved in the deaths of her husband, Aegeus, the king of Athens, and his son. Most dramatically, it also depicts the reunion, though such is not the appropriate word, of Medea and Jason and the final end of the twenty-year-long, tragic narrative. Cullen clearly envisioned the two dramatic scenes to flank *Medea* proper and therefore form a three-act play. The writing and the characterizations of the two additional parts remain consistent with the central play and so indicate even more strongly that Cullen desired a fully produced and staged drama that would provide for a "standard" theatrical experience. As it turned out, he was frustrated in this desire, as "Byword for Evil" was mounted at Fisk University, but only in the spring of 1945, just months before his death.

Some of the reviews of *The Medea and Some Poems* began to sound a negative note about Cullen's career. Eda Lou Walton, writing in the *New York*

Herald Tribune, for example, said that the volume showed that "Cullen is just a little too much the product of our American colleges. His earlier work was more his own." Yet, referring to the tragedy, Philip Blair Rice, in the *Nation,* judged that "where Oxford dons have so often failed, an American negro [*sic*] writer has succeeded." The translation of the play enjoyed an extended life to some degree when Virgil Thomson wrote music for some of its choruses. This work premiered in March 1943 at the Museum of Modern Art, where one listener described it as "somber and beautiful."[22]

Though the greatest concentration in Cullen's poems deals with love and desire, he also wrote one poem that dealt with emotion in general. This is "Any Human to Another," one of his most unusual poems, attempting as it does to say something about how people are joined by emotions of all kinds, but especially through grief. In one sense the poem presents a variation of the theme of "No man is an island": no one is allowed

> A little tent
> Pitched in a meadow
> Of sun and shadow
> All his little own.

It is not simply that our emotions are positive and negative, in "sun and shadow," but that they are inherently connective of people. Cullen pronounces that

> Your grief and mine
> Must intertwine
> Like sea and river.

The ending presents images of military triumph—a sword and a crown—but the images are not badges of honor but of fate, as the lines tell us what "must" happen.

> Your every grief
> Like a blade

Shining and unsheathed
Must strike me down.
Of bitter aloes wreathed,
My sorrow must be laid
On your head like a crown.

Though grim content pervades the poem, the tone is more stately than funereal. In a way the poem celebrates a fellowship of sorrow, and the chivalric imagery to which Cullen often resorted heightens the sense of a lost era, a fading ethos that is maintained only by accepting the inevitability of loss.

Near the end of 1933, Cullen received a request from Hughes, then in Carmel, California, asking him to donate a manuscript of one of his poems, to be auctioned off. The organization behind the auction was the Committee for the Defense of Political Prisoners. (Another similar organization, the International Scottsboro Committee, was more focused, and it would ask Cullen to serve on its board, as either a member or an honorary officer.) Mainly directed at the case of the Scottsboro boys, nine young black men falsely accused of rape and being held in prison under a death sentence, these committees were drawing on the support of artists and writers. Hughes followed up his first request by sending a more formal letter to Cullen on the committee's letterhead. He added in the margin, "Your work is greatly admired out here. An original of one of your poems would be a great help. Yeah, man! So please send it." Cullen did, and it went for twenty-five dollars. In his poem composed for the situation, called "Scottsboro, Too, Is Worth Its Song," Cullen revealed more than a trace of bitterness as he compared the outcry over Sacco and Vanzetti to the then rather muted protest about an equally egregious miscarriage of justice.

Here in epitome
Is all disgrace
And epic wrong,
Like wine to brace
The minstrel heart, and blare it into song.

Surely, I said,
Now will the poets sing.
But they have raised no cry.
I wonder why

The poem ends without punctuation of any kind. It would be one of the last poems Cullen wrote on a political subject, but its understated tone speaks forcefully about Cullen's political sensibility.

Some of the artistic and cultural efforts that arose in the Renaissance involved many people, but came to very little in the long run. One short-lived progressive organization that drew on Cullen's participation was the Committee for Mass Education in Race Relations. This was started in 1934, largely through the efforts of Charles S. Johnson. In June of 1934, Johnson invited Cullen to become a member of the committee and to take an active part in its productions. These productions were to take the form of movies that would deal with racial issues, the scripts being written by well-known African American authors and presented in a forthrightly didactic way. Hughes would write a script around his famous poem "The Negro Speaks of Rivers," and Bontemps would portray "Martin de Porres," the patron saint of people from mixed races and those who sought racial harmony. Johnson assigned the topic of the "Negro church" to Cullen and Owen Dodson, with whom Cullen was already collaborating. But the two men took a different direction. Their script, written but never filmed, dealt with the questions of black migration and the world of industrialized labor. *They Seek a City* depicts the story of a black farmer who comes to a large city only to discover the competition between workers and the difficulty moving from chopping cotton to a mechanical lathe. Meanwhile, the immigrant's son goes to school where he reads about world unity. Not so subtly, but distantly, the prospect of a bright future for industrial workers hovers in the man's eyes, even as he settles into the routines of urban society. The story ends on a quiet note as the boy says, referring to the ideal of universal peace, "How did it turn out, Pa?" The father struggles with his answer: "All according to . . ." The boy enquires further, "According to what, Pa?" The father laughingly replies, "I forgot the answer—went away just like that but I'll get it again." And the two sit down to supper. This ending shows that Cullen remained averse to using straight propaganda in art, yet retained his own progressive hopes. In a sense the script is a grim version of Sam Lucas's north-ward journey.[23]

In 1934 Cullen's poems were gathered in his last full volume, his novel was published, and some of his dramatic projects were being labored over. He realized that, having lived quite near the poverty level for a number of years, he would need to go on a vigorous campaign to secure a teaching position at an African American college. In mounting his effort, he appealed to virtually all the senior spokesmen of the Renaissance. During this period some black leaders had gone on to teach at the university level: Charles S. Johnson was at Fisk, Benjamin Brawley was at Shaw, while Alain Locke, Carter Woodson, Sterling Brown, and others continued at Howard. A strong sense of a new cultural energy, as represented by the Renaissance, was being implanted at what were later referred to as "historically black" colleges, though the schools also served as a place of asylum for various race leaders. As locales of black leadership, the colleges played a limited but expanding role; nevertheless, white educators overwhelmingly held the presidencies of these colleges until the 1920s. Changes were occurring, however. This made it seem logical that Cullen, especially considering his literary skills and advanced degree, should choose college-level teaching. Years later, some even opined that his failure to find a position at an institution of higher learning indicated his lack of ambition and a retreat from public life. The failure was not, however, of Cullen's making.

In January 1934 Cullen relayed his efforts to Dorothy West, saying, "I am so penurious that I am sending out s.o.s. calls all over the country for a teaching job, rescue may well be effected by some institution way down south, so that we shall be far removed from one another more than ever. The situation I was hoping to have in Raleigh did not come through, not enough funds in the school to pay their current debts, to say nothing of providing a salary for a poet who would probably be a very poor instructor anyway." In the same month Cullen inquired about a position at Atlanta University. Hale Woodruff had started teaching there in 1931, just after returning from Paris, and would go on to influence a generation of younger painters. In the same week Cullen wrote to Montgomery Gregory, who had left Howard and become a principal at a public school in Atlantic City. But the system there was not hiring, due largely to the defunding of public education during the Depression. Cullen wrote as well to Lincoln University in Pennsylvania, where Hughes had graduated five years earlier. A small institution in Austin, Texas, Samuel Huston College (named after a man from Iowa, not the famous Texan), made Cullen an offer, though the salary was extremely meager.

Cullen also focused some of his search on larger colleges. Walter White volunteered to help, and wrote Mordecai Johnson, the first black president at Howard, to see if a position could be made available. None was forthcoming, as the budgetary problems there were serious, since congressional committees still stringently controlled the school's finances. Then what seemed a stroke of good fortune occurred. In June 1934 Dillard University in New Orleans made Cullen an offer. Several of his friends wrote to congratulate him, and some assured him that the city was not typical of the Deep South, and he would not be as oppressed by Jim Crow as he would be in other locations. James Weldon Johnson declared it "next to New York, the most interesting city east of the Mississippi." The college administration sent him his teaching schedule for the fall 1934 term; he would be teaching a literature survey course and a course in modern poetry. Just at this time, the reverend became ill, and Cullen asked if his starting date might be postponed. But the postponement was not enough, and by the turn of the year Cullen faced the necessity of declining the offer. Unable to leave the ailing reverend, Cullen was forced to change his focus to employment in New York City.

This in effect meant only one thing, that the teaching job he had for many years shied away from was to become his anchor for the next decade. Cullen's attitude toward teaching contained a number of different emotional dispositions. Just after graduation from college, he had told his friend Brown that he lacked the sense of firm belief that he felt teachers should possess.

> I do not feel that teaching will go hard with you, nor that you will allow it to give you any unnecessary concern—I feel that your sense of humor will stand you in good stead. With me it is different; I should be considerably concerned with the souls of the young things; I should even persuade myself that these dubious appendages were really there—and then how could I teach with all that was in me? Souls are so delicate; more so in our time than ever before. They need but to be breathed upon

to be sent headlong down the devil's path, granting again that there is really such a person and such a personal path over which he rules. I hope you see my predicament, and how perilous it would be for me to teach. And then I might, as a matter of recreation, want to indulge in a poem or two. Can you not see the great danger there?[24]

Because Cullen's letters to Brown are often playful, here there is more than a bit exaggerated. Yet the recourse to the spiritual imagery indicates that Cullen placed an extremely high value on education. When the prospect arose of turning to teaching for his livelihood, Cullen had resorted to asking Jackman more than once to obtain the necessary licensing information and applications. But this time the stakes were higher, and the prospects more delimited.

In fact, his preparation in the theory and practice of pedagogy had begun a decade earlier, as he listed for the admissions office at Harvard in 1925 the courses he had completed at NYU.

You will note that the four educational courses which I took in my senior year are not included in this catalogue, for the reason that they were pursued at a different branch of New York University, however, in strict conformance with the University custom. The four courses in question were: The history of education, educational psychology, principle[s] and problems of education, and elements in the methods of teaching high school English. Each of these courses gave two credits per semester, and each lasted a year.[25]

By all accounts, Cullen would go on to be a highly successful teacher, and though he earlier resisted the reverend's plan for him to obtain the PhD degree, he apparently happily accepted teaching at the junior high school level. Still, the concern he expressed to his classmate Brown ten years earlier—that teaching might interfere with his composing poetry—brought substantial weight to bear during his final decade as a writer.

Conflicted though he may have been about turning to the classroom for his life's work, he had diligently pursued his French courses while in Paris. During this time he also read and took notes on recent work on pedagogy. A book by Charles H. Judd, entitled *The Psychology of High School Subjects*, urged teachers instructing in any foreign language to realize that learning takes place through the ear. This emphasis on the lecture-recitation mode was complemented by injunctions not to let the students see the printed text of the lesson, to teach the class and not individuals, to appeal to the eye only at "the proper time," and to eventually involve some muscular appeal—the last perhaps a reference to mimicking actions associated with certain vocabularies. An article by Alexander and McMurray, titled "The Training of Modern Foreign Language Teachers for French Secondary Schools," supplemented these rules.[26] When he took the New York City Board of Education test for teachers in December 1931, he scored 77.85 points out of a hundred, easily enough to qualify him for a certificate.

In January 1932, the principal at P.S. 139—Frederick Douglass Junior High School—had written to tell Cullen he was looking forward to hiring him. However, the New York City public schools were in the grip of the Depression and a consequent hiring freeze in the early 1930s, again due to the lack of proper funding. But fortunately a part-time appointment opened up, and after serving for twenty-three days as a substitute at P.S. 184, he began the spring, 1935 semester as a full-time teacher of French at Frederick Douglass. Ten years later he could inform Jackman that he had received his certificate of competency, referring to the previous seven years of teaching as being "on probation I suppose." He summarized his feelings: "I think the Bd. of Ed. is getting battier every year." The decade and more of work in the huge bureaucracy of a public service had sustained him economically, but it wore him down in other ways.

At this same time Cullen found himself involved in another form of public service. On March 19, 1935, a riot erupted in Harlem. The combination of Depression-induced unemployment and poor housing conditions for Harlemites had magnified the economic impoverishment that gripped the country. The Federal Housing Authority had joined forces with local bankers to expand the practice known as "redlining." This meant people with low incomes were forced to live in the same neighborhoods, and the resultant concentration of people who were denied full social opportunities meant that conditions in Harlem slid downhill rapidly. Fiorello La Guardia's reform government was nonresponsive, as the mayor admitted that racial prejudice was something he could not defeat politically, due in large measure to the way the city had relied on ethnic politics in the preceding decades. The widened cultural horizons of the Renaissance had contracted severely in economic times that were unprecedented, and especially harsh for African Americans. All along 125th Street people marched and picketed, protesting especially against white storeowners who refused to hire black employees; "Don't shop where you can't work" became the slogan of the boycott that started near the end of 1934.

The events that triggered the riot remained somewhat murky, but a young boy was caught shoplifting, and though the police released him, a crowd began to hear rumors that he had been injured or even killed. When an ambulance was called the gathered crowd became angry and began to hurl rocks and other objects. Considerable property damage resulted, and it was decided that an official investigation should be initiated. Two months after the riot, La Guardia announced the creation of a Mayor's Commission on Conditions in Harlem. Shortly thereafter, a subcommittee of the commission began to examine issues involving public education. The rather bureaucratic question of whether the Harlem Evening High School for women should be merged with the one for men surfaced as one such issue. Cullen was appointed to the board of the subcommittee, and larger questions began to be taken up by its members. For example, the subcommittee discovered that no elementary school had been constructed in Harlem since 1925, despite the marked growth in population. This and other points were detailed in a six-page report.[27] However, the bureaucracy became disturbed when the report was released, anonymously and surreptitiously, to the *New York World-Telegram*. This ignited a scandal, and some suspicion fell on Cullen as the source of the "leak."

Meanwhile, by the mid-1930s, Cullen had imperceptibly but inevitably become more a schoolteacher than a poet. It was not an identity that he altogether resented, and he had much to offer to his students. James Baldwin, later to become one of the most famous African American writers, enjoyed his experience of being one of Cullen's students at Frederick Douglass Junior High.[28] But he was not the only student of Cullen to leave behind a sense of the poet as teacher. Elvyn Davidson was a student of Cullen's for two years in the 1930s before he took a competitive exam that allowed him to attend Stuyvesant High School; in fact, he credited Cullen with helping him pass the exam. Prior to that he saw how Cullen set high standards for his students. Reflecting decades later, he characterized the situation:

We had a teacher, when I first went to 139 that had just started a program called Rapid Advance. And . . . our teacher was a man named Countée Cullen, who was a black poet. And he said . . . I'll take sixty boys in this class he said I'll make them good students. And out of that sixty, I remember now, only one turned out bad. Every one of the fifty-nine little boys either doctors, lawyers, policemen, judges, different things. But only guy out of that class that turned out to be a drunk.[29]

Putting aside for the moment the class size, Cullen was determined to carry forward the sense of excellence that he had absorbed at DeWitt Clinton so that it would carry the day at P.S. 139. He was able to do this because of a distinctive approach to teaching.

Because he [Cullen] . . . had a method of teaching which [was] probably unusual. He uh, taught us . . . there's nothing that you can't read and there's nothing that you can't do. There's nothing that you can't figure out. And he says we're gonna teach you how to memorize things. And what he would do, take out the class and we'd walk around a block, a city block and come back. He'd say I want you to write down everything you saw . . . And we did that every day for a month and at the end of a month we were supposed to be able to draw every building and write down every street number and everything we saw in that building in the windows. . . . And at the end of the month everybody in the class could tell you exactly everything he saw in that window. He worked on your memory. He said you have to learn how to memorize without being aware that you're memorizing. I want you to look at something and be able tell me what you saw. I want you to read something and tell me what it says in your own words without repeating what . . . Don't read this way, you read straight down a page. He taught us how to read fast, how to comprehend, how to give back what you read. [If] . . . hadn't been for him I don't think I probably could've made it through school, but . . . He taught us . . . I went from Seven A to Eight A to Nine A in like a year's time. And graduated from nine B . . . Junior high school [is] supposed to be three years, but everybody in class did it in two, which I [did] and everybody did it.

The method testified to Cullen's seriousness as a teacher, and even though he often felt the burden of the long hours and the overly full

19. Cullen at the lectern, probably taken when he was a teacher at Frederick Douglass Junior High, a position he took in the early 1930s and held until his death.

classrooms, he never relented in his efforts to give the students his best efforts. Davidson summarized the experience: "He was our mentor, our teacher, our confidant."

Cullen proved sedulous as a teacher, and even after he obtained his permanent license he took summer courses in Paris to maintain and improve his French. But the model of the "visiting poet," or the academic poet who enjoys a university position, was not available to him, since such positions became widespread only after the war. However many— or however few—poet-teachers there are recorded in literary history, Cullen did not manage to flourish at both enterprises. Back in the mid-1920s the pressure of public readings and his scholarly and editorial endeavors already overwhelmed him. Despite the writing habits he had developed in his early years, he couldn't produce poetry to the measure of a regular calendar. Paris and the Guggenheim years allowed him to go deeper into his sense of rich but troublesome emotions, yet despite his summer sojourns in France, the regularity of the school year and the settled domain of the reverend's house had resulted in other interests, other forms of expression. His three long narrative poems—"The Shroud of Color," "The Ballad of the Brown Girl," and "The Black Christ"—had recorded his experience of race, in different modes that were related to the quest, the ballad, and the folktale. His novel saw him trying out some of the realism that he discovered and shied away from that summer of 1922 in Pleasantville. Chances are he didn't have a crystal clear program for himself as a writer. His place in the classroom, however, enervating as it may have been, would not be his only realm.

On the second to last day of 1935, the Federal Theatre Project for New York sent a letter to the Lafayette Theatre in New York requesting permission to produce a play called *St. Louis Woman*. The production was planned for February 20th, the following year. Unfortunately, it would be a full decade before this production was realized, and the intervening ten years were to be a steady trial for Cullen and his ambition to become a man of the theater.

6

Codas and Finales, 1936–1946

The final ten years of Cullen's life resonate, from some points of view, as a diminuendo. His daily life centered on his time-consuming job as a public school teacher of French at Frederick Douglass Junior High, on 140th Street. With the summers off he could still travel to Paris, which he did avidly, but after the late 1930s the beginning of the war closed off that option. His teacher's salary remained short of handsome, but it alleviated the threadbare existence of the immediate post-Depression years. His marriage to Ida Roberson in 1940 was a signal event, especially as it led to his moving his residence from Harlem to the staid precincts of White Plains, in Westchester County, north of the city. Married life did not eliminate his attraction to men, and he carefully and discretely maintained a long intimate attachment to Edward Atkinson, as well as continuing to rely on Jackman for many kinds of affection. Beneath the placid surface, however, literary thoughts and ambitions continued to attract and realign his efforts and imagination. The stage remained perhaps the main magnet, and his dreams of full-scale productions of his dramatic writing drew him to a range of projects. Approaching his late-thirties, he turned to writing children's books, led perhaps by the memory that some—Yolande and Dorothy West, among others— had always seen in him something childlike, a gentleness but also an aesthetic longing that always included a touch of fantasy. Some projects came to very satisfying ends, while one of his largest and most time- and energy-consuming commitments, the Broadway staging of *St. Louis Woman,* would be realized only after his death.

Many commentators and critics have noted that in his last decade Cullen wrote but half a dozen poems. His lyric muse became a fitful visi- tor as early as 1927, when his duties at *Opportunity* began to take up time and energy. The hoped-for productivity intimated by the Guggenheim year bore melancholic fruit, and that in decreasing amounts. Though his poems stayed with the subjects of love and loss—and the themes of life's cruelties and the paradoxes of fidelity—his poetry was no longer that of a young man. The self-reflexive lyrics tell us how high his ideals about poetry remained, yet they only occasionally speak about how he might adjust to weakened inspiration. Some suggested that his youth and his fame had produced a stasis, but his "late" poetry is in many ways fully mature work. The children's books enabled him to continue with the pleasures of wordplay, while his dramatic endeavors allowed him to pursue the reaches of emotion and social awareness. Racial questions continued to occupy him, and some of his dramatic undertakings indi- cate that the scars of past insults and the prospect of continuing ones were never less than immediate and deeply felt. The ten years prior to his passing saw the country stumble toward another world war, and Cul- len used some of his personal prestige and effort to work against the more obviously destructive instincts let loose in international affairs. And every now and then, the shadowy flames of his poetic skills flared.

But the beginning of 1936 marked one of the more dispiriting re- sponses to Cullen's poetry. It occurred in a short unsigned review in the *New York Times* for January 12 and addressed the volume *Medea and Some Poems.*

> Countée Cullen has written a version of "Medea" for Rose McClendon with choruses that will be sung to Vergil [sic] Thompson's music. It is an interesting experiment in reducing a Greek tragedy to the content and colloquialism of a folk tale, with characteristic Negro sentiment

and rhythm. (Creon says: "I'm not really a hard man, Medea. In fact, I am just about my own worst enemy.") But the story, or at least a story, comes through with a sense of pathos, if not of tragedy. The poems are less important.

Here, where he might least have expected it, Cullen had to face the issue of the conjunction of race and art and to see it stripped of nuance. The lines the reviewer quoted were not, and were not meant to be, "characteristic" of either "Negro sentiment or rhythm." To end the acerbic review with those last five words not only compounded the insult but also overlooked lyric poetry full of emotion and interest. Of course, the reviewer—this time understandably—could not know of the greater sadness, that six months later Rose McClendon, famous as the leading African American actress of her generation, would pass away. So before Cullen's *Medea* could be performed, the death of the star, who would have had the title role, left the production in doubt.[1]

Still, Cullen continued to assemble his plans and talent for the sake of seeing one of his dramatic compositions professionally staged. He resolved to adapt his novel into a three-act stage play, called *Heaven's My Home* in one version, but in another he changed the title to *One Way to Heaven*. The idea of dramatizing his novel may have begun with, or at least was commented on by, Rowena Jelliffe, who was the director of the Gilpin Players, but when she saw the script she felt the problem was that the play had "two divergent streams of action." This judgment contributed to the way Cullen proceeded. The story was considerably shortened, and some other changes were made—the opening action was set in the living room of Constancia (now renamed Sheila), for example—and a theatrical agent circulated the play, but no Broadway producer elected to take it on.[2] It was given at least one performance, at the Hedgerow Theatre, in a small town in Pennsylvania, during the fall of 1936. This performance received the briefest of mentions by Alain Locke (he characterized it as "middle class Negro comedy"), in his annual *Opportunity* review of African American writing. The review of the *New York Times*, which ran on September 28, was almost as short:

As the first of a series of Negro plays planned for this winter, the Hedgerow Theatre at Rose Valley, under Jasper Deeter's direction, presented tonight the world premier of "One Way To Heaven," a play in ten scenes by Countée Cullen.

A mixture of satire and comedy, the play revolves around the conversion of the rather stubborn Mattie Johnson, played by Goldie Ervin, [and] her marriage to Sam Lucas, eventually exposed as a revival meeting racketeer.[3]

In the novel it is hardly the case that Sam is "eventually" exposed, and part of the effect of the novel comes from our seeing him as crooked from the start and, yet, to some measure identifying with him. The revision took away much of the sting in the novel and perhaps brought it accurately into Locke's category. The phrase "world premier" might well have provoked Cullen to laughter, for the play was apparently never again staged in his lifetime.

Sometime in the later part of the 1930s Cullen conceived of an idea for another play (which remained untitled and undated), this time one that would deal directly with the issue of race, but he apparently never wrote any of it. He did, however, write up four pages of notes in which he spelled out the idea for the play, its "object," its "premise," its "action," and a concluding "comment."[4] This was likely shown to people, perhaps even his theatrical agent, Leah Salisbury, but the fact Cullen never supplied a title for the play may indicate that he declined to circulate his proposal widely. Stating its object, Cullen began abruptly: "to smile and sneer at much of present-day American civilization, concentrating especially on the over-sentimentalized value placed on sex, and upon the ludicrousness and ridiculousness of black-white race relations." This would be driven by the play's premise: "All action takes place on the understanding that present black-white race relations are reversed, the whites being the subject race. Thus, Roosevelt in the White House becomes a Negro president of a Negro people—the backgrounds of each race having also been switched." The thoroughness of the reversal is clearly necessary to make the "smile and sneer" reaction occur. Cullen goes on: "white speech will become the jargon which is used by Amos and Andy on the radio, and the Negro characters will speak of having had white mammies, white children will be pickaninnies, etc."

The action, which Cullen noted that he had not worked out in detail, involves a "wealthy New York society woman, with a Colony Club accent and with exaggerated grande dame mannerisms," who is on her way to South America to get a divorce. The plane she's on crashes, but not before she, her maid, and her lawyer parachute to safety on a tropical island. On the island there is a savage "white" race that has a garbled view of America but turns out to be friendly. Based in part on *Robinson Crusoe,* the play features a radio set that washes ashore, which becomes the source of further farcical accounts of goings-on in America. Cullen enthusiastically describes the "skeleton framework" as providing a "superb vehicle for burlesque and satire." He was convinced the framework could be made to play, though it would obviously require "hard work." Trusting in large part his assumption that he could get Ethel Waters to play the central role, he saw no reason why "the play cannot be as funny and exciting and interesting (in a different way, of course,) as 'As Thousands Cheer,' and certainly, into the bargain, more literate." The musical revue *As Thousands Cheer,* with songs by Irving Berlin, was staged in 1933 and became a solid hit; Cullen had it in mind because it was the first time Ethel Waters had been given equal billing with white performers. With a considerable flourish, Cullen summarized his viewpoint and revealed some of his personal attitude about racial questions: "My sense of humor may not be average, but I can think of nothing funnier than the white race shown as a naked, heathen savage, and against a background of burlesque-cultured Negroes who represent the height of civilization as it exists today." It remains clear from this that Cullen envisioned a Juvenalian satire rather than an Horatian one. At the same time, his belief in its workability rested very heavily on obtaining Waters's cooperation, knowing that if "she would agree to appear in it, any manager would be glad to have it as a production." But such a production never materialized.

Another incomplete project that engaged Cullen was a play called *They Seek a City.* Written as a radio script, an unsigned copy of it survives in the Cullen archive. However, the play may have been exclusively the work of Owen Dodson and is listed as such in a bibliography devoted to his published and unpublished work.[5] Dodson was a poet and playwright and was probably introduced to Cullen by Jackman or Charles Sebree, who illustrated Cullen's first children's book and with whom Dodson had a long-term relationship. Cullen's translation of *Medea* had impressed Dodson, so much so that he would later rewrite Cullen's version and append his name as coauthor. Dodson admired Cullen a great deal, and in the many revisions to *They Seek a City* may have turned to him for advice; this would explain why the script ended up in Cullen's archive.[6] This particular script apparently resulted from the project masterminded by Charles S. Johnson in 1934, the Committee for Mass Education in Race Relations. The project foundered for lack of funds, though considerable effort and consultation went into fund-raising attempts. The purpose of Johnson's Committee for Mass Education was to use the mass media— at first, concentrating on films—as an instrument to eliminate racism and the burdens caused by active prejudice against African Americans. Johnson himself suggested several scenarios, but none of these poets ever realized any film based on such a script.[7]

Even as Cullen faced difficulties bringing his efforts in writing for the theater to some practical conclusion, various forces contributed to the maintaining of his reputation as a leading poet. By the end of the 1930s his place as one of the central voices of the Renaissance was attested to in many ways. Some garnered much notice, and others took place further from the center of the cultural world. In the spring of 1939, for example, his poems were put to music by Kurt Pahlen, an Austrian-born composer, and sung in German along with poems by Hughes. This was part of an evening at Town Hall, where the Mwalimu Festival Chorus presented a program of African music that included Negro spirituals and a choral rhapsody by Samuel Coleridge-Taylor, then one of the best-known African American composers. The conductor for the evening was Manet Harrison Fowler, an African American singer, musician, and educator from Fort Worth, Texas, who in 1928 founded the Mwalimu School in Texas, later relocating it to Harlem. The school was associated with the Harlem Renaissance, providing educational opportunities in the arts for Harlem's residents.[8] Eight months after the Mwalimu concert, Jules Bledsoe, an African American baritone who was recently returned from a successful European tour, sang one of Cullen's poems at another Town Hall concert; Bledsoe himself had written the setting. Throughout his career Cullen received numerous requests to put his poems to music, and the composers who did so form a long and impressive list: William Schuman, Virgil Thompson, and Emerson Whithorne, among others.

In his writing projects that took shape in a dramatic mode, Cullen more than once resorted to collaboration. Some time in the late 1930s he began to work with Hughes Allison. Allison enjoyed only one production of his dramatic work, a play called *The Trial of Dr. Beck,* produced by the Federal Theatre Project, which ran for twenty-four performances in August 1937. He and Cullen were able to develop in some detail plans for a radio serial, perhaps spurred by Johnson's Committee for Mass Education. The first page of Cullen's proposal for this serial—called *The Sunny Side of the Street*—says that Cullen and Allison have "collaborated before in writing about Negro life," though there appears to be no record of this. The proposal, containing "outlines, character sketches, scripts, etc.," takes pains to describe the aesthetic framework and goals by which the coauthors have been guided. They want to create a "springboard" (a term they repeat a number of times) that will allow them to launch a story of Negro life; their primary audience will be Negroes, but they remain aware of the possibility of having white members in the audience. Considerable attention is paid to how the Negro audience would react negatively to the use of stereotypes, especially the overuse of dialect and the presence of characters who are "buffoons." Though not easily assimilated into the category of "racial uplift," the script is written in a way that ensures that "there must never be any implication which might be construed as a *racial failing.*" To this end the authors describe themselves as "step[ping] cautiously and conscientiously to our story's construction." This self-conscious aesthetic ideology introduces the proposal and takes up six pages, out of a total of twenty-seven. In some ways, it reiterates the aesthetic argument that Cullen had with Hughes in the wake of the publication of *The Weary Blues* and *Color.*

The proposal contains the outline of a narrative, mostly derived from the character sketches. The locale is Newark, New Jersey, and the main characters are a Negro family: the father had been killed in a hit-and-run accident, and the mother is left with her four children, ages ten to twenty years old. She runs the family business, a music shop, left her by her husband. The main action centers on the eldest child, her daughter Ella, and the choice she must make between two suitors. A subplot involves a villainous gambler, named Chain, who was the driver behind the wheel of the car that struck and killed the father. Overly familiar today, after three or more generations of predictable television serials and soap operas built on family life, the material shows little dramatic promise and is too strongly influenced by a careful sociological approach (at one point the proposal even cites the then current population of Newark). Of all the various dramatic works by Cullen that deal with the problems of racism, this is by far the most reserved, even anodyne.

Cullen, however, had not done with writing about the issues of race, and again he turned to a fellow playwright for collaborative help. Whether or not he and Owen Dodson had collaborated on *They Seek a City*, they plainly coauthored a one-act play called *The Third Fourth of July*. Though never staged in Cullen's lifetime, the play was published, under both men's names, in 1946.[9] It originated when Mura Dehn, an expert in jazz and African American dance, approached the two poets with an experimental idea. She thought that a poem illustrated with dance sequences could be performed at the New School for Social Work. Resembling in some ways the untitled satire on race relations, this short play plunges into the questions about race that many saw as most troubling to American society. Depicting a black family and a white one living next door to each other, the play anticipates the incipient issues of segregated housing that came to be a major social problem in postwar America. Using the national holiday—depicted in three succeeding years—as its temporal structure, the play called into question all of the unfulfilled promises of the American experiment and its commitment to democratic values. The play thus confronts the issue of race and democracy, which was contemporaneously the subject of work by both Locke and DuBois, among others. Both these men questioned how America could hope to spread democracy in the world after the war if it remained a racist society within its own borders.[10]

Cullen and Dodson mounted their criticism of racism in America in equally unflinching terms. Their play begins with two narrators, who function much as a Greek chorus, though one is white and the other black. Throughout the play all the characters wear either black or white masks, the color for each actor being the opposite of his or her actual skin color. This reversing of the index of skin color, which recalls the satire meant for Ethel Waters, pervades the play. Beginning with the notion of an unfulfilled dream, the narrators recall broken promises: for the black, it is the question of segregation, while for the white, it is the promise of peace. A dance interlude, the first of several, begins as two families, one white and one black, take possession of neighboring houses. The white family taunts the black with racial epithets, but the daughter of the black family, Pearl, stands up to the abuse, and another dance—

called a "DANCE OF HUMILIATION AND HATE"—successfully silences the taunts, and then a "DANCE OF DEFIANCE AND LIBERTY" ensues. The narrators return to open the next scene and discuss what all this portends, and the white narrator ends by suggesting that everyone must, by fighting for freedom, rise above the barriers of color.

The next scene shows the interiors of the two houses as both families in parallel go about their daily activities. But the mother of the white family resorts again to racial taunts. Then a complicated balletic fantasy occurs as the white daughter and her black counterpart watch while their thoughts are dramatized by a chorus of dances. Confusion ensues as the two daughters mistakenly exchange their masks, and each ends up in the house of the other family. Though each daughter insists she is no different because of her skin color, the families are horrified. The girls rush out only to confront each other in the street and take back their "proper" masks. The final scene takes place on the "third" Fourth of July, opening with the black narrator lamenting the implacable burdens of war:

> War is a clock.
> No matter how long it runs
> Or how short
> It takes away your sons
> Until it runs down.

Then a messenger attempts to deliver a telegram, containing news that the black family's son had died in battle. Finding no one at home in the black family's house, he goes to the white family's house to leave the telegram there. The white family's mother at first thinks it concerns her son. Upon discovering the truth, she must then go and deliver the tragic news to the black family, who is seen returning home "as if from a picnic," full of good cheer. Before she hands over the telegram she removes her mask, and both mothers end by weeping together. This is followed by a blackout, and the concluding action then shows the white son returning from the war. He is able to bring about a reconciliation between the two mothers, removing their masks, and his own. This revelation prompts both families to celebrate the Fourth, and the play ends with all singing a chorus in praise of the "four freedoms." This refers, of course, to Roosevelt's State of the Union speech in 1941, where he enunciated the four freedoms: freedom of speech, freedom of worship, freedom from want, and freedom from fear.

The play would require several things in order to work well, not least a high degree of choreographic skill in making the dance sequences succeed in conveying what Cullen intended. The use of heavy symbolism and the presence of a strong didactic tone mean that the play resembles to some extent the agit-prop drama of the 1930s, even as the dance sequences give it a highly aestheticized feel. Despite considerable difficulty in producing some of the desired effects, however, the play is not meant as a drama restricted to the page. Though published only after his death, it clearly shows Cullen's thoughts on racism and his political and social feelings, even as it anticipates the questions about postwar segregation and the persistence of Jim Crow laws. Taken together with the satire for Ethel Waters and *The Sunny Side of the Street, The Third Fourth of July* testifies to Cullen's desire to use various dramatic formats to express himself. Furthermore, if he had had better luck in getting these works staged, he would have become known as a playwright concerned with race as the central problem of his time. By remaining largely unknown, these plays failed to remove some of the charges against Cullen, namely, that he was less interested in racial issues than in a desire to deal in "universal" values and truths. This false dichotomy became calcified, to the detriment of his reputation.

Cullen continued to engage with his fellow poets in a number of different projects, but some of these presented more problems than possibilities. He fitfully dealt with Claude McKay in the later 1930s, after the older poet had returned to New York from his years of self-imposed exile. Their relationship failed to be as fruitful as they both seemed to want it to be, for even though both used traditional forms for their poetry, their political and emotional registers were quite distinct. For a long time McKay had been quick to anger, and on at least one previous occasion his heated remarks focused on Cullen's sense of semantic nuance. A decade earlier, in 1927, Cullen had commented on McKay's poetry, using the pages of his preface to *Caroling Dusk* to do so: "Claude McKay is most exercised, rebellious, and vituperative to a degree that clouds his lyricism in many instances, but silhouettes most forcibly his high dudgeon." At this time McKay was facing unusual penury, and indeed he had lived in near poverty for many years, and so was understandably sensitive about his reputation back in America. Living in Marseilles and resenting any negative reception at the hands of African American critics, he took the occasion to tell Jackman just how bitter his feelings were toward a number of reviewers, starting with a sarcastic characterization of Braithwaite, before going on to others.

> I have had the distinguished attaché of the Boston Transcript up and at me in "Crisis" and the honorable Oxonin [sic], Doctor Locke, and now comes your friend, Mr. Cullen, who in the Anthology of Negro Poets cannot find anything more appropriate than the journalistic word "vituperative," synonym of the police court term "abusive," to express his opinion of my hortatory poems. Even the worst of my white critics, the Stoddards and Dixons, have never used such a contemptible word as "vituperative" to show their disapproval of such of my poetry in which a race cries out against murder and suppression.[11]

The reference to the notorious white supremacists Stoddard and Dixon typifies McKay's exaggerated polemic and only exposes how his argument proceeds unchecked. He summarized his attitude by saying, "I am disappointed in Mr. Cullen's adjective. It speaks volumes and it is interesting and illuminating that it came from the author of 'Heritage.'" Jackman answered this by trying to reassure McKay that Cullen meant no disrespect or negative critical judgment, but McKay's rejoinder continued along the same lines. "Any cub reporter knows that 'vituperative' is 'abuse.' . . . If Mr. Cullen doesn't know the common meaning of the word it shows an amazing ignorance." Using a cub reporter as the example, McKay refers to the jargon of journalism and so fails to acknowledge that his own poetry clearly has occasional vituperation in it and was clearly meant, from time to time, to be abusive toward various targets.

For all the prickly manner that McKay could exhibit, toward foe and friend alike, Cullen, and Jackman as well, managed to maintain a working relationship with him. In 1938 the relationship seemed to open up a positive horizon, as Cullen was invited to coedit a journal. He and Claude McKay, always someone who wanted to extend the readership for African American writers, were to be named coeditors of *The African: A Journal of Literary and Social Progress*. Unfortunately, the project was never realized. The Universal Ethiopian Students Association (UESA),

20. Claude McKay. Upon his return to America in the 1930s, McKay entered into a number of projects with Cullen. Photograph by Carl Van Vechten.

whose home office was in New York, would provide the chief support. The association was already publishing a journal with a different name: *The African: Journal of African Affairs*. The proposed change in the journal's subtitle may have originated at the suggestion of McKay and Cullen, but in any case it forecast a more culturally focused approach. As for UESA itself, it utilized a complex body of thought about the mythical status of Ethiopia to advance a progressive social and political policy. But there were contradictions as well, since the association supported claims, made by and in the name of Haile Selassie and the state of Ethiopia, that were imperialistic. One historian has characterized the journal as looking toward the future of African peoples: "Although the publication cannot be characterized as radical (in the socialist sense), or conservative (in the culturally nationalist sense) one thing the UESA makes clear is its commitment to a Pan-African, anti-(European)-colonial, and a Black Nationalist vision."[12] Cullen made a real effort to energize the journal, calling on favors from his friends. For example, he wrote Dorothy West almost immediately, asking her to review Richard Wright's recent book, *Uncle Tom's Children* (1938), but what may have promised to be interesting ended up only as an unrealized project.

Whatever befell the UESA project, McKay and Cullen were able to cooperate, at least briefly, on another project in 1937. This was the scheme, something of an offshoot of the Federal Writers' Project, devised by McKay to form a Negro Writers' Guild. The guild would assemble with the main purpose of advancing the work of its members and improving the conditions that black writers faced in the literary world at large. This attempt foundered when a controversy arose over the admission of a white woman writer to the group, as some members wanted the guild to be for Negro writers only. McKay persisted in his organizational efforts, however, and on his second attempt to gather his peers—among them Cullen—he was able to devote considerable energy and thought to the guild, making James Weldon Johnson the president and drafting a constitution that would, among other things, restrict membership to African Americans. McKay, however, lacked the skills and the friendly, or at least tolerant, temperament that would serve to keep the organization going, and it soon dissolved. Cullen seemed less offended by McKay's often overbearing manner than did other of their contemporaries. On the other hand, McKay, suspicious to the point of paranoia, seldom took Cullen into his confidence, at one time telling him that he, McKay, had a good job prospect, but couldn't reveal when and where it would begin.[13] Both poets suffered from stomach ailments and high blood pressure, and in the early 1940s they shared their various diagnoses with one another. McKay's style as a poet earned considerable praise for its use of traditional poetic forms, such as the sonnet, to express his radical social and racial views, but sharing this stylistic trait with Cullen didn't make for any exceptional closeness between the two.

As McKay's politics veered toward conservative positions in the late thirties and early forties, Cullen's remained much more liberal. Near the end of their lives the men moved in opposite directions, from their earlier views as well as from each other. McKay did not let this stand in the way of his offering Cullen various opportunities to collaborate. In May of 1938, he suggested that the two of them should write a play together, a suggestion unlikely to charm Cullen immediately, given his experiences in trying to get his own plays produced. (An undated letter included an outline of a possible source for a play: the story, called "Menelik, of Abyssinia," would center on the man who was the fabled and embattled emperor of Ethiopia.) Even as he had told Cullen he couldn't give him the details of his new job, he asked Cullen for the loan of twenty dollars. A month or so later McKay had gone off to New Milford, Connecticut, to a cabin in the woods, to recuperate from a stroke and work on his writing. Another scheme was hatched: he, Cullen, and Hughes would together compile an anthology of their own poems. Each poet would select from his work, but the other two, so as to make sure all the most impressive and successful poems were included, would then vet the selections.[14] Though the editorial scheme was ingenious, there exists little evidence to show what happened, though the straitened circumstances of most publishers at this time may be explanation enough. A few years later, in October 1944, McKay denounced his earlier communist sympathies and joined the Catholic Church before he died, at the age of fifty-eight, in 1948.

When the second half of the 1930s saw many writers turn leftward in their political sympathies and become engaged in activist efforts to influence public opinion, Cullen also participated in a number of left-wing political activities. By the end of May 1939 virtually everyone knew there would be another world war, as the German army had been built-up aggressively to the point that any other course had clearly been ruled out. The Munich Pact was eight months old, and the notorious Hitler-Stalin nonaggression pact was but a few months in the future. Many American artists and intellectuals were signing various manifestos, some of which took opposing views that argued ideological—and nonideological— points. John Dewey, then the leading American philosopher by virtue of his founding role in pragmatism, felt strongly that such manifestos, if they were to argue coherently for a new world order based on democratic values—as did Cullen's position in *The Third Fourth of July*—had to oppose not only German and Italian fascism, but Russian totalitarianism as well. Dewey proclaimed the signatories of his document were "independent of control, whether open or secret, by any political group," signaling unequivocally that no front group was manipulating them. Franz Boas, whose anthropological work had done so much to resist notions of racial superiority, had earlier circulated a manifesto, but many refused to sign it because of its silence on the repressions operating in Russian communism. Dewey made it clear that his manifesto (actually described by the New York Times as a "call to organization signed by ninety-six artists and scientists") was not a repudiation of Boas, but he wanted his stand to be clear: no "front group" was guiding him. In May 1939, Cullen was approached to sign with Dewey's group, and he chose to do so. The poet's signature on Dewey's manifesto makes it apparent that his political views remained progressive.

A month or so later, on June 26, Cullen met with a group of fellow poets, including William Carlos Williams and Kenneth Fearing at the George Washington Hotel, at 23 Lexington Avenue, a favorite stopping place for well-known writers. The League of American Writers sponsored the meeting, which they billed as a Symposium on Poets and Poetry. This was in fact one of the "front groups" singled out by an anonymous member of Dewey's group—the Committee for Cultural Freedom—as being a target of Dewey's manifesto. Cullen's signing with one group and meeting with another that implicitly opposed it should not be taken as a sign of indecisiveness on his part, let alone duplicity. But what it does show is that he was known to many white writers, some of who belonged to disparate or overlapping organizations, and they courted his allegiance. Dewey's signatories included almost no African American writers except for George S. Schuyler and Dorothy Thompson, neither of whom had been supportive of the Renaissance; Schuyler, having gained his reputation by being a scold about "racial" art, continued as a conservative voice until the 1970s. Cullen's participation in various forms of cultural expression, from signing manifestos and adding his voice to symposia, demonstrated how he was still convinced that politics and culture could function as overlapping fields of effort. He also knew that the two fields were neither analogous nor synonymous. In this sense he retained some of the hopes and cautions of the Renaissance throughout the 1930s.

On January 1, 1937, Ida Roberson arrived in New York City, taking up permanent residence there after having decided to divorce her husband, Robert Lee Parker. Born in Tulsa, Oklahoma, in 1903, she had married Parker when she was just eighteen years old. Their daughter, Norma, was born the next year. Many years later Ida would devote herself to championing the work of African American artists, and she obviously had a keen aesthetic sense from the beginning. Her brother, Orlando, had come to New York as an aspiring singer and succeeded in landing a place as the lead vocalist in Claude Hopkins's orchestra. He also worked for a while as a manager of a popular drinking establishment, Vincent's Tavern, on 163rd Street. She turned to him when she decided to dissolve her marriage and start over in Harlem. Shortly after arriving in New York she met Cullen, who was a regular bridge player in a game hosted by Orlando. Their courtship started soon thereafter, and it grew quite serious in the next three years. By 1940 her divorce was concluded, and by that time the couple had already made plans to marry.

Though Cullen may not have remembered it clearly, an earlier meeting occurred between the poet and the woman who became his second wife: this was ten years earlier, during a brief visit to New York when Ida went to a party at the Dark Tower salon, where Lionel Hampton was providing the music. She had gone for a night out with her brother, Orlando, and her two sisters, and she recalled A'Lelia Walker saying to her, "I wish I had a family like that." (Cullen apparently later recalled meeting Ida's sister, but not Ida.) Though Ida was married to Parker at the time, she later vividly recalled the charged atmosphere of Harlem and the handsome young Cullen and so was delighted to meet him again a decade later.[15] Meanwhile, Orlando, living throughout the late 1920s and 1930s in Harlem, provided a chance for Ida to hear gossip about the Renaissance and the social goings-on in Harlem, so that her earlier impression of the social scene prepared her for her return in 1937.

In early 1940 Cullen proposed to Ida, and she gladly accepted. Cullen offered her a ring he had brought back from Paris and then introduced her to the reverend. The couple went out for drinks to celebrate their engagement, and Cullen told her, "I know this is right," as she later recalled him saying. They were married on September 22, 1940, in the living room of the reverend's house, and then spent a few days in Asbury Park for their honeymoon. Jackman acted as best man, and the maid of honor was Hallie Mitchell, the reverend's sister-in-law. The reverend wanted the couple to move in with him at the parsonage, but Cullen demurred and for a while they stayed with Orlando in his apartment near the Polo Grounds. The summer of 1940 was the first time Cullen had

21. Ida Cullen. A woman of considerable beauty, she was deeply attached to Countée.

to forgo his trip to Paris, and he spent that summer vacationing at Old Orchard Beach in Maine and the following summers in Pleasantville, frequently at work on his children's book. By 1942, however, the reverend had grown weak, and Ida and Cullen took him in to their apartment at 435 Convent Avenue. Not long thereafter the search for larger quarters began, and two years later the three of them moved to the house at 41 Grand View Boulevard, in Tuckahoe, a quaint village carved out of the town of White Plains, north of New York City. It was a short trip from the center of New York City to the village's charming train station, and Cullen frequently traveled back and forth on the commuter rail line.

POET WEDS AGAIN [Oct. 5, 1940]

MR. AND MRS. COUNTEE CULLEN

Mr. and Mrs. Countee Cullen, newlyweds pictured above, are now at home at 940 St. Nicholas Av. The bride is the former Miss Ida Mae Roberson, of this city and Kansas City, Mo. The groom is the internationally known poet and French teacher. This is the second marriage for the principals, who took vows here on Friday, Sept. 27, and honeymooned in Asbury Park.

22. Ida and Countée's wedding photograph, 1940, as it appeared in a New York newspaper.

Ida was impressed with Cullen's deep love for the theater, something she shared with him from the start. Cullen and Ida also loved going to concerts together, and they often played bridge with friends. Though their marriage only lasted five years, it seemed a thoroughly happy one for both of them, and in her later reminiscences Ida clearly expressed her devotion to Cullen. He opened up to her about his early childhood in

Harlem, giving her details about his grandmother and her need to take in foster children in order to make ends meet. Cullen also revealed that he would often comfort some of the children younger than he. He told Ida he couldn't recall anything about his own mother, but that he did send her twenty-five dollars a month; this started after she had contacted him once she saw a feature story about him in the newspaper. He knew that it was very "fortunate" that the reverend had taken him in when his grandmother died, and he admitted that the reverend was greatly disappointed when the marriage with Yolande failed. For her part, Ida felt very close to the reverend—whom she referred to as "Pa"—and worked for him in a secretarial role for three years, beginning shortly after she moved to New York.

Cullen very likely did not share with Ida his continued attachment to Edward Atkinson. An actor in a number of stage productions in New York City, Atkinson had been on intimate terms with Cullen for a number of years.[16] Cullen maintained their covert relationship throughout the early 1940s by having a regular weekly "night out," usually on Fridays, in order to play cards and meet with his friends. Van Vechten hosted a party for Atkinson in August 1943, as Atkinson was about to join the army. Cullen wrote to Van Vechten to thank him for the festivities and described how Atkinson had overindulged: "I know few people who could have been so prettily drunk," Cullen quipped. Later Van Vechten photographed Atkinson in his costume as Edward III, and this became the nickname by which Cullen often referred to him. During the last years of his life, and even after he had moved to Tuckahoe, Cullen occasionally worked in the Canteen, a USO-type meeting place for the armed forces personnel who were numerous in New York City during the war. Jackman was aware of this relationship, and often served as a go-between, passing messages back and forth between Cullen and "Edward III."[17]

Van Vechten grew closer to Cullen during the early 1940s, in part because of Van Vechten's growing interest in photographing African American personalities and cultural figures. In May 1941, for example, Van Vechten sent Cullen his photograph of Rose McClendon costumed as Medea, and, writing back to thank him, Cullen said he had never seen McClendon on the stage but exclaimed, "How excellently she would have portrayed *Medea!*" Almost a year later Cullen asked Van Vechten to send him a photograph of a "friend," perhaps Atkinson. Meanwhile, Van Vech-

23. Edward Atkinson, taken at the Canteen. Cullen's nickname for him was "Edward III," after one of Atkinson's roles. Photograph by Carl Van Vechten.

ten had started amassing the collections of manuscripts and other documents that he would eventually bequeath to the Beinecke Library at Yale, and he implored Cullen to retrieve some of his poetry manuscripts from the reverend's attic storeroom. Later in 1942 a Van Vechten photograph of Atkinson dressed in Persian finery reached Cullen, and he exclaimed, "He looks every inch a Shah!" Cullen reassured Van Vechten that he, Cullen, would be sure to be fingerprinted and obtain a photo identification card so he could work at the Canteen, presumably at Van Vechten's urging. Van Vechten also interceded with Irita Van Doren, the editor of the book section of the *New York Herald Tribune,* to have Cullen do some reviews, "a very acceptable source of necessary new income," but nothing came of this. Throughout these last years, Van Vechten, a sedulous recorder of African American culture, remained appreciative of Cullen's contributions of his personal material to the Beinecke.

Cullen's annual trips to Europe, and chiefly Paris, continued throughout the late 1930s, often in the company of the reverend and Jackman as well. As early as August 1937, Cullen was involved enough with Ida to send her postcards from Paris. The following summer he stayed in the Hotel St. Pierre, but took a separate room from the reverend, writing to Ida about his dancing and drinking rum, buoyed in part by a heavily decorated Paris that was busy celebrating a visit from England's king and queen. A year later he let Ida know he was sailing home from Paris on the *Ile de France*. In the next summer, however, as Europe went to war, he went to Old Orchard Beach in Maine to work on details about the impending publication of *The Lost Zoo* and waited to hear when Ida's divorce would become final. Ida remembered that around this time Cul-

24. A triple portrait, taken at the Canteen, circa 1943, showing, from left, Langston Hughes, Arna Bontemps, and Harold Jackman. All three men played large parts in Cullen's life. Photograph by Carl Van Vechten.

len recalled how he was struck by the "good Broadway material" in Arna Bontemps's novel and so had approached him about the idea of collaborating on a stage musical based on *God Sends Sunday*. Ida knew just how deep Cullen's love for the theater was, but she may not have had any idea of the struggles and frustrations that would come of what seemed such an attractive idea.

The Children's Books

As the 1930s drew to a close Cullen began to consider seriously the project of a children's book. Hughes and Bontemps had collaborated on such a work, based on Hughes's travel to Cuba, and it had achieved a certain success. Bontemps would likely have encouraged Cullen to follow suit. As for his predilections, Cullen had always been fond of cats. And in his interview with James Baldwin, who had been his student at Frederick Douglass Junior High, Cullen spoke of how his students always wanted him to read his work and discuss it with them.[18] When he did so, however, he felt they would be better served, and better entertained, by hearing fanciful stories rather than love lyrics. Since he had gone beyond lyric poetry in translating Greek tragedy, there might be some rightness in venturing in the other direction, so to speak. Given his broad and deep knowledge of literary values, Cullen obviously saw that such an effort could go well beyond the commonplace. What resulted was a striking display of inventiveness and a nuanced approach to the question of narrative authority.

Cullen demonstrated his commitment to children's literature by capturing a sincere feeling about a range of experience generally considered limited or merely fanciful. He also reached back to classical sources, basing his book on tales in which animals are central; this links him to the allegorical mode employed by Aesop, who prototypically joined the playful and the didactic. Jackman, in perhaps a purer aesthetic vein, had begun urging Cullen to write a children's book as early as the late 1920s, and even supplied Cullen with a work on the psychology of cats.[19] Cullen was also unusually attached to the cats of Steve and Sophie Green while he was visiting with them in Paris. When it came to publishing his translations of French poems, Cullen chose two by Baudelaire, both on the subject of cats. Widely divergent in sensibility as he was from Baudelaire, Cullen nevertheless appreciated the duality in the species:

Lovers that burn and scholars cold
Dote equally in their appointed time
On subtle cats which do them both combine–
Quiet as scholars and as lovers bold.

The duality here attracted Cullen, but he was even more strongly drawn to the way the cat in his imagination could be both subtle and altogether reticent. In creating his alter ego, so to speak, Cullen made Christopher Cat into an interlocutor much like himself, but if anything even more in control of his words and his unexpected linguistic ability.

The parodic framework of the book adds to this fascination with the feline sensibility, in which Cullen borrows, more or less wholesale, the biblical story of Noah's ark. Topping off the multiple levels on which the book can be read is the use of Christopher Cat—Cullen's purported pet feline—as the story's narrator, resulting in a complex and nuanced literary work. Referring to the accepted axiom that children's literature has a dual audience, of children and adults, one expert in the field describes the ambivalence of Cullen's work:

> The Lost Zoo has proved to be of uncertain status . . . , and for those adults who initially mediate between the text and adult buyers and child readers, reviewers. Even more uncertain is its status for those other readers at whom it is directed—the "not too young" who are represented in the subtitle by italics. It is arguably the ambivalent nature of this work in terms of its audience, its genre, its possible readings, and the subtlety of its coded racial messages that has led to its neglect by those adults for whom it was in part intended, although it is still in print in an inexpensive edition for children.[20]

Cullen interjected the phrase "not too young" out of what may have been his need to signal a subversive impulse, one that would allow him to write a children's book that would display not only his high linguistic inventiveness but raise questions about status and identity as well.

Part of the aesthetic satisfaction of the book comes from the way it uses an almost casual prose introduction—explaining how the author and Christopher Cat have come to speak to and understand one another—and the coda, also in prose, in which the author playfully, though with some frustration, tries to have Christopher explain a bit more about the missing animals. The tone in these prose passages combines playfulness and moral instruction, the latter kept very low key, in a way that cleverly echoes that of the verse passages that describe the various animals. Perhaps the most direct didactic passage is when the author questions Christopher about whether or not he had previously mentioned an animal called a "Pussybow," which is a hybrid of a cat and a dog. Christopher, with considerable vanity, denies ever mentioning any such, for to be part of such foolishness is beneath consideration. The author apologizes:

> "I'm sorry," I blurted out as fast as I could. "You're right and I'm wrong. I'm convinced that you never told me a word about the Pussybow. I must have invented him. I'm sorry and I apologize."
>
> "Your apology is accepted," Christopher purred, as he arched his back higher than usual and waved his tail in triumph, "but I can't help saying that if you and the general run of humankind thought twice before speaking once, you'd probably make fewer mistakes and have fewer reason for always going around apologizing to one another." (92)

This stands out as one of those rare moments when a writer with a certain temperament—in this case Cullen's often remarked upon reticence—allows one of his or her characters to offer what amounts to approval of the writer's character. At the same time, as Christopher is also Cullen's mouthpiece, we are being given a lesson in self-control and the important value of tasteful utterance.

Delight clearly remained high on Cullen's agenda, especially when it came to having a chance to characterize the hitherto unknown animals. Again and again his sense of irony manifested itself, for each animal happily combined traits that either demonstrated imaginative physiology or were simply comic, or some combination of the two. A good example of the former is the two-headed "Hoodinkus":

> Whatever way the animal went,
> One head alone could be content;
> The other head must nurse
> Its disappointment and its wrath

The while it churned a dusty path
Traveling in reverse! (67)

As the animal ages it has learned to "quarrel less," and so

Had for many years contrived,
Until a certain note arrived
To live in peacefulness.

25. The cover of the book jacket, designed by Charles Sebree, for *The Lost Zoo* (1940), Cullen's first book for children.

THE HAHAHA

So merry was the Hahaha;
"Tra-la," he sang, "tra-la-la-la."

26. One of Charles Sebree's depictions of a creature from *The Lost Zoo*.

The note that arrives is Noah's invitation to the animals to board the ark and escape the flood. Cullen inventively contrives a way to explain how each unknown animal misses the boat, literally, and so the narrative always has a point to make. But pointedness is only part of the story;

on occasion Cullen is content to be merely humorous. Here is the last animal to be described, the "Ha-Ha-Ha."

> Round as a wreath of Christmas holly,
> There never was a beast so jolly,
> Not one who found life such a jest!
> He laughed the buttons from his vest,
> The spectacles laughed from his nose,
> And all the toenails from his toes. (83)

Each animal has at least a mildly allegorical meaning. The "Ha-Ha-Ha" fails to take anything seriously; the "Hoodinkus" is the person consumed

THE SLEEPAMITEMORE

I'm such a sleepy, sleepy chap;
I'm having such a pleasant dream.

27. Another of those who missed the departure of the ark in *The Lost Zoo*.

by ambivalence; the "Sleepamitemore" is a lazy ne'er-do-well. Equally pertinent, though subtly advanced, is the notion that each represented a moral caution: "Sleepamitemore" warns against sloth, "Lapalakes" shows the danger in gluttony, and so on.

With a children's book, the role of the illustrations was even more important from a commercial point of view that it was with poetry. So, as he had done with *Color*, Cullen saw to it that an artist whom he admired illustrated his book. The dancer Katharine Dunham introduced Alain Locke to a set designer whom she had come to know and admire, Charles Sebree. Locke, in turn, introduced Owen Dodson, his Howard colleague, to Sebree, who would become one of the best-known African American visual artists after the war. Cullen was then introduced to Sebree, who happily agreed to do the illustrations for *The Lost Zoo*. With this assignment in hand, Sebree left Chicago and moved to New York City.[21] Eventually Sebree tried his hand at playwriting and moved around sporadically, always involved with groups of other innovative artists, but in 1939 he was willing to devote considerable time and effort to the imaginary animals of *The Lost Zoo*. He and Cullen corresponded frequently, going over details and working out deadlines and payments. Sebree was often strapped for funds, and Cullen was required to send him partial payments throughout the months leading up to the final manuscript. At one point he pleaded for help from Cullen, being so impoverished that he had left the YMCA without paying his bill.

In February 1940 Sebree sent Cullen the manuscript with passages underlined that he thought would be more pertinently illustrated. In the middle of March he said he had "a feeling that this venture will click." The complication presented itself here, however, that a librarian suggested to Cullen that the illustrations be done in color, and this, the publisher insisted, would increase production costs and so diminish royalties. In August Cullen urged Sebree on, saying, "Remember that Alain Locke is expecting great things from you, and so am I." Cullen did all he could to move things along, even sending Sebree rather crude sketches of how he thought some of the animals should look. Sebree responded sympathetically and knew that a creature like "Wakeupworld" should have "just that amount of strangeness about him which should arouse the curiosity of the children." Eventually, all the crises were managed and the book appeared by the close of the year, and Cullen read from it to a group of delighted children at the 135th Street library at the end of November.

Given the level of imaginative play in *The Lost Zoo*, it is tempting to read the book at a deeper level. There are passages that suggest Christopher expresses an intelligence and sensibility that lies just beyond the social boundaries. (He has conquered the biological ones.) As such, he could be exemplifying the strictures that govern racism. The book's narrative is triggered by the author's visit to a zoo, where he imagines that he has seen all the animals. But Christopher points out that the category "animal" extends beyond the human's imagination. Furthermore, Christopher demands even more than his already unusual measure of human qualities—he wants to become an author himself. Christopher speaks most frankly to his "owner" about what is "unheard of": "That's what people always say when you don't want to do the fair things by us animals. *You never heard of such a thing!* You never heard of those lost animals either until I told you of them; but that didn't keep you from writing about them. And although it may surprise people at first to see my name on a book, they'll gradually get used to it" (21). This doesn't say exactly what we hear at the end of "Yet Do I Marvel," that it is a curious thing, "to make a poet black, and bid him sing." But if every author reflects and refracts a version of him- or herself in the book, here and in his poem Cullen enacts a version of the almost unthinkable act of becoming a writer.

The other way *The Lost Zoo* resonates involves not only the sensory delight and moral instruction it contains, but what it leaves out. Though Cullen clearly invokes the biblical story in treating Noah in a proper way, he omits any sense of the divine retribution and providence that the Old Testament advances. The animals exist in and shape a narrative that is totally secular. The lost animals are wondrous and in that regard they partake of the preternatural. But they are not gifted with any high spiritual power or symbolism. They are, if anything, "human, all too human." To the extent that Cullen chafed against the reverend's high-mindedness, he decided to craft a book that teaches and delights without invoking an eternal or transcendent framework.

Two years later Cullen's second children's book, *My Lives and How I Lost Them*, appeared, with illustration by Robert Reid Macguire. He was an artist, designer, and illustrator who first exhibited his work in New York City in 1928. The early part of his career was spent mostly in interior design, but by 1940, he began concentrating upon painting and illustration. Cullen, for his part, continued the conceit of Christopher's human abilities by having the title page read "by Christopher Cat, in collaboration with Countée Cullen." The form of this book, however, lacks the inventiveness of its predecessor. There is a brief prelude as Cullen and Christopher discuss things and stumble upon the expression of a cat's having nine lives. Cullen doubts it; Christopher affirms it. What follows is an extended first-person narrative, by Christopher of course, relating how he has lost the first eight of his lives. The incidents relayed in this effort are, of course, not actual deaths, but rather severe injuries or threatened demises that only serve as transitions to a new narrative context. Christopher also has five siblings (his tender mother having borne three sets of twins), an overbearing father, and a rakish uncle, called Tom Cat, who makes a late appearance. Occasionally, this cast of extra characters contributes to a feeling the book is padded, a feeling that extends to some of the incidents as well. There is a poetry recital by Christopher and some of his siblings, but even there the writing is rather bland, as Cullen fails to slip in any clever observations about a social format or aesthetic occasion he knew well. Though the writing overall proceeds in a fairly direct and relaxed manner, Christopher's acting as the book's narrator surprisingly limits rather than enhances the element of play. Cullen was obviously at pains to maintain the illusion of Christopher as author, but in the end the reader is unlikely to be satisfied at the artistry, since both the adult and juvenile contexts lack conviction and drive. The cautious side of Cullen won out in this case.

Even as Cullen was enjoying a measured success with his children's book, and even as the long travails of *St. Louis Woman* were to extend through several years, he once again considered a position at a black college. Charles S. Johnson, now well installed at Fisk, had always been one of Cullen's chief supporters, and this continued into the war years. In the summer of 1944 Johnson invited Cullen to visit him in Tennessee, and Cullen obliged, giving two poetry readings and deciding what to do about the offer of a permanent teaching position there. Johnson combined his part of the offer, which would be to participate in an Institute for Race Relations that he had inaugurated, with that of one from Dr. Jones, the head of the English department. Cullen hesitated, since such an arrangement would not lighten his teaching load. After returning to Tuckahoe,

Cullen finally rejected the offer, and his letter to Johnson spelled out his financial situation.

> After much talk with Ida, much figuring how I could make all ends meet if I came to Fisk, I have been obliged to decline Dr. Jones' (and what pains me more) your offer of a position at Fisk. There are two considerations against my acceptance of the offer, and both, we feel, are strong enough for you to hear of sympathetically. I could not come to Fisk and at the same time keep my home here, and we are both disinclined to give up a place into which we have sunk all our available funds. The second reason is that Fisk does not have a pension fund. If I were a single man, that latter consideration would not deter me, but married as I am, it is of great importance to me.[22]

Cullen had cashed in a life insurance policy in order to afford the down payment for the Tuckahoe house, and he may have felt that his shaky health made caring for Ida after his death a more proximate concern. It may have been that other considerations were involved as well: the failing health of the reverend, and Ida's reluctance to leave the New York City area. In any case, once again Cullen was unable to take a position that was more in line with his accomplishments as a writer, and so he returned, with a mixture of stoicism and genuine commitment, to his younger students at the junior high school. Added to those long days in the classroom would be the countless hours of struggle to see *St. Louis Woman* finally come to Broadway.

St. Louis Woman

Cullen decided to collaborate with Arna Bontemps, whom he had known for years, on a musical meant for a full-scale Broadway production. Bontemps, a year younger than Cullen, was born in Alexandria, Louisiana, but spent much of his childhood in Los Angeles, before eventually coming to Harlem in 1924, encouraged in his writerly vocation by Wallace Thurman, and by having placed a poem in *Crisis*. At A'Lelia Walker's Dark Tower salon he met many writers, especially Hughes, with whom he collaborated on several projects and remained a lifelong friend. The standard joke around Harlem was that he resembled Hughes to such an extent that Cullen's father couldn't tell them apart.[23] The father of six, Bontemps became well known for his children's books and probably would have encouraged Cullen's efforts in that regard. Eventually, he ended up at Fisk as the college's head librarian, teaching writing and publishing frequently. Though a gifted writer himself, he often collaborated with others, Cullen and Hughes chief among them. He thoroughly enjoyed being a writer, blessed with a temperament that was always friendly and upbeat, despite the financial worries that plagued him and his family until he was able to secure a stable academic appointment. He and Cullen shared a propensity to put on too much weight, a trait remarked on by any number of their friends.[24]

Choosing Bontemps's first published novel, *God Sends Sunday*, as the basis of the musical made considerable sense. As for the standing of Bontemps's novel among readers in the Renaissance, Hughes weighed in on the subject just a year before he died, in a reminiscence of Harlem's literary scene, beginning with himself:

> I published *Not Without Laughter* in 1930, just as the Depression set in, so my first novel did not sell very well. A year later, Arna Bontemps published his first novel, *God Sends Sunday*, a little novel of great charm that had very little sale. During the remainder of that decade, nothing much exciting happened, literarily speaking, except for the debut in 1934 of the long-burgeoning talent of one of the most sparkling of Negro writers, Zora Neale Hurston.[25]

Hughes unfortunately omits mention of *One Way to Heaven*, which appeared the year after *God Sends Sunday*, an omission due more to Bontemps and Hughes maintaining a decades long friendship than any lingering animosity toward Cullen.

Bontemps's book has several colorful locations, including a Louisville racetrack, a New Orleans cakewalk, and a farm on the outskirts of Los Angeles. With Augie, a small Negro jockey, the story has a central character of large ambition and ego who nevertheless squanders his talent as he loses his moral bearings. The nearly picaresque structure of the book's plot offers any number of scenes that could be colorfully and musically presented, as Cullen pointed out to Ida. There is folk material (Augie's sister believes in conjuring), urban dazzle, and rural charm (the Los Angeles farm, however, is the scene of Augie's final downfall.) What at first Bontemps and Cullen didn't take fully into account was the complete lack of redemption or morally uplifting sentiment in the story. Augie kills two men, loses the wealth and social status that he had earned as a successful jockey, and, at the novel's end, he takes off for Mexico to avoid arrest for killing his rival for the affection of a farm girl decades younger than he. The first half of the novel presents Augie as almost preternaturally lucky, while the second half shows him as victimized by several forces. Contrasted with Cullen's *One Way to Heaven*, Bontemps's book is much grittier, and the society and characters it depicts remain starkly bound by the canons of self-defense and the rules of self-aggrandizement. Unfortunately, the scandalized reaction to the prospect of mounting the novel as a Broadway musical wouldn't erupt until just before the production was realized—but that would take place only after several years of convoluted starts and stops.

Cullen and Bontemps apparently began their collaboration in the mid-1930s; they even took a long bus ride to Cleveland in late 1933 to discuss a possible production with the Gilpin Players.[26] By the late 1930s, however, the form and fate of *St. Louis Woman* was being handled in part by Hughes, who was enlisted by Bontemps, presumably because of his experience writing scripts. From early 1937, and for a few years after that, the two men corresponded about their respective revisions of the play and the chances of its being produced, either in Los Angeles, at the Federal Theatre Project,[27] or in New York. Hughes felt the royalty and credit arrangements should be formalized, since he was likely still sensitive after the complications of his disputed rights to *Mule Bone* and the break with Zora Neale Huston, who had claimed Hughes plagiarized her work.[28] Writing from California to Bontemps in January 1937, Hughes raised the question of making sure all was settled: "Are you and Countée going to get together on that agreement for a sharing of all rights outside Federal Theatre with Muse and I, or do you want us [Muse and Hughes] to draw up a tentative agreement out here and submit it to you all?"[29] Muse was Clarence Muse, an experienced actor and screenwriter whom Hughes had enlisted for help with the lines the script needed in order to make the comedic elements pay off. Eventually, Hughes, sensing resistance from Bontemps—and possibly Cullen—agreed to leave Muse out of the rights altogether.

Throughout their collaboration Bontemps and Hughes were both facing grim economic circumstances and were preoccupied with dozens of publishing chores between them, including Bontemps's ghostwriting of W. C. Handy's autobiography and Hughes working on advances and frequent poetry readings just to stay solvent. Added to this pressure was the task of getting the latest revised versions typed up and mailed off to the agents—Leah Salisbury in New York representing Cullen, and Lieber and Harcourt Brace dealing with *God Sends Sunday* for Bontemps. Bontemps was settled for a while in Chicago, while Cullen remained at his teaching job in New York, and Hughes went to California for a long stay. So it was a year later, on March 7, 1939, when Hughes reported that the play "was coming along fine, and the Federal Board [in Los Angeles] likes our revisions very much." Bontemps, however, replied ten days later with depressing news, having heard negatively from Salisbury: "Leah Salisbury has at last written me. The letter just came, and it sounded like a knell for our easy-rider [i.e., Lil' Augie]. The hope of getting Salisbury, Lieber, Harcourt-Brace, Countée, Clarence, you and me together on a sort of Munich accord with the play as the pawn now seems to me almost too much to hope for. I can't see much hope for Czechoslovakia, under the circumstances." The allusion to the events that would soon provoke a world war were of course meant as bitterly ironic, but Bontemps probably knew negotiations were troubled, if not at an impasse. Salisbury was nevertheless hopeful as far as getting a producer went, as she told Bontemps that she felt "Broadway [was] Negro-minded again."

Meanwhile, Bontemps and Hughes had traveled together to Los Angeles, in part to give talks along the way in various venues about the children's books they were coauthoring. While in Los Angeles, Bontemps and Hughes arranged for Clarence Muse, who served on the board of directors of the Federal Theatre, to secure a grant from the board for Hughes to go on working on the script. This led to a confidential agreement that Bontemps worked out and sent to Hughes, which gave Hughes "a division of royalty," assuming the play would be produced. Hughes was animated by this and went on to work hard in revising, telling Bontemps the play was "75% a new show." Muse convinced the theater to stage the play, but, with an uncannily ominous development, many on the board felt the play was "beneath them and proposed staging an opera instead."[30] As things turned out, the Federal Theatre Project never mounted the play, since in 1939, Congress canceled the project because it was felt that the plays being produced under its auspices were full of seditious material. Hughes tried to keep alive the dream of a staging of *St. Louis Woman,* and in September 1939, he sent Bontemps a list of instructions on how to handle submission of the script, along with a number of other projects, to various people who might be able to place it with a producer.

As far as Cullen was concerned, he felt that Hughes was entitled to a flat fee for his work on the script. But he was adamant about the question of royalties, no percentage of which he felt Hughes deserved. Cullen wrote to Bontemps stating this unequivocally in late 1938. A few months later Arna had received the latest revision of the play's prologue from Hughes, and he told Cullen he thought it was Hughes's best work, and therefore he was deserving of some percentage of the royalties. Cullen's response went unrecorded. For the next six years Cullen and Bontemps maintained a fruitful working relationship, and both men kept faith with the project. By the time the production of the play was assured and the early preparations were underway—in early 1945—the question of sharing royalties was dwarfed in importance compared to the immense uproar that broke out over the content of the play.

The fate of *St. Louis Woman* seemed destined never to be settled smoothly.[31] It was on November 15, 1944, that the peak of good news occurred, as Cullen wrote to Bontemps to say the play had finally gotten a producer: Edward Gross. This meant a measure of monetary reward, as a contract came that provided for option rights and payments to both men. But almost immediately—and until the end of Cullen's life, a mere fourteen months away—the problems came in all sizes and shapes. W. C. Handy heard from the trade press of a play to be called *St. Louis Woman,* and he wrote Cullen to object, albeit at first in a friendly tone. But he persisted, claiming the title would "damage his interests" as it would draw attention away from his classic, "St. Louis Blues." Then there arose the question of royalties to be paid to Harcourt, which held the copyright on *God Sends Sunday.* Throughout the seemingly unending negotiations Leah Salisbury acted as Cullen's agent, but not as Bontemps's. This angered Bontemps on occasion, especially as she was in the habit of dropping all references to the musical being based on *God Sends Sunday.* Bontemps was by his own admission very sentimentally attached to his novel and hoped to see it reprinted one day, so he felt justified in insisting on this point of recognition. He also asked that his name be put above that of Cullen, as he had obviously written more of the script. Cullen agreed wholeheartedly, and generally the working relationship between the two was a model of coauthorship, always a path through troubling obstacles.

The script sustained constant pressures. The producer wanted the main character to be a boxer instead of a jockey, so Canada Lee could be the star. Scenes were rewritten to eliminate dialect, and in response to concerns about "low" material, Lil' Augie was made to propose marriage to Della. Even good developments had a negative side. When Gross decided to take the material to Metro Goldwyn Mayer to work out a film version, the play suddenly was reenvisioned as a thoroughgoing musical. In earlier versions Bontemps and Cullen anticipated using some musical numbers, and Cullen had at first supplied lyrics for ten songs, but Gross rejected them all. The rejection may have been spurred by the offer of songwriting by two of the best talents in American popular music: Harold Arlen and Johnny Mercer. Bontemps was weighed down with his position as librarian at Fisk, and of course Cullen was hard-pressed despite his public school teaching. The men tried to get together physically for rewriting, and almost did so before Christmas 1944. But only after the turn of the year was it possible. Cullen attempted to get a month's leave from the board of education and was turned down. He even appealed to the mayor, whom he had met during his time of the Commission on Conditions in Harlem, but even that influence was unavailing. He told Bontemps he could not give up his summer school teaching, as the extra salary was necessary for solvency. The coauthors often appeared as hard-pressed as their characters.

Most ironic of all the disappointments Cullen would suffer, however, was that the musical had been scheduled to open in the fall of 1945, which meant that Cullen would have been able to see it. But the opening was postponed. Successful tryouts took place in New Haven, and then Boston, in the Schubert Theatre. The casting presented the usual headaches. Ruby Hill was eventually tapped for the lead, and Rex Ingram and the Nicholas Brothers, all top headliners, were cast as well. Pearl Bailey made her stage debut as Butterfly, and her rendition of "Leavin' Time" became a classic, as did the standards, "Come Rain or Come Shine" and "Any Place I Hang My Hat Is Home." Lemuel Ayers, whose long career

28. The cover of the program for *St. Louis Woman,* 1946.

included work on over thirty-five Broadway productions, designed the scenery, and Rouben Mamoulian, fresh from his successes with *Oklahoma* and *Carousel,* was the director. At one point there was a plan to replace Ruby Hill with another actress, but the cast revolted and threatened a walkout until the plan was dropped.

More rain than sunshine was to come. After the details were set, but before the production opened, word spread that its content and tone were not going to be altogether edifying. Before long all the Harlem tongues were wagging, and what developed was a full-scale scandal. Cullen was outraged that leaders in the black community would object to the content of the play. After all, they had hailed with pride the triumph of *Porgy* years earlier, and *Strange Fruit* also had "low" characters, and it was currently enjoying a successful run. Fredi Washington, at the time a leading black actress, had not only rejected the lead role in *St. Louis Woman,* but she made a public display of her disapproval, giving an interview to *People's Voice,* a popular newspaper. In September 1945 Hughes met Cullen on the street, and his rage was virtually uncontainable. Hughes described the scene to Bontemps:

> I ran into Countée at a newsstand with the new PV [*People's Voice*] in his hand, and he had just read what Fredi said, and he was trembling like a leaf more from anger than grief—mad not sad! And he grabbed me and cried for me to take heed to a letter that he pulled from his pocket to read. And in it Fredi told how since she could not sing but Isabel [Fredi's sister] could sing, being free from Adam [her husband] the lead for her now in a play would be the thing, and Fredi closed by saying how fine the script was—like wine! And Countée cried, "It's a disgrace!" And shook the letter in my face, and said, "Sure's you're born, it's because Lena Horne has the lead in the play, and not Isabel, and I say, Fredi can go to hell!" He was in a state.[32]

The dispute over who would get the lead role only added to the heated discussion about the morality of the play. Lena Horne had been approached to play the lead, a choice that would possibly lead to a movie version, but those who found the material objectionable dissuaded her from taking it. Bontemps was able to keep his temper better than Cullen, for he wrote Hughes in his own defense about the content of *God Sends Sunday:* "Actually, this new version of SLW, while still a folk tale, is certainly not to be classed with the anti-Negro stuff. Neither, in my opinion, is the book. It is all rhythm and color, of course, but nothing to low-rate a heads-up brown skin on the Avenue."

Not all the race leaders were against the play, and at least one lamented the outcry that seemed to be echoing throughout Harlem. In late September, Charles S. Johnson told Cullen that people shouldn't judge the work without seeing it, and that "if *St. Louis Woman* is the important thing to be feared in race relations, may the Lord help us all." The heated wrangling over the possible negative impact of *St. Louis Woman* did not remain only in the public eye, however. Steps were taken to control the situation in private. Cullen seems to have assumed the lead in this. In August of 1945 Walter White wrote Cullen to tell him that he had requested from Howard Dietz, the famous lyricist, a copy of *St. Louis Woman* so he could read it. Cullen replied two weeks later, denying the request, but with an explanation. He told White that the reverend's illness had meant that he had had to return from Los Angeles, where he was at work on the play, and so he had no final typed copy to offer White. Instead, the two men agreed to have a reading of the play, followed by a discussion, to take place at Walter White's home on September 14.

The fact that many of those who objected to the play had not yet read it only inflamed the situation further. Cullen hoped to draw on the collective good sense of many notables. His invitations to the discussion at the White's house were extended to Aaron Douglas, Alain Locke, Dorothy Peterson, George Schuyler, Edward Perry, Charles S. Johnson, and others.[33] Locke, Johnson, and Schuyler were not able to attend. Van Vechten subsequently expressed to Cullen his regret that he wasn't invited. White asked Roy Wilkins of the NAACP, among others, to attend. They agreed the play would provide "good theatre," but at the end of the reading the tally was only nine in favor and six still opposed. Bontemps, meanwhile rather safely removed to Chicago, but mindful of the possibility of increased royalties, tried to give the events a positive spin. He told Cullen that "the controversy will give us both country houses if it keeps up long enough," and this wry crack was supported by his belief that the "fight is going our way." Still, the evening's discussion proceeded with a good deal of enmity. Cullen was convinced that White was set against the play before he heard it read, and that he was so agitated by it that he jumped up and walked around two or three times even as the reading progressed. Cullen told Bontemps that White's attitude was "strange, violent, and almost vicious." He declined to look at the drawings for the sets and costumes that Cullen had brought along to bolster his case. As was so often the case throughout his life, Cullen faced the tangle of issues involving race, art, and audience with very little hope of any resolution that would be free of harsh contention.

Whether or not amity prevailed, the show did go on. In the *New York Journal*, George Jean Nathan, then one of the country's leading drama critics said, "In a season historically remarkable for its many unhappy new musical shows, 'St. Louis Woman' comes as a comparative bluebird." The play ran for 113 performances.

Years later Walter White, one of the most renowned Renaissance leaders, remembered the dispute well enough to feel he had to tell his side of the story. Of course he was in many ways at the heart of the dispute, and people attacked him for hypocrisy, claiming that his daughter had been given a role in *Strange Fruit,* another play with "low" material, just in order to keep White quiet about the matter. This account is from his autobiography:

> Some of the Negro newspapers, using the occasion as a political grindstone, were less kind. I had opposed the making of a sordid moving picture called *St. Louis Woman,* and defended Lena Horne's refusal to play in it. It had been planned to produce the story first as a play and then as a picture. Although written by two able Negro writers, Countée Cullen and Arna Bontemps, who were my friends, it had pictured Negroes as pimps, prostitutes, and gamblers with no redeeming characteristics. Even one role supposed to portray a decent person—that of a pious churchgoing woman—represented her as having had several children, each by a different father without benefit of clergy. I had been shocked on reading the script to find every cliché and stereotype of the minstrel Negro included in it.

What might seem mere prudishness on White's part derived from a context in which race relations were being affected by the rise of motion pictures and other forms of mass media but in ways people didn't always comprehend. The Federal Theatre Project, from which the play had originally received much support, originated in the fact that African Americans had no access to Hollywood and the movie industry, and their roles in Broadway and other commercial theaters were all too often scarce in number and prestige. White continued his explanation:

> My disapproval had angered a number of people, particularly some of the Negro actors and actresses in Hollywood who feared the loss of em-

ployment through the abolition of movie stereotypes of Negroes as perennial and incurable buffoons or feeble-minded menials.

While I would have written *Strange Fruit* quite differently had I been fortunate and able enough to write so successful a best seller, its story and motivation were vastly different from that of *St. Louis Woman*. Lillian Smith had written her tragic story of racial hate in Georgia as honestly as any author had ever put word to paper. Considerable as were its faults it had an integrity and realism which were totally absent from *St. Louis Woman*. My enemies and critics, happy to find what they believed to be inconsistency between my attack on *St. Louis Woman* and my support of *Strange Fruit,* charged that Jane [White's daughter] had been given the role only to silence criticism from me.[34]

White's account makes clear how strong were the feelings of the black community about the issue of racial uplift and the role assigned to authors (by some in the community) in promoting it. Cullen's position had been clearly stated as far back as his dispute with Hughes a decade earlier. Now he was in the unusual, and quite ironic, position of being the author whose work was attacked as too "low" in material and style of presentation.

A number of people remarked on the possibility that the manifold frustrations Cullen faced seeing *St. Louis Woman* to its final version contributed to his early death. The episode where he fulminated against Fredi Washington supports such a possibility, considering that high blood pressure played a role in his final affliction. However scientific or medically accurate such an explanation is, there persists the irony of his being denied a chance to see his efforts fully realized, an irony that is painful, even tragic. Cullen's posthumous reputation usually involves noticing his reserve, his commitment to a rigorous sense of artistic discipline, and a rather academic set of themes. *St. Louis Woman* stands out from the usual broad strokes that depict Cullen, since the musical is full of African American material from folk strands and urban stylishness and a bright melodic spirit. These elements often appeared in Cullen's portrait, when his friends described his boyishness, good humor, and love of dancing. The dark poetry of his later years came forth from both a sense of pained experience and that tradition of his "soul's high song." But there was more to be told.

One bright spell broke through all the frustration and anxiety of the work on *St. Louis Woman,* however. As consuming as it was, in terms of time and energy, Cullen had bent himself to it with great seriousness. Then an opportunity came along that would draw Cullen to cross the country and work directly with those who were controlling the development of the script for the musical. The play's producer, Edward Gross, once a classmate of Cullen's back at DeWitt Clinton, was willing to pay for Cullen and Bontemps to come together to work with Mercer and Arlen in coordinating the lyrics and the script. But they ended up working separately in Los Angeles, as Bontemps could get away in May and Cullen's schedule only permitted him to come in July. However, this gave him the rare chance to enjoy the environment of Hollywood and Southern California. He took to it with a surprisingly unchecked pleasure. He told Jackman in July 1945 that Los Angeles "was a wonderful city, and I could live here all the time." The weather was the most of it, but his enthusiasm went beyond meteorology: "This is really the place for me, and I haven't any doubt that sometime in the next five years I'll wind up here for good, intent on buying a house large enough to have a permanent room for you!" His dream included Ida: if she were to join him, he "would call this an ideal summer although I might not get much work done." But work was going well, as he attended rehearsals and revised two scenes to the "apparent satisfaction" of the producer and the lyricists. He was still looking forward to meeting Lena Horne, who, for the time being, was slotted in as the lead, and he felt Butterfly McQueen—"so funny with that strange voice of hers"—would be chosen, though in the end she wasn't. All in all, his Hollywood sojourn was a source of great and much-needed productivity and relaxation.

One measure of his high spirits at this time was his proposal to Hughes that they work together on a dramatic adaptation of *One Way to Heaven.* With the proposal for the anthology of their poems, along with McKay's, in his mind, and aware of Hughes's increasing commitment to, and success with, dramatic writing, Cullen had thought out several points in this context. Even as he was leaving for Los Angeles he wrote Hughes with the idea.

> I would like to make a contract with you for our collaboration on changes in the script ONE WAY TO HEAVEN. Here are the propositions I want you

to consider. I suggest that we give the script that we do a time limit of five years before the producers. If at the end of five years no one has taken the script, I am to be free to try another revision unless you and I have done another in that time. Secondly, I suggest that inasmuch as the story will be taken from a novel written by me that all returns to be divided on a sixty-forty basis, the twenty percent edge to me being given because of the novel. In our work on the ST. LOUIS WOMAN I have had to give Bontemps a twenty-five percent advantage because of the novel.

But it wasn't only the business end of the arrangement that excited Cullen, as he went on to suggest specific revisions that Hughes might pursue, based in large measure on his experience with *St. Louis Woman*.

If the above is agreeable then here are further suggestions: You have the script, and I believe you told me that you also have an entree to Wildberg. Try to see him personally to get him to read the script. Tell him that Canada Lee has been crazy about the play for a long time and would like to play Sam and that Frederick O'Neil likes it well enough to want to do the part of the Reverend Drummond. Point out to him that the script is something unique as far as Negro plays go and would be a distinct novelty. . . . Tell him that if it interests we will be willing to work along any lines of change that he may suggest. Failing to interest Wildberg my next suggestion would be this: Discard the entire society set-up in the play and try to work out a synopsis using only the Sam and Mattie story and reducing the characters to no more than six or eight. . . . I think our script reduced to a minimum of characters and sets would have a better chance of production. If you decide to accept the above propositions I hope you will do as much as you can while I am away, and then we can work together as soon as I get back.[35]

Some of Cullen's thinking here reflects what others—Locke, for instance—probably told him about the double plot, and he knew that drama made demands different from those of the novel, of course. But what seemed like such a good idea for another collaboration would end up being only one more unrealized project, one more heavy stroke of irony, adding to the wounds Cullen bore over his desires as a man of the theater.

Cullen was unable or unwilling to put the war out of his mind. For him—as for Locke and DuBois and many other black people—the war proceeded with a false promise at its core. Though ostensibly waged for the "four freedoms," as *The Third Fourth of July,* his radio play, made clear, the conflict nevertheless would be hollow if it failed to bring about justice in racial terms. Fighting for democracy abroad while denying it to citizens at home was frustratingly hypocritical, so Cullen wrote a poem directly on the subject: "Apostrophe to the Land."[36] It is not a successful poem in aesthetic terms, as the rhymes are clumsy and the symbolism so standard that it becomes clichéd. However, attacking the "worm" of racism and lynching, Cullen rather daringly spells out that the enemies of democracy—the Axis powers of Germany, Italy, and Japan—understand that the Allies are weakened by their racial policies. The poem sees the possibility of eliminating this racism, and so "the cheated cropper [will] thrive / And draw his first free breath," but only if racism and fascism are equally defeated. If no "gifted Galahad" arrives to win the war, then "our own flag . . . shall . . . remain / The garment of the Worm." The poem ends with a qualified, "unless."

> Not till the hedges fall, the moats
>   Be mirrors for the stars,
> And fair hands drop from darker throats
>   Shall we extinguish Mars.
>
> O land of mine, O land I love,
>   The Worm gnaws at your root;
> Unless that Worm you scotch, remove,
>   Peace will not be the fruit.

The feeling remains clear even as the rhetoric, probably beholden in part to that of the reverend, beckons toward that of prophecy. Cullen's political view contains an ineradicable patriotism, but it also speaks unreservedly against the failures of democratic idealism.

Work on *St Louis Woman* took a heavy toll, further weighted by the controversy it generated. Occasional headaches tempered Cullen's enthusiasm even as he took delight in Los Angeles, but he seemed not to regard them as too ominous. But his lucky streak broke after only a few weeks of California sunshine: the reverend had become rather gravely ill, and Ida went into the hospital for an operation. She had been told she needed one back in the summer, and Cullen didn't want to travel to the West Coast while his wife was in need of medical care, so the operation was postponed until October. Cullen had no choice but to return to Harlem after July, weeks earlier than he had planned. The reverend underwent major intestinal surgery, and in the later parts of 1945 he required considerable attention. Knowing that his time would not be greatly prolonged, he had grown intent on finishing his autobiography, *From Barefoot Town to Jerusalem*.

Reverend Cullen officially retired from the Salem Church on April 4, 1942, after more than four decades of service. The idea of writing his autobiography might have occurred to him sooner, but by career's end he certainly knew what he wanted to say. The most striking parts of it dealt with his conversion experience, when he was cast into doubt and uncertainty as to his vocation. The story is viewed, to be sure, from the vantage of later years, when such doubts had been eradicated. But the humility that enveloped the doubt persisted, at least as a rhetorical framework, and it lends charm to the book. When he first arrived to take over his pastoral duties in Harlem, the front of the building was so small and undistinguished that he walked past it three times until he at last noticed a small slate tablet in the window identifying the church. Countée is mentioned several times, especially during the recounting of the 1927 trip to the Holy Land, and the reverend allows his pride in his son's accomplishment full expression. He even includes two of Cullen's poems, "To My Father" and "Dad," though both keep the spotlight on him.

The reverend's condition in 1945 was grave enough for him and Ida to call Cullen back from Los Angeles, yet it also spurred him to work more continuously on his autobiography, and since the book wasn't published until shortly after his death, his concern was valid. The character expressed in the book was quite solid, however, and the reverend crafted a spiritual autobiography that would have surprised the poor people among whom he was raised back in Maryland a half-century earlier. He dedicated the book to his wife, Carolyn Belle Mitchell Cullen, as he wrote out her full name, and praised "her charming, heart-warming, magnetic voice in song." Two frontispieces adorned the volume, one of the reverend and the other of his successor, Reverend Charles Young Trigg. Reverend Cullen often praised his staff and helpers. In mentioning James Gowins, the church's treasurer, for example, he said the man had served for decades and never lost track of a single dollar.

Many passages in the book read as homilies, preached from a lifetime of dedicated service and fervent belief. The clerical life for the reverend might have been either a "profession" or a "calling"; it was apparent that for him it had been the latter. He describes his Creator in humble terms that take on some of the lyricism of the pulpit: "For me He is sitting in glory, seated there on the throne, and He promised never, never, never to leave me; no, never to leave me alone." The narrative portions of the book stand out with a strong and powerfully direct quality, though often the story is interrupted to present a list of people to whom he is indebted. There are, in effect, two speakers in the book: a pastor steeped in fideism and a masterly manager of an organization. Neither of these, however, shut out certain opinions, some of which may have been passed on to his adopted son. Somewhat surprisingly, for example, he exempts the Jewish landowners in Harlem from the charge of gouging their renters, saying instead that it is the black community itself that drove up costs by being too eager to obtain fancy housing. He also testifies that "I never held, or allowed to be held, a political meeting in Salem Church." This again was surprising, considering his activist role in the NAACP and other organizations, which he describes in some detail.

The specific reason for Ida's operation in October was never spelled out to Cullen's friends—even to Bontemps—and coming as it did when the reverend was quite ill added to his anxiety. But years later Ida gave an account of a medical emergency that may have been related to this operation. Without giving any exact dates, Ida recounted how she and Cullen had gone into Manhattan one afternoon to attend a poetry reading at the Forty-Second Street Public Library. After the reading, Cullen sensed that a thunderstorm was coming (Ida described him as always sensitive on this point), and so, rather than enjoy an afternoon in the city, they rushed to Grand Central Terminal to take the train back to Tuckahoe. On the way back Ida developed severe abdominal cramps. By the time they reached Tuckahoe, she was in such pain she could hardly walk. Cullen took her home immediately and called the doctor. The next morning, when the doctor, William Proctor, who had his office on Main Street in Tuckahoe, was able to come and examine her, Ida was told that she had

had a miscarriage. The doctor tried to console her, saying "you can always try again." Cullen knelt by the bed and told Ida "we're going to have a little girl and call her Carolyn," the name of his adoptive mother.[37]

Throughout the early 1940s, Cullen was beset with headaches, gastric problems, and high blood pressure, all afflictions worsened by the strains he was facing. He had often missed his turn at the Canteen because of such illness. However, despite persistent medical difficulties, he suddenly needed to be hospitalized because incipient kidney failure had brought on uremic poisoning. The last two days of Cullen's life took place in January 1946 at the 124th Street hospital in Manhattan. Ida attended him throughout. She later recalled how he vouched that she was the best wife any man could have and how solicitous he was in planning for her welfare after his death. Since none of his books were in print at the time, he felt he had left her in a precarious state. He suggested that she could tour throughout the country and read his poetry, thus making money from such appearances and perhaps helping to get the poetry back into print. For her part, she asked him, "are you crazy?" She knew he himself never enjoyed reading in public.[38] Cullen succumbed to a cerebral hemorrhage at Sydenham Hospital on January 9, 1946, at 3:15 in the afternoon. The final rites were conducted eleven days later, at the Salem Methodist Church, and he was buried in Woodlawn Cemetery.

Coda

Before his death Cullen had been at work on a volume of his poetry, which would appear a year after he passed away; it was called *On These I Stand,* and it selected poems from all the previous volumes and added six previously unpublished poems. The title of the collection suggests thoughtful resolve and perhaps a touch of defiance. He clearly knew that the arc of his career as a lyric poet bent downward, but he also knew that his early success was not unmerited. Still, he proved to be his own most demanding editor. Of all the previous volumes, *Color* was most severely culled, going from more than seventy poems down to only twenty-five. *Copper Sun* was also all treated stringently, as all the poems from the "Juvenilia" section and several from the sections "Varia" and "At Cambridge" were dropped. *The Black Christ* went from forty-seven to twenty-four poems. Though he omitted the translation of the tragedy from *Medea and Some*

29. Cullen in his early forties, striking a reflective pose.

Poems, he included all the other poems from that volume, thereby giving his readers another chance to hear these dark utterances. As an act of critical evaluation, *On These I Stand* is perhaps too harsh, and, like its maker, perhaps too self-denying.

The passing of a poet is often the occasion for special grief, especially so for Cullen, who died at the relatively early age of forty-three. Alain Locke's final written words on Cullen's life and work came in an annual review he wrote for *Phylon,* one of the many he produced for two decades as a sort of contemporary history of African American letters. These annual reviews were careful critical assessments, and Locke contextualized his observations and judgments in broad and balanced terms:

> Sadly enough, the significant poetry volume of 1947 is a valedictory rather than the hailing of new talent. Countée Cullen's, *On These I Stand*, is only a self-culled anthology with six fragile unpublished poems added. They sadly tell the story of a dimmed talent, and its cause, which was not the decline of technical power but a personal retreat from the world of significant outer experience without any compensatory opening up of a world of internal experience. This narrowing of social vision and immersion in the mere charm and magic of words whispered its way out to lines of sentimental deftness, like "Goodnight, dear friends and gentle hearts," while yet capable of such magnificent bursts as these from his translation of Baudelaire's "Death to the Poor": "Ec-static sleep / In easier beds than those we had before, / Death is the face of God." Ironically Cullen's widest social vision was in his youth; there it was based on a sensitive heart and a passionate love of race. No intellectual maturing replaced it when it lost its youthful ardor. Cullen shrank from reality, perhaps, because it wore the frightening mask of prejudice. Even our poets of the virile school, Langston Hughes, Sterling Brown and Waring Cuney speak only intermittently at present. These are fallow years for Negro poetry.[39]

Locke's temper here is morose, and his claiming that "perhaps" Cullen shrank from reality suggests he chose to offer little if any appreciation for the poet's circumstances and his attempts to work in theatrical idioms. For Locke, lyric poetry was the supreme art. Somehow, though, he failed to hear the deep cries in the poems Cullen included in *Medea*.

Owen Dodson, with some characteristic melodramatic touches, recounted Locke's final physical good-bye to Cullen, in the form of his attendance at Cullen's funeral.[40] The reverend himself had rearranged the funeral at the last minute, replacing the plan to have Dorothy Maynor sing and substituting someone with a "stubby, wobbly voice." Though his students from Frederick Douglass attended, few of Cullen's poems were recited; only one telegram from a prominent writer, Clifford Odets, was read aloud. When Locke approached the open casket for a final viewing, he stood and looked for a long time. He ended with an ambiguous gesture: "Raising his right hand, he brought it to his forehead and made a sharp distance between life and death." Other writers were present to serve as the pallbearers: Hughes, Bontemps, Jackman, and Dodson. After a heavy rain the ground at Woodlawn was muddy, and Dodson remembers almost slipping and fearing that such an accident would have been a "desecration of the new age of craftsmanship, lyricism, and raised consciousness."

Another senior voice of the Renaissance went on record to eulogize Cullen. W. E. B. DuBois, writing in *Crisis,* rendered an assessment partly negative, partly honorific, and dominated by a sense of incompletion. Using a very sweeping context, DuBois brought forth his usual sternly didactic tone:

> The opportunity then for literary expression upon which American Negroes have so often turned their backs is their opportunity and not their handicap. That Countée Cullen was born with the Twentieth Century as a black boy to live in Harlem was a priceless experience. . . . Yet, as I have said, Cullen's career was not finished. It did not culminate. It laid [a] fine, beautiful foundation, but the shape of the building never emerged.

The decline of production, as it was often called, that Cullen experienced in the last years of his life has drawn forth a variety of explanations. One of these even suggests that it resulted from Cullen's inability to maintain an identity as a racial poet.

> Cullen's refusal to accept race as a basic and valuable segment of his total identity was an evasion which prevented him from further straightforward and clear development. Race did not have to be a circumscribing point of view. Nor was Cullen compelled to do as Langston Hughes did and make it the conscious subject of all he wrote. Race was, however, an inescapable aspect of his identity which, in spite of all he said to the contrary, did affect him. . . . Cullen's racial equivocations were rooted deeply in the Harlem Renaissance itself. For the decade of the 1920s was a period of racial confusion and contradiction. Blacks were in vogue, but the values many New Negroes lived by, and the goals they sought, were white. Blacks were forced to play racial roles they did not find comfort-

able in order to achieve recognition from whites. Few New Negroes overcame the limitations of the period and were able to assert and maintain their own more solid racial and personal integrity. Langston Hughes was one of those few. Countée Cullen was not.[41]

This claim—that "the goals they sought . . . were white"—gives too much credit to the dichotomy of white and black. A desire to write poetry that aspires to represent universal values cannot be described as merely

30. Cullen, always a natty dresser, shown here in a studio photograph, wearing a chalk-stripe suit.

"white." Cullen's entire career stands as a counter to such a description. He never pretended or assumed that his racial identity failed to "affect" him, and what we could call his "racial equivocations" were rooted in many things: temperament, personal experience, and artistic questions. One of his most famous poems even made it clear that he was equivocal about being a poet.

Two decades after Cullen's death, Hughes—whom some saw as Cullen's counterpart, others as his antithesis—recalled a specific sense of what he and poets like Cullen were doing:

> Cullen died at the age of forty-three. Among the most beautiful of his poems was "Heritage," which asked, "What is Africa to me?" Had the word *negritude* been in use in Harlem in the twenties, Cullen, as well as McKay, Johnson, Toomer, and I, might have been called poets of *negritude*.[42]

Invoking the worldwide poetics of *negritude* may be ahistorical if taken in the strictest sense, but Hughes's willingness to extend the term to Cullen outweighs any such qualification. Cullen's singular genius stood out in the eyes of his fellow poets, and his popular reputation derived from a community's lasting sense of his sincerity. Finally, and for more than two decades out of a lamentably short life, Cullen did answer the call to sing, even when he found it transcendently curious.

Notes

Introduction

1. From *Rhythm,* a British magazine that appeared from 1927 to 1939. See the reprint in *The Duke Ellington Reader,* ed. Mark Tucker (New York: Oxford University Press, 1993), 46–49.

2. Darryl Pinckney, "The Sweet Singer of Tuckahoe," *New York Review of Books,* March 5, 1992.

3. See David Levering Lewis, *When Harlem Was in Vogue* (New York: Oxford University Press, 1981), 76, where the reverend is rumored to have been "a menace to the choirboys." See also chapter 1, note 17, below. A substantial body of criticism on Cullen's poetry uses the methods of "queer theory" and has offered genuine and useful insights into the work. This critical approach assumes, correctly I believe, that Cullen was actively homosexual throughout his life, and his experience in this regard of intimacy and longing is expressed in many of his poems.

Chapter 1

1. Thomas Wirth, who is currently editing all of Cullen's correspondence, shared the census record with me. It is possible, of course, that the Henry Porter listed in this census was in fact Cullen's grandfather. Furthermore, Henry and Amanda Porter—assuming they were Cullen's grandparents—may have taken in the young boy because neither of his birth parents was able to care for him, and the grandparents allowed the census taker to assume the boy was their son.

2. In a taped interview with Ida Cullen, in 1971, she said she decided not to reveal this information while Cullen was alive. (Amistad Research Center at Tulane University, audiotape 3, Ida Cullen Papers. Further references will be given as ARC-TU.) Harold Jackman sent an undated letter containing reminiscences of Cullen to Sister Mary Margaret (Krejer), FSSJ (Franciscan Sisters of Saint Joseph), a nun who wrote a well-researched thesis about Cullen in 1962. Her research notes and documentation are contained in a single box at the Schomburg Research Center of the New York Public Library. (Further references to this material will be given as SMM-Schomburg.) In his letter, Jackman also said that Cullen pointed out the house in Harlem where he lived with his grandmother. "I do not remember when Coun-tée Cullen first told me that he had a mother living in Kentucky. I do remember, however, one evening when we were taking a stroll in Harlem, and as we approached a building on West 134th Street near Seventh Avenue, he turned and said, 'That's where I lived with my grandmother.' He went on to say that his grandmother took care of small children in her home." Jackman ends by saying, "Through the years Countée kept in touch with his mother, and when she died the following month after his marriage [to Ida] in 1940 he went out to her funeral." The letter is signed by Jackman and dated August 27, 1960.

3. This information, along with the registration form mentioned later, is in SMM-Schomburg.

4. Cullen would later receive a letter at the time of the public notice that followed the success of his early poetry. In it, Robert Weyh, a former teacher of his from P.S. 27, wrote, "I wonder if your thoughts ever stray back to the days of Public School 27, the Bronx, and in particular, to the old workshop where you were one of my stars. And to that time, too, when I coached you in your Graduation Oration." Box 6, folder 1, ARC-TU.

5. A photostatic copy of the clipping is in SMM-Schomburg.

6. These details are also on audiotape 3, ARC-TU, where the oval portrait is in box 23, folder 9.

7. The bill and its envelope are in box 6, folder 15, ARC-TU. Her burial plot is listed on the bill as being in the Cemetery Association section EE, grave number 3, range B.

8. These details were gathered by two diligent students, each of whom wrote a thesis on Cullen. The first thesis, "Countée Cullen: A Biographical and Critical Study," written by Mrs. Beulah Reimherr at the University of Maryland for a master's degree in 1960, relied on an interview with Ida Cullen. Sister Mary Margaret's thesis in 1962 relied on a proxy interviewer, Miss Frances Barchat, who was in Louisville and spoke to several people who knew Elizabeth Lucas. The recollections this interviewer recorded are internally consistent and match up with the documents. Copies of both theses are at the Amistad Research Center, as part of the collected notes of Clifton Johnson, the center's first director.

9. The address is listed as 335 East Liberty Street, Louisville, KY. The book is in box 16, folder 24, ARC-TU.

10. Thomas Wirth uncovered both death certificates.

11. Assuming the dates recorded are accurate, this John Henry Porter would have been born in 1865. By contrast, Elizabeth Lucas was born in 1885. Obviously, Cullen's birth mother was a generation younger than the Porters with whom Cullen was living in 1917, at 190 West 134th Street.

12. This is also the house, at 190 West 134th Street, that Cullen pointed out to Jackman as the place "where he lived with his grandmother." SMM-Schomburg.

13. One of the poems in *Color*, a single quatrain, is called "For My Grandmother."

> This lovely flower fell to seed;
> Work gently sun and rain;
> She held it as her dying creed
> That she would grow again.

Reminiscent of Ben Jonson's epitaph for his son, this softly accented lyric tactfully naturalizes the Christian consolation.

14. In box 18, folder 21, ARC-TU, a completed form from the Surrogate's Court is signed by Reverend Cullen, but it is undated. It names the reverend as the "General Guardian" of Countée Cullen. The lack of a date may support the rumor that the adoption was never fully legalized.

15. The details of Reverend Cullen's life are drawn in large part from his autobiography, *From Barefoot Town to Jerusalem*. See the following note.

16. In the early 1940s Cullen himself typed the manuscript of the otherwise undated autobiography for the reverend, who supplemented the book's narrative with an extended series of diary entries and other documentation; the entire book is 128 pages. A copy is in the ARC-TU.

17. Such details are part of an urban myth and indeed rather typify that form of gossip and innuendo. For example, Jean Wagner speaks of the reverend's "homosexual tendencies" and suggests that his "adoption of the future poet may have been motivated by feelings that were more than pastoral." Calmly ignoring any standard of evidence or proof, and continuing in a vicious circle, Wagner then says, "These facts are widely known, though because of their nature they have never been put in writing." See *Black Poets of the United States: From Paul Laurence Dunbar to Langston Hughes* (Urbana: University of Illinois Press, 1973), 287. This is a translation of Wagner's French doctoral dissertation, and it probably is the first place where the rumors about the reverend are recorded.

18. The poem was one of the very few that Cullen wrote in free verse. In his anthology *Caroling Dusk* (1927), he characterized himself as "a rank conservative, loving the measured line and the skillful rhyme."

19. Michael L. Lomax's "Countée Cullen: A Key to the Puzzle," in *The Harlem Renaissance Re-Examined* (New York: AMS Press, 1987), 213–22, argues that the poet never came to a definitive view of race and how it affected him as an artist. "Cullen's refusal to accept race as a basic and valuable segment of his total identity was an evasion which prevented him from further straightforward and clear development." This "key" is a monocausal explanation that seems wrong on more than one count.

20. These details are drawn from the high school's newspaper, which Cullen would edit in his final year at DeWitt Clinton. As was the case with Alain Locke, who

was born as Allen, Cullen apparently relied on a tradition that saw in a French pronunciation a sort of literary rechristening of the self. In the present work, "Countée" is used throughout, as Cullen obviously preferred this spelling and all his friends used it as well. When the unaccented version appears in citations of titles of books and articles, it is silently corrected.

21. The correspondence with Brown, which extends throughout Cullen's high school and college years, is in the Givens Collection at the University of Minnesota (hereafter cited as GCUM). My thanks to Cecily Marcus for her assistance in obtaining copies. A few letters from Brown to Cullen survive; they are in box 1, folder 13, ARC-TU.

22. A few years later, on July 22, 1925, while still corresponding with Brown, Cullen allowed as to how he destroyed some of his early poems. "I am sending you, later on, some verses, some of which of you may have seen, others of which are new to you. There may be some duplicates among them; I am too lazy to sort them out. When you have finished with them, throw them away, unless you want to keep them for reference for the biography you are to do of me when I pass into the far beyond. Last month I destroyed thirty of my children, poems I had written in my youth. It was a heart-rending affair. My tears almost quenched the flames in which they were consumed." ARC-TU.

23. The famous actor sent Cullen a handwritten note congratulating him on the prize.

24. In *Crisis* 24, no. 6 (October 1922): 272. The magazine's regular feature, called "Horizons," often displayed young African Americans of promise and achievement. Cullen's fame as a poet of the Harlem Renaissance was solidified and advanced by such public notice.

Chapter 2

1. David E. Goldweber discusses Keats and Cullen in "Cullen, Keats and the Privileged Liar," *Papers on Language & Literature* 38, no. 1 (Winter 2002): 29–48.

2. James W. Tuttleton first told the story of Cullen's time at New York University in "Countée Cullen at 'The Heights,'" in *The Harlem Renaissance: Revaluations* (New York: Garland Publishing, 1989), 101–37.

3. The text of the speech is available in *My Soul's High Song: The Collected Writings of Countée Cullen,* ed. Gerald Early (New York: Doubleday Anchor, 1991), 547–50.

4. Cullen also wrote a detailed letter on May 4, 1923, to William Brown about the experience of writing the Town Hall address and the aftermath. "I have received letters from several people whose opinions I deeply respect commending my speech. I spoke from notes and did not have my speech written out, so I can't send it to you now. But Miss Fauset, literary editor of the Crisis, has written asking for the speech which means that I shall have to attempt to write it out. In case I can remember enough of it, I will send you a copy. The papers carried slight articles about the meeting, but quoted me in such a way as to gain me some notoriety and ill feeling among my own people. The papers made me say that the chief concern of the New Negro was 'less dependence on the deity.' The quoted words are mine all right, but

they were qualified greatly in my speech. As a result, when I attended a large dinner the next evening, a gentleman who had always been very effusive in his greetings, refused to speak to me. I am not certain whether notoriety is something in which to glory, or to deplore. I also wrote a poem for the occasion which, as made-to-order poems generally are, is very bad. Several persons have looked at me askance for that, because I said age had failed."

5. Fauset's letters to Cullen are in box 2, folder 9, ARC-TU.

6. The correspondence between Cullen and Yolande is found at the Beinecke, JWJ MSS, box 1, folders 9–15 (hereafter cited as JWJ MSS).

7. "For him to be humble who is proud / Needs colder artifice." Cullen's artifice manages to speak "through his acquiescent mask / Of bland gentility."

8. Cullen's early letters to Jackman are in box 1, folders 19–20, JWJ MSS. Jackman's to Cullen are in box 2, folders 21 to box 3, folders 1–2, ARC-TU.

9. The correspondence between Locke and Cullen, of great interest for both figures, is in the Alain Locke papers at the Moorland Spingarn Research Center (ALL-MSRC), at Howard University, 164–22 /35–40.

10. Hughes's letters to Cullen are in box 2, folder 19, ARC-TU.

11. These poems are in box 2, folder 19, ARC-TU.

12. Though Cullen published this poem in *Color,* Gerald Early did not include it in *My Soul's High Song.*

13. From *The Collected Poems of Langston Hughes,* ed. Arnold Rampersad (New York: Vintage Books, 1994), 82.

14. This letter, dated March 12, 1924, is in the Witter Bynner papers at Harvard. Bynner responded on June 20 with a detailed critique of the manuscript, in which he said, "In these judgments you will see that I have usually found the poems in which you touch on your race much surer poetry than those which reflect your course at college. You, like other poets, are happier in expression when life, rather than literature is the well-spring." He closed the letter with stern advice to the younger poet: "Let me know that you are not too much disappointed, and let me see the book again. I adjure you, by all gods, both black and white, not to publish it as it stands."

15. The letter about the visit is dated January 7, the one about pulling strings was sent on October 14, and the one about Villard is dated June 13, 1924. All are in ARC-TU.

16. Cullen reprinted the poem to Holmes in *Copper Sun.* The letter to Locke suggesting the approach to Holmes is in ALL-MSRC, dated November 10, 1924. Holmes wrote to thank Cullen for the commemorative poem, in a letter of February 10, 1927. "Many a humble soul otherwise unworthy of fame has snatched immortality from the jealous hands of the gods through being addressed by a real poet, and I had a happy glimpse on last Thursday night that this might be my destiny." ARC-TU.

17. Most striking perhaps is a letter from Cullen to Locke dated October 31, 1924: "L.R. [Llewellyn Ransom] was here Wednesday night—until late. I was painfully distressed, and he was very kind. But I am not certain whether it was mere kindness, or what I most desired it to be. It may be cowardly in me, but I am depending upon you to find out for me. Even Wednesday's desultory relief was invigorating and inspi-

rational. A permanent understanding would eliminate my problem. I can think of no solution that would suit me be better—not even H. J. [Harold Jackman]. I know you will do your best. Love."

18. Carl Van Vechten, *The Splendid Drunken Twenties: Selections from the Daybooks 1922–30*, ed. Bruce Kellner (Urbana: University of Illinois Press, 1993), 60.

19. See *Remember Me to Harlem: The Letters of Langston Hughes and Carl Van Vechten, 1925–1964*, ed. Emily Bernard (New York: Knopf, 2001).

20. The letters from Cullen to Van Vechten are in the box 2, folders 26–27, JWJ MSS.

21. He also sent a handwritten version to William Brown.

22. This letter was dated August 8, 1924, and is in the Brown Collection in Minnesota. The letter also speaks of Cullen's wrestling with Millay's "frankness" and generally admiring her innovative use of the sonnet form.

23. A different reading from the one that follows here is by Houston Baker, *A Many Colored Coat of Dreams: The Poetry of Countée Cullen* (Detroit: Broadside Press, 1974).

24. Jon Michael Spencer has traced this particular aspect of religious thought in the African American community, in "The Black Church and the Harlem Renaissance," *African American Review* 30, no. 3 (Fall 1996): 453–60. Also of interest is Peter Powers, "'The Singing Man Who Must Be Reckoned With': Private Desire and Public Responsibility in the Poetry of Countée Cullen," *African American Review* 34, no. 4 (Winter 2000): 661–78.

25. Referring to the cultural phenomenon of a desire to establish at least an imaginary homeland in Africa as rooted in "racial romanticism," George Fredrickson, in *The Black Image in the White Mind* (New York: Harper and Row, 1971), 327, says that it "became something of a national fad, resulting in part, curiously enough, from patronizing white encouragement of the 'New Negro' movement and the 'Harlem Renaissance.' 'The New Negro,' as perceived by many whites, was simply the old romantic conception of the Negro covered with a patina of cultural primitivism and exoticism fashionable in the 1920's." However, even if part of the lineaments and importance of the imaginary Africa was due to "simply the old romantic conception," there were political and social issues that were entwined in all the widespread references and depictions. See also Norma Ramsay Jones, "Africa, as Imaged by Cullen & Co.," *Negro American Literature Forum* 8, no. 4 (Winter 1974): 263–67. For a full and important assessment of the poems by Cullen that appeared in Locke's *The New Negro* and their attitude toward Africa, see George Hutchinson, *The Harlem Renaissance in Black and White* (Cambridge, MA: Harvard University Press, 1995), 410–12.

26. The literature on the relations between African American artists and the African diaspora has grown voluminously. But Emily Bernard offers an apt summary in her article "Nomadic Memory," *Black Renaissance/Renaissance Noire* 3, no. 1 (Fall 2000): 123–32. "In the Harlem Renaissance, the construction of diasporic identity is centered on the concept of reappropriation. Origins, translated through memory, are recovered and fill the gaps created by historical dislocations in the African diaspora. In this theoretical framework, a mythical dimension is given to African cultures, and

Africa becomes a place of longing, a locale articulating desire and identity (although they refer consistently to it, very few African-American artists or intellectuals of the Harlem Renaissance traveled to sub-Saharan Africa)" (129). Despite the absence of travel to Africa, many African American artists incorporated a range of diasporic themes, motifs, and images.

27. David Bergman offers an especially strong reading of the poem, centered on Cullen's homosexuality. He quotes a passage near the end of the poem, and then offers his gloss:

> Heathen gods are naught to me—
> Quaint, outlandish heathen gods
> Black men fashion out of rods,
> Clay and brittle bits of stone,
> In a likeness like their own.

"Clearly heathen gods, far from being naught to Cullen, are very precious, especially if they look like the 'strong bronze men' who haunt his imagination. The price for Christ is renouncing those rods fashioned by the men into gods, these phallic deities, and Cullen seems highly reluctant to pay it. The poem ends with the prayer, 'Lord, forgive me if my need / Sometimes shapes a human creed' (253). Christianity of the puritanical sort practiced by black churches does not allow Cullen the human need for humans. Its strict separation of spirit and matter does not satisfy Cullen's more pagan (and homosexual) requirements. Africa becomes both the despised Sodom and the long-sought Eden of the homoerotic against which Cullen stuffs his ears and for which his heart sings. In such ways Africa is far more problematical for the gay than for the heterosexual black American writer." See David Bergman, *Gaiety Transfigured: Gay Self-Representation in American Literature* (Madison: University of Wisconsin Press, 1991), 277.

28. See Van Vechten, *The Splendid Drunken Twenties*. Invaluable for details about various events, mostly parties and dinners, peopled by everyone in the arts at the time, this book is the source for much of what we know about Van Vechten's friendships with various and sundry figures.

29. A recent book about the word *nigger* gets this event wrong. In Randall Kennedy's *Nigger: The Strange Career of a Troublesome Word*. (New York: Vintage Books, 2002), 188, he says, "The title [*Nigger Heaven*] alone alienated many blacks, including some who knew the author personally. Van Vechten had, for example, selected some lines of poetry by his friend Countée Cullen to serve as the epigraph for his book, but when he told the poet about his proposed title, he turned, in Van Vechten's words, 'white with rage.' And soon their friendship ended." Of course their friendship did not end; it lasted until Cullen's death.

30. The story appeared in the *Brooklyn Daily Eagle* on February 10, 1924.

31. This was in a letter dated October 10, 1925, in ARC-TU.

Chapter 3

1. White's book was published by Haldeman-Julius Publications in Girard, Kansas; this excerpt is from the chapter called "The Negro Artist Emerges," 9.

2. These observations by Cullen are from letters he wrote to Jackman while at Harvard. See folder 20, JWJ MSS.

3. The remark was in a letter from James Rockel, dated April 1957, in SMM-Schomburg.

4. In box 4, folder 10, ARC-TU. Braithwaite also wrote Cullen, months before he arrived in Harvard, requesting his Cambridge mailing address. In the same letter he included a proof of one of Cullen's poems, to be included in the annual anthology.

5. Cullen asked Braithwaite either for a poem or two, or a "short disquisition on Negro Poets." This letter, dated October 7, 1925, is in the Braithwaite papers at Harvard. As for the special issue of *Palms,* Cullen included many of his friends and acquaintances—like Hughes, McKay, and James Weldon Johnson—along with Locke's review of *The Weary Blues.* The small magazine, published in Mexico, was run by Idella Purnell and Bynner, who likely arranged for Cullen to edit the special issue.

6. A good study of Braithwaite is Lisa Szefel, "Encouraging Verse: William Stanley Braithwaite and the Poetry of Race," *New England Quarterly* 74, no. 1 (March 2001): 49–61.

7. Sydonia was a music student at a conservatory in Boston; Cullen would later dedicate "Advice to a Beauty" to her in *Copper Sun.* It read in part, "Sweet bird, beware the Fowler, Pride." To Fiona Braithwaite, in the same volume he dedicated "Pity the Deep in Love." Here the love poet also evoked a sense of danger, but one different in tone and focus:

> Pity the deep in love;
> They move as men asleep,
> Traveling a narrow way
> Precipitous and steep.

These two tones of caution and pity recur often in Cullen's love poetry.

8. Thomas's letters to Cullen are in box 2, folder 23, JWJ MSS 7, and in box 5, folder 17, ARC-TU. His to her do not survive.

9. The letter from Cullen, dated May 7, 1926, is in the Mencken papers at the New York Public Library. Mencken's letter to Cullen is in ARC-TU.

10. This letter shows how the friendship between Cullen and Brown maintained the same familiar tones and even kept alive the dream of collaborating on a popular song.

11. The review appeared in the magazine's May issue; the letter from Johnson to Cullen is dated March 18, 1926.

12. An analysis of the work by Whithorne is in Will Earhart's "Saturday's Child by Countée Cullen & Emerson Whithorne," *Music Supervisors' Journal* 13, no. 5 (May 1927): 79. "There is no question about the great power of the work: but criticism might be directed against the *genre.*" The critic, though claiming the poems showed "more than a trace . . . of Poe's genius," felt the work used "modern cacophonies" to "invade . . . obscure psychological realms filled with murky vapors."

13. This letter is dated September 9, 1924. Cullen apparently referred again to Walrond when, a few weeks later, on October 27, he wrote Locke about his frustrated state: "How long will it be before you see L.R. again? If it will be over a week, you

might enclose a sealed note to him in your next letter to me, with instructions for him to read and destroy in my presence. Please pardon my urgency, but I must have an adjustment as soon as possible, or I shall be driven to recourse with E.W. and that I fear." L.R. is apparently Llewellyn Ransom, and E.W. would be Eric Walrond. In his letters to Locke, Cullen used the term "adjustment" to mean sexual relations. Both letters are at ARC-TU.

14. The review appeared in *New Republic* 39 (July 9, 1924): 192. It said that the novel was "not really 'younger generation Negro' stuff. . . . Toomer's insouciant 'Cane' in this respect is miles above it. . . . Mediocre, a work of puny, painstaking labor, *There Is Confusion* is not meant for people who know anything about the Negro and his problems. It is aimed with unpardonable naiveté at the very young or the perfectly old."

15. Cullen kept many of these; they are in box 16, folder 7, ARC-TU.

16. The review, which mentioned the work of several Negro writers, was in *New Republic* 42 (August 31, 1927): 195–200.

17. This piece appeared in the *Independent*, a leading black newspaper, on September 24, 1927.

18. The account of this trip is based on letters from Cullen to Jackman, in the folder 20, JWJ MSS, as well as the diary entries that conclude the reverend's autobiography. See chapter 6 for further details from Reverend Cullen's autobiography.

19. This letter, dated May 15, 1925 is in ALL-MSRC.

20. The review appeared in *Opportunity* 4 (February 1926): 73. A pointed and helpful comparison of the two poets, which focuses on this review, can be found at http://xroads.virginia.edu/~MA03/faturoti/harlem/collage/artistic.html.

21. The question of which writers might most authentically use folk or jazz material would bedevil the Renaissance and its commentators for many years. Here is what the always surprising Zora Neale Hurston wrote to Cullen about Hughes's jazz poems: "By the way, Hughes ought to stop publishing all those secular folk-songs as his poetry. Now when he got off the 'Weary Blues' (most of it a song I and most southerners have known all our lives) I said nothing for I knew I'd never be forgiven by certain people for 'crying down' what the 'white folks had exalted,' but when he gets off another 'Me and mah honey got two mo' days tuh do de buck' I dont see how I can refrain from speaking. I am at least going to speak to Van Vechten." This is dated March 11, 1926, and is in ARC-TU.

22. This letter is in box 1, folder 20, JWJ MSS. Someone—probably Jackman himself, who in 1951 donated the letter to the Beinecke—has changed the date from January 6, 1925, to January 6, 1926; the latter date is clearly correct.

23. An informative article on this subject is Robert C. Hart, "Black-White Literary Relations in the Harlem Renaissance," *American Literature* 44, no. 4 (January 1973): 612–28.

24. Some of Cullen's review was devoted to unalloyed praise, which, while put in elevated diction, captured Hughes's spirit well: "this poet represents a transcendently emancipated spirit among a class of young writers whose particular battle-cry is freedom. With the enthusiasm of a zealot, he pursues his way, scornful, in subject matter, in photography, and rhythmical treatment, of whatever obstruction time

and tradition have placed before him. To him it is essential that he be himself. Essential and commendable surely." This is then followed by "yet the thought persists that some of these poems would have been better had Mr. Hughes held himself a bit in check." Charles S. Johnson wrote Cullen to say that the review was "an honest and discriminating criticism of the book."

25. The essay is frequently reprinted and is readily available in *The Portable Harlem Renaissance Reader*, ed. David Levering Lewis (New York: Viking, 1994).

26. Of course the question of whether the audience for African American poetry was primarily white or black readers, or both, was always on the table. When Hughes arranged for Cullen to review *The Weary Blues*, he wrote to say that his publishers, the Knopfs, were very happy, and then added "they also said they would like you to review it for some white publication, too."

27. Of course, there are several viewpoints that would see Cullen and Hughes as sharing literary values, chief among them that of J. Saunders Redding, in *To Make a Poet Black* (Ithaca, NY: Cornell University Press, 1988), a reprint of the 1939 edition. Redding outlines the two necessities that face black poets, one of ends and one of means: the chief end is "the need to adjust himself to the American environment" and the chief means is to write for two audiences, black and white ("opposed when not entirely opposite"). The latter "necessity has grown almost to the point of desperation." For Cullen and Hughes, "these two necessities can be traced with varying degrees of clarity—now one and now the other predominant—like threads through the whole cloth" (3).

28. Among many instances of where Cullen and Hughes were presented as contrasted types, there is a contemporary view, recalled years later by Marvel Cooke, who worked at the *Crisis*, where she replaced Jessie Fauset. She recounts the following in an interview:

> *Currie:* . . . we should say Countée Cullen was a poet, right?
> *Cooke:* Yes.
> *Currie:* Was he ever in any of your writing groups?
> *Cooke:* No. No, he led a very strange life. He was a very sweet person. It was rumored that he was homosexual. He just didn't seem to make it, you know, with the virulent crowd that we went with. I liked him very much. He used to come to our house after we were married to play a French gambling game called *ballotte*. He taught Cecil and me how to play *ballotte*. He used to come quite often. I liked him.
> *Currie:* But he also never got the recognition that, say, Langston Hughes got.
> *Cooke:* No, no, he didn't. Well, Langston was more a people's poet, you know. Rugged and yet a great poet.

See http://wpcf.org/oralhistory/cook.html; the passage occurs in the second session. My thanks to James Davis for calling this to my attention.

29. This is the view Locke advanced in his *Race Contacts and Interracial Relations*, a series of lectures he gave at Howard. They are discussed in *Alain Locke: Biography of a Philosopher* (Chicago: University of Chicago Press, 2008), coauthored by the present writer and Leonard Harris.

30. For more information on Gladys May Casely-Hayford, see *Shadowed Dreams: Women's Poetry of the Harlem Renaissance,* ed. Maureen Honey (New Brunswick, NJ: Rutgers University Press, 1989).

31. Cullen's reply to Hughes is dated November 18, 1926, and is in ARC-TU.

32. The letter, dated March 5, 1927, is in ARC-TU.

33. For background on the magazine and several details, see Chidi Ikonne, "*Opportunity* and Black Literature 1923–1933," *Phylon* 40, no. 1 (1st quarter, 1979): 86–93. On its founder, see Patrick J. Gilpin, "Charles S. Johnson: Entrepreneur of the Harlem Renaissance," in *The Harlem Renaissance Remembered,* ed. by Arna Bontemps (New York: Dodd, Mead and Co., 1972).

34. This is from the memorial held at the Countée Cullen branch of the New York Public Library, on September 12, 1951, in SMM-Schomburg.

35. Ikonne claims at one point that for Cullen's experience as an editor "his apparent dissatisfaction with the success of the magazine seems to reflect that of the magazine itself." The annual poetry contest, for example, was suspended for two years because of the flood of poor submissions.

36. Both editorials are cited in Ikonne, "*Opportunity* and Black Literature 1923–1933."

37. This is from the May 28, 1927, issue of the *Courier;* Cullen had been invited to Pittsburg to read his poems. His agent often sent along a press kit so the visit could be well publicized.

38. Named for the great Russian poet, playwright, novelist, and short-story writer Aleksander Sergeyevich Pushkin (1799–1837), the Pushkin Award, distinguished from the other *Opportunity* awards, was expected to attract "the most ambitious and most mature work of the Negro poet," and contestants were requested to submit only their very best work to this competition. The letter is dated November 19, 1925, and is in ARC-TU. Cullen was not awarded it, though his good friend Arna Bontemps was.

39. For an excellent overview of the context in which *Opportunity* existed, among other literary magazines, see Abby Arthur Johnson and Ronald M. Johnson, "Forgotten Pages: Black Literary Magazines in the 1920s," *Journal of American Studies* 8, no. 3 (December 1974): 363–82.

40. *My Soul's High Song* reprints only one "Dark Tower" column, from the April 1928 issue. The other columns have never been reprinted.

41. See the article by Kate Dossett, "'I Try to Live Somewhat in Keeping with My Reputation as a Wealthy Woman': A'Lelia Walker and the Madam C. J. Walker Manufacturing Company," *Journal of Women's History* 21, no. 2 (Summer 2009): 90–114. Dossett convincingly corrects the stereotypes of the mother—Madame C. J. Walker—as a hardworking entrepreneur and the daughter—A'Lelia Walker—as a bon vivant. The *New York Times* of April 24, 1994, reported, "Before A'Lelia Robinson's death in 1931 she leased 108 West 136th Street to the city, which established a series of health clinics in the house. . . . The Walker town house, then owned by the city, was demolished in 1941—the Landmarks Preservation Commission was established in 1965—for the Countée Cullen Branch of the New York Public Library,

which was built to ease the pressure on the existing branch library at 103 West 135th Street. The 135th Street building had become a center of black studies in the 1920's; today it houses part of the renowned Schomburg Center for Research in Black Culture."

42. Dossett, "'I Try to Live Somewhat in Keeping with My Reputation as a Wealthy Woman,'" 104.

43. The play was not well received. It was notably misunderstood by the critic for *New York Herald-Tribune* as being against miscegenation, and Cullen said so, defending his friend Duff, a white pacifist, who worked briefly on the editorial staff of the left-wing journal *The Liberator*. Cullen said that despite the "united chorus of condemnation by accredited critics, we consider it ["Stigma"] a gallant endeavor."

44. Allen (1891–1955) was a pacifist and left-wing writer. Cullen's citation of him anticipates the poet's leftish leanings as they would develop in the next two decades.

45. In *A Bio-Bibliography of Countée P. Cullen* (Westport, CT: Greenwood Publishing, 1971), Margaret Perry argues that "this . . . was a poem about racial prejudice." She then adds, somewhat contradictorily, that Cullen "treated the tale with objectivity and avoided obscuring the poem's meaning with his own feelings."

46. The letters and the typed version of the ballad are in GCUM; unfortunately, the third of the five pages of the typescript poem is missing.

47. Herbert S. Gorman, "Countée Cullen Is a Poet First and a Negro Afterward," *New York Times,* August 21, 1927.

48. This appeared in *New Republic* 42 (October 1927).

49. Quoted in Perry, *A Bio-Bibliography,* 57.

50. For an account of *FIRE!!* and how it fit in the context of other journals, see Abby Arthur Johnson and Ronald Maberry Johnson, *Propaganda & Aesthetics: The Literary Politics of African-America Magazines in the Twentieth Century* (Amherst: University of Massachusetts Press, 1979), 77–85. Wallace Thurman's contribution to *FIRE!!,* besides his editing duties, was a statement of aesthetics that emphasized artistic freedom: "Any author preparing to write about Negroes in Harlem or anywhere else . . . should take whatever phases of their life that seem the most interesting to him, and develop them as he pleases" (cited in *Propaganda,* 80).

51. Though similar to other of his poems, this lyric shows Cullen at his most openly, even aggressively, medievalizing in his use of the language and conventions of courtly love, its prototype in Edenic bliss, and its romantic afterlife. "We played a gay, fantastic game / Of our own making." The length of this poem, its recourse to the self-conscious making of illusions, and its dedication ("Yolande: Her Poem") mean it deserves special attention. In David Goldweber's "Cullen, Keats, and the Privileged Liar," *Papers on Language & Literature* 38, no. 1 (Winter 2002): 29–48, we are told that "the strength of illusory pride" operates throughout Cullen's poetry. This strength arises out of a recognition that life and mortality demand recourse to illusion, but of the three sorts of illusion—religion, suicide, and poetry—the third is the one most favored by Cullen. Goldweber's article is one of the deepest and most thorough of those that treat Cullen's poetry comprehensively. At once relying too much on Cullen's debt to Keats and yet stressing Cullen's own strengths, the argu-

ment has a Nietzschean flavor (without directly using that term or framework) when it suggests that "whatever the case, lies enable us to smooth over the cold, brutal harshness of reality" (37). The end result, however, is that Goldweber—despite almost completely ignoring the issue of race in Cullen's work—sees the poetry in terms that are modernist, even existential (again without using such a terminology). These terms, in fact, seldom occur in critical readings of Cullen, though a thorough reading of the poetry invites such a framework.

52. See chapter 4, note 13.

53. This letter is dated September 14, 1927, and is in the McKay Collection at the Beinecke.

54. This is dated June 6, 1927, and is in GCUM.

Chapter 4

1. The letter and Cullen's reply are in box 2, folder 13, ARC-TU.

2. These details are in the letters from Yolande to Cullen in the box 1, folders 11–15, JWJ MSS. Cullen's letters to Yolande in this period unfortunately do not appear to have survived.

3. One account sees the scale and symbolism of the wedding as coming from DuBois's attitude about race and eugenics. In "W. E. B. DuBois's Family *Crisis*," *American Literature* 72, no. 2 (2000): 291–319, Daylanne English cites DuBois's own account of the wedding in his magazine and argues that, "with an elegant, full-page photograph of the bride (captioned 'Mrs. Yolande DuBois Cullen'), the *Crisis* becomes, quite literally, her wedding album, and thus her father's family album. . . . DuBois takes the editorial-paternal opportunity to ponder 'the problem of marriage among our present American Negroes' and asks, 'Should we black folk breed children or commit biological suicide?' With sixteen bridesmaids and thirteen hundred invited guests, the wedding represents, for DuBois, the foundational moment of a eugenic dynasty for 'black folk.' He describes, rapturously, the guests leaving the ceremony, exulting that 'it was a new race' . . . The elaborate, bourgeois trappings of the wedding suggest just how DuBois pictures that 'race'" (306).

4. The letter is dated June 6, 1927.

5. Several clippings are in box 16, folder 11, ARC-TU.

6. The envelope for this letter is dated April 19, 1928, and it is in box 1, folder 15, JWJ MSS.

7. The letter, dated May 11, 1928 is in the DuBois collection at the University of Massachusetts–Amherst Library, hereafter referred to as DuBois-UM. In it Cullen also seeks his father-in-law's advice about using a speakers' agency to handle arrangements for his poetry readings when he returns to America from his Guggenheim. The agency usually handled events for white-only audiences, and Cullen wanted to see if they would not book him in places where "colored audiences" would be admitted.

8. The letters from DuBois to Cullen are mainly in ARC-TU. The letters from Cullen to DuBois are in DuBois-UM, though some of the letters written by DuBois have

carbons, which are also in DuBois-UM. All the letters between Cullen and Yolande are in box 1, JWJ MSS.

9. The official French documents are in box 7, folder 7, ARC-TU.

10. The synopsis is in box 19, folder 25, ARC-TU.

11. One of the more nonresponsive reviews of the book occurred in *Poetry*, where the reviewer said, "In this poem one may see charm and skill, and a complete unimportance." See Bertha Ten Eyck James, "On the Danger Line," *Poetry* 35, no. 5 (February 1930): 286–89.

12. For an in-depth reading of the poem, which offers a confident interpretation of the climax, see Qiana Whitted, "In My Flesh Shall I See God: Ritual Violence and Racial Redemption in 'The Black Christ,'" *African American Review* 38, no. 3 (Fall 2004): 379–93. The article by Peter Powers (see chapter 2, note 24) also offers a full reading of the poem. I have relied on these essays for details about the theological resonances in the poem, though my interpretation differs from both. The prospects of a rhymed narrative poem were not especially bright, as even Locke felt Cullen was risking a lot with such a form. He wrote Cullen on April 22, 1929, saying "It is good to hear from you directly, especially any such news as the completion of a nine-hundred line poem. If it wasn't yours, I am not sure that I would ever read all of it. After 'John Brown's Body' and 'Tristram,' I vowed that the next long poem would be read in Heaven. Still, 'The Black Christ' sounds Miltonian enough to be intriguing" (MSRC).

13. A different treatment of the theme of Christ as humanized and sacrificial victim is "A Thorn Forever in the Breast." This strange sonnet begins by sounding like a fairly standard lover's complaint: "A hungry cancer will not let him rest / Whose heart is loyal to the least of dreams." But in the sestet the subject is transformed into Christ crucified:

> there to meet his doom
> Between two wretched dying men, of whom
> One doubts, and one for pity's sake believes.

Cullen bleakly combines his religion and his sense of love poetry into a virtually nihilistic moment.

14. The following information about the "Roberta" to whom Cullen dedicated the book and the poem was gleaned from the papers of Clifford Johnson and generously given to me by Thomas Wirth. "Roberta Bosley is sometimes referred to as 'one of the Bosley girls' and as a cousin of Countée Cullen. She was a bridesmaid in his wedding to Yolande DuBois. Cullen dedicated 'To a Brown Girl' in *Color* and 'Youth Sing a Song of Rosebuds' in *Copper Sun* to her, and, as previously stated, *The Black Christ and Other Poems* was dedicated to her along with Harold Jackman and Edward Perry. In 1940, Roberta Bosley was chairman of the James Weldon Johnson Literary Guild in New York City, and she worked as a community relations officer for the Riverdale (New York) Children's Association in 1947." Cullen may have used the term "cousin" out of affection rather than kinship; and if she were one of Yolande's bridesmaids, she was also one of the "Moles," and probably knew Yolande from Fisk or from Baltimore. In the July 1922 issue of the *Crisis*, Carl Van Vechten said (222) that the

complete manuscript of Cullen's *The Lost Zoo*, which he was giving to the Beinecke as part of the James Weldon Johnson Collection, was reassembled from drafts donated by Harold Jackman and Roberta Bosley. Also, Cullen mentions a Roberta in a letter to Jackman of August 14, 1924, suggesting that she, Jackman, and Walrond all join him in Pleasantville. A final note: Bruce Kellner, in his edition of Carl Van Vechten's *The Splendid Drunken Twenties: Selections from the Day Books 1922–1930* (Urbana: University of Illinois Press, 2003), 129, identifies Roberta Bosley as a model for sculptor Richmond Barthé.

15. Another poem in this volume, "Nothing Endures," uses a dimeter line as well.

16. One critic has seen the relation between Cullen and modernism as a "dynamic" in which his work did not aggressively refute tradition and sentimentalism, nor did it satisfy the new generation of middle-class readers seduced by mass culture. "If after only a decade Cullen no longer enjoyed the high regard he did as Harlem's poet laureate, it is because he got ensnared in this dynamic and the contradictions it engendered for black poets. Caught between a modernist reaction against traditional poetic conventions and a bourgeois desire to win cultural legitimacy by demonstrating competence in them, Cullen eventually became 'the symbol of a fast disappearing generation of Negro writers' [that] Thurman predicted and his work dismissed as just the kind of 'third-hand Keats' [Ezra] Pound lamented: effeminate and raceless because it is traditional and popular and vice versa." See Jane Kuenz, "Modernism, Mass Culture, and the Harlem Renaissance: The Case of Countée Cullen," *modernism/modernity* 14, no. 3 (2007): 507–15.

17. On April 13, 1924, five hundred prominent writers and other notables honored W. E. B. DuBois at a dinner, and the program included a poem by Witter Bynner, "To DuBois and His People," and one by Cullen, "The Fledglings and the Eagle" (which he never republished). Bynner retitled his offering "Hymn to the Dark Race," and sent it to Cullen in July, closing the poem with the lines

> England, O England let it please us
> That our Father hears us, sees us,
> We are dying, we are Jesus,
> We are never dead.

Cullen responded, "I would like your poem better than I do, if it did not express a philosophy which has practically been carried to such an extent that we are just about dead." This rather bold charge suggests Cullen didn't appreciate that the dying of the race, even if based on sentiments of Christian meekness, could be seen as a triumph. But he was able to soften his critique by suggesting an emendation: "Pardon my temerity, but it seems to me that should you change, 'we are Jesus' to read 'but like Jesus,' your effect would be better." The shift from the glorious dying of the race to its perseverance is crucial.

18. This is from a letter dated June 20, 1924, sent from Santa Fe, where Bynner had already relocated. It is in the Bynner papers at Harvard.

19. Though Bynner's critical judgment arose from his temperament and taste, there was likely another particular factor operating as well. Bynner had just finished

his translation of *The Jade Mountain,* an anthology of three hundred Chinese poems, and the dominant tone and restrained style of these lyrics differ considerably from Cullen's rather troubled emotions.

20. For background on Charles Cullen and his work beyond Cullen's books, see Caroline Goeser, "The Case of *Ebony and Topaz:* Racial and Sexual Hybridity in Harlem Renaissance Illustrations," *American Periodicals* 15, no. 1 (2005): 86–111. There is also this description, from Bruce Nugent: "Charles Cullen is White, blonde, and insipid. I knew Charles without knowing any connections between Charles Cullen and Countée Cullen. I knew Charles when I was a bellhop at the Martha Washington Hotel and Charles lived right across the street from there. And because of his interest in art and my interest in art, we got to know each other. I'm being cruel when I say 'insipid.' He just wasn't as exciting as other people whom I knew. And he was more conventional—on the surface—than most people I knew. But then, everybody was more conventional on the surface than I knew." From an interview in 1982 with Bruce Nugent by James Hatch, in *Artists and Influences* (New York: Hatch Billops Collection, 1982), 81–104.

21. Several letters referring to this situation, one that would have surprised many in New York, but which seems to have remained fairly secret, are in box 2, folder 21, ARC-TU.

22. The rumor of the appearance at the funeral was told to me by Thomas Wirth. I have been unable to discover any facts in the matter.

23. Hughes remarks in his autobiography, "Harold Jackman, a handsome young Harlem school teacher of modest means, calmly announced one day that he was sailing for the Riviera for a fortnight, to attend Princess Murat's yachting party." See *The Big Sea* (New York: Hill & Wang, 1993), 227.

24. Lord Dunsany was the nom de plume of Edward John Moreton Drax Plunkett (1878–1957), 18th Baron of Dunsany and Anglo-Irish writer of fantasy plays.

25. Alden Reimonenq made this identification in "Countée Cullen's 'Uranian Soul Windows,'" *Journal of Homosexuality* 26, no. 2 (1993): 143–66. The entire article is of interest, as Reimonenq claims that Cullen and Perry "were lovers in the late twenties and thirties before Cullen took his French lovers" (157). It was Perry, then appearing in a production of *Porgy,* whom Cullen visited when he went to London in April 1929. Reimonenq also describes Llewellyn Ransom, Donald Duff, Ralph Loeb, and others as Cullen's lovers before he went to France.

In September 1929, Perry arrived in New York, having sailed from Cherbourg on the *Majestic.* His New York City address was 300 West 138th Street. This information, from ancestry.com, was supplied to me by Thomas Wirth. In the same year, and for several years thereafter, Perry served as a social reporter for the *Afro-American.* His accounts of parties and celebrations in Harlem appeared under various titles in the newspaper, such as "Social Whirl" and "Manhattan Madness." His own name was often among those of the partygoers, and he was once described as the "noted young writer, artist and social personage." In addition to his acting talents, he worked for a while as the personal manager of an aspiring pianist, David Fontaine, once arranging for him to give a drawing room recital at an apartment on Sutton Place. Attendees included not only Cullen but also Walter Damrosch and DuBois. As for Fontaine himself, "On Saturday nights pianist David Fontaine would regularly throw stylish flat parties for his many gay friends." See http://www.queerculturalcenter.org/Pages/Bentley/Spectacle.html, for an account by Eric Garber centered on Gladys Bentley and the homosexual culture in the Renaissance. In the early 1950s Perry served as the social director of the Shangri-La Country Club in Napanoch, New York, and as the social escort for an elaborate escorted tour of Europe. See the *Afro-American*, November 28, 1931, and December 26, 1931.

26. This column appeared in the *Afro-American*, October 19, 1929.

27. A telling contrast with Cullen's experience can be seen in *Memoirs of Montparnasse* (1970), a roman à clef by John Glassco, a young Canadian poet who at first aspired to join the surrealists. He arrived in Paris at almost exactly the same time as Cullen and stayed for about two years, eventually returning to Montreal suffering from a quite dissolute lifestyle. Claude McKay appears in the *Memoirs* under the name Jack Relief. See the New York Review of Books reprint, 2007.

28. This is from a letter of March 11, 1924, at box 2, folder 19, ARC-TU.

29. The paperback reprint is Claude McKay, *A Long Way from Home* (New York: Harcourt, Brace, 1970), and the passage cited is on 311–12.

30. A recent study of the "colony" is by Theresa Leininger-Miller, *New Negro Artists in Paris: African American Painters and Sculptors in the City of Light, 1922–1934* (New Brunswick, NJ: Rutgers University Press, 2001). An earlier work, of considerable breadth, is Michel Fabre, *From Harlem to Paris: Black American Writers in France, 1840–1980* (Urbana: University of Illinois Press, 1991).

31. A good account of Woodruff's career is given by Donald F. Davis, "Hale Woodruff of Atlanta: Molder of Black Artists," *Journal of Negro History* 69, no. 3/4 (Summer–Autumn, 1984): 147–54.

32. Hale Woodruff's own recollections are of interest here; see Oral History Interview with Hale Woodruff, November 18, 1968, Archives of American Art, Smithsonian Institution. Apparently, Woodruff made his visit before Cullen arrived in Paris in 1928, but he may have arranged the meeting between Cullen and Tanner.

33. See Leininger-Miller, *New Negro Artists in Paris,* chapter 6, for more details.

34. These three columns, plus one he wrote on his trip to London at this time, are reprinted in *My Soul's High Song,* 551–68. All the columns appeared between January and April 1929.

35. The diaries are at box 12, folders 1–3, ARC-TU.

36. "Profit" is Cullen's phonetic spelling of Elizabeth Prophet, who was for a time intimately involved with DuBois, having earlier divorced her first husband and sailed to Paris with little financial means.

37. In Leininger-Miller, *New Negro Artists in Paris,* 46–47.

38. The correspondence with the Greenes is in box 2, folder 14, ARC-TU. It is not known how Cullen first met them.

39. Nevertheless, after nearly twenty months years abroad, Cullen wrote to Locke on April 23, 1930, about what many African American writers experienced: "I am enjoying Paris immensely. It is a marvelous place to be, but I am getting a bit

homesick and will welcome the moment of leaving for New York. I miss Harlem and the colored people tremendously."

Chapter 5

1. The letters from West to Cullen are in the Amistad Research Center; those from Cullen to West are in the Dorothy West Collection at the Radcliff Library, Harvard University.

2. Douglas (1899–1979) had arrived in New York in the heyday of the Renaissance and went on to be one of the century's leading African American artists. He headed the Artists Guild in the 1930s, lobbying for fuller support and recognition from the WPA. Rudolph Fisher (1897–1934), a physician who fell victim to the x-ray technology that he used in his research, was one of the more promising and widely published fiction writers of the Renaissance.

3. See Alan Reimonenq, "Countée Cullen and Uranian Soul Windows," *Journal of Homosexuality* 26, no. 2 (1993): 143–66.

4. Cullen included the sonnet in *The Medea and Some Poems*.

5. An account of the incident from one of its chief participants is given by Langston Hughes, *I Wonder as I Wander* (New York: Hill & Wang, 1993), in the chapters in the section headed "Moscow Movie." This is a reprint of the edition first published in 1956.

6. A letter from Dr. Kugel describing Mrs. Cullen's last days is in box 3, folder 5, ARC-TU.

7. This poem figures in the analysis of Cullen's melancholia offered by Esther Sanchez-Pardo, *Cultures of the Death Drive: Melanie Klein and Modernist Melancholia* (Durham, NC: Duke University Press, 2003), 366. Relying heavily on the theoretical language of Kleinian psychology (its first two hundred pages offer a dense historical and analytic view of Klein and her relation to Freud and psychoanalysis), the book claims of "Tribute" that "this protective and beneficial image of the mother (her face, or breast) is what in Cullen's poetry usually remains outside figuration. As I have attempted to demonstrate through my reading of Klein, the foreclosure of the image of the (good) mother is determinant in the production of melancholia." That much of Cullen's lyric poetry arose out of the melancholic side of his temperament is obvious, but given the lack of knowledge about his early years, the chances of a trustworthy psychoanalytic investigation would be limited. This study, however, does offer a thorough interpretive scheme—involving discussions of modernism, racism, homosexuality, and other topics—and deals with much of Cullen's work.

8. One critic says that West's writings and her overall literary efforts "reveal an astute and active political awareness." But it is also argued that the three standard categories of politically conscious writing overlap in West's case. "Her work suggests a proclivity toward the 'proletarian' aesthetic as she challenged readers of the publication(s) she edited to break through geographic and class stratification in order to promote community. West's interest in 'proletarian' ideology may stem from her own activism and joint heritage of 'folk' and 'bourgeois.'" See Sharon L.

Jones, "Reclaiming a Legacy: The Dialectic of Race, Class, and Gender in Jessie Fauset, Zora Neale, and Dorothy West," *Hecate* 24, no. 1 (1998): 155–64.

9. Satire dominated not only Wallace Thurman's *The Infants of the Spring* but Richard Bruce Nugent's unpublished novel, *Gentleman Jigger.* Both novels, exulting in the tradition of the roman à clef, even make use of the same incidents, which feature sharply parodic portraits of Renaissance figures. Nugent's narrator, Stuartt, refers to an award ceremony at a literary contest dinner where he depicts Cullen acidulously, under the pseudonym of Burton Barclay, in these terms: "mostly Stuartt remembered Burton Barclay and wondered how such lyric poetry could emanate from that round and rubicund figure, made more ridiculous-seeming by the sweeping tails of the evening clothes he had worn to grace his reception of the first prize. He looked like a little brown pig." See Thomas Wirth, ed., *Gay Rebel of the Harlem Renaissance: Selections from the Work of Richard Bruce Nugent* (Durham, NC: Duke University Press, 2002), 169.

10. The Great Migration has been deeply explored by Isabel Wilkerson, *The Warmth of Other Suns: The Epic Story of America's Great Migration* (New York: Random House, 2010).

11. There has been relatively little extended commentary on the novel. One exception is an essay that draws heavily on several theoretical models; see David Jarraway, "No Heaven in Harlem: Countée Cullen and His Diasporic Doubles," in *New Voices on the Harlem Renaissance: Essays on Race, Gender, and Literary Discourse* (Madison, NJ: Fairleigh Dickinson University Press, 2005), 214–37.

12. These reviews are in box 16, folder 11, ARC-TU.

13. This is mentioned by Amritjit Singh, *The Novels of the Harlem Renaissance* (University Park: Pennsylvania State University Press, 1976), 83. This study offers little by way of structural or thematic analysis.

14. In his full-length critical study, *Countée Cullen* (Boston: Twayne, 1984), 72.

15. The annual review, which originally appeared in *Opportunity,* is reprinted in *The Critical Temper of Alain Locke,* ed. Jeffrey Stewart (New York: Garland, 1983), 215–20. Singh misquotes the phrase to read "a high life and high society."

16. Padraic Colum, the best known of the Irish poets at the meeting where Cullen was a guest, sent Cullen a note thanking him for sending a copy of the poem. See box 1, folder 17, ARC-TU. The meeting took place in London.

17. David F. Dorsey, Jr., explores Cullen's classical allusions in "Countée Cullen's Use of Greek Mythology," *CLA Journal* 13, no. 1 (September 1969): 68–77.

18. Cullen's version is discussed at length by Lillian Corti, in "Countée Cullen's Medea," *African American Review* 32, no. 4 (Winter 1998): 621–34. Highlighting the themes of the play, Corti compares Cullen's effort with those of Linda Brent, Harriet Beecher Stowe, Kate Chopin, and Toni Morrison, all of whom have stories that depict babies in a slave society who are killed by their mothers. She goes on to suggest in conclusion that perhaps Cullen "deliberately wished to explore the question of violence as an instrument of political action. . . . The bitterly disappointed black poet chose to dramatize the agony of a tormented soul torn between the desire to spare the innocent and the passion for revolution." The essay is at pains to make the

translation into a full-blown autobiographical document explicative of Cullen's life in the mid-1930s.

19. Dodson continued to take a strong interest in Cullen's translation. As reported in Richard Coe, "The New Negro Dramatist," *Transition*, no. 11 (November 1963): 29–30: "Novelist, poet and teacher, Dodson has done much over the years to further the Negro playwright. For the late Countée Cullen's adaptation of Medea, he recently staged an original variation, Medea in Africa, wherein the Greek heroine is portrayed as a 19th century Ethiopian princess whose Jason is a white South African miner." This was the 1959 production, staged at Howard University.

20. This is from the 1906 edition. The translated play was produced on stage at the Savoy Theatre in London in 1907, where it received a remarkably negative review by T. S. Eliot (reprinted in *The Sacred Wood*, 1922), who concluded that "it is because Professor Murray has no creative instinct that he leaves Euripides quite dead." This production starred Sybil Thorndike and was broadcast on the radio by the BBC in 1925.

21. This translation is from 1910 and was widely reprinted.

22. See box 16, folder14, ARC-TU.

23. The forty-seven-page script is inbox 18, folder 12, ARC-TU. Folder 11 contains the scripts by Hughes and Bontemps.

24. This letter is dated July 22, 1925, and is in GCUM.

25. This letter is dated June 29, 1925, and sent from Pleasantville, as Cullen was preparing to start his Harvard classes. A photocopy is in the Miscellaneous American Letters and Papers at the Schomburg Center.

26. These notes are in box 13, folder 8, ARC-TU.

27. The riot was also the focus of a special issue of the *Survey Graphic,* the same journal that ten years earlier had published the issue that, in book form, became *The New Negro.* Alain Locke edited both issues, which together form a trajectory of the Renaissance. Locke titled his essay that introduced the later issue, "Harlem: Dark Weather Vane." It appeared in August 1936. See Charles Molesworth and Leonard Harris, *Alain Locke: Biography of a Philosopher* (Chicago: University of Chicago Press, 2008), for further discussion.

28. See chapter 6 for a discussion of Baldwin's interview with Cullen, which took place in 1942.

29. From an interview with Elvyn Davidson as recorded by the Veteran's Oral History Project at the Center for the Study of War and Society, in the Department of History at the University of Tennessee. G. Kurt Piehler and Jason Bowen conducted the interview on April 4, 2000. After World War II, in which he served in Japan and Italy, Davidson enjoyed a successful career as a surgeon. His interview is of great interest. It is available at http://web.utk.edu/~csws/interview.html.

Chapter 6

1. Some early preparations for a staging were made before McClendon's illness and death. Van Vechten photographed her in a costume designed for the role for Medea.

2. A copy of the script is in box 8, folder 14, ARC-TU. On the title page the authors are listed as "Countée Cullen and Harry Hamilton," and the copyright is given as 1935. In box 9, folder 5, a virtually identical script is entitled *One Way to Heaven*, with only Cullen's name listed as the author. Apparently, Cullen took enough of Hamilton's advice in the revision of the novel into a play that he was willing to share authorial credit.

3. A flyer announcing the performance is in box 17, folder 6, ARC-TU. Locke's mention, which lists Cullen and Bontemps as coauthors, was in his review, "God Save Reality!," in *Opportunity* 15 (January and February, 1937), 8–13. It appears that Locke did not actually see the performance but spoke of the play only from a manuscript of it, probably given to him by Cullen. The review in the *New York Times*, datelined Philadelphia, is on page 35.

4. The typescript is in box 10, folder 16, ARC-TU.

5. James V. Hatch, Douglas A. M. Ward, and Joe Weixlmann, "The Rungs of a Powerful Long Ladder: An Owen Dodson Bibliography," *Black American Literature Forum*, 14, no. 2 (Summer 1980): 60–68.

6. The story of the protracted revision process for *They Seek a City*, which may or may not have involved Cullen, is told by James Hatch, *Sorrow Is the Only Faithful One: The Life of Owen Dodson* (Urbana: University of Illinois Press, 1995), 125–27. I have relied on this biography for other details about Dodson.

7. The scripts by Hughes and Bontemps are in box 18, folder 11, ARC-TU; *They Seek a City* is in folder 12.

8. Fowler (1895–1976) was also a painter; her papers are part of the Beinecke's James Weldon Johnson Collection. Kurt Pahlen (1907–2003), an amazingly prolific composer, conductor, and musical educator, was born in Vienna and trained in the classical European tradition.

9. This account comes from Hatch, *Sorrow Is the Only Faithful One*, 132.

10. DuBois published a book called *Color and Democracy* in 1945, and Locke edited a special issue of *Survey Graphic* called "Color: The Unfinished Business of Democracy" in 1942. The argument about the duty of democratic nations to end racism was also put forward by Cullen, in his poem, "Apostrophe to the Land." See below for a discussion of the poem.

11. This letter is dated March 10, 1928. It is in the McKay Collection at the Beinecke.

12. See the informative article by Hillina Seife, "A New Generation of Ethiopianists: The Universal Ethiopian Students Association and *The African: Journal of African Affairs*, 1937–1948," *African and Black Diaspora: An International Journal* 3, no. 2 (2010): 197–209. "What distinguishes the UESA as Ethiopianist as opposed to more generally anti-colonial nationalist Pan-African, like many other organizations of the period is that the group supported Ethiopia and Haile Selassie I at almost all costs, championing both the nationalist and imperialist nature of the modern Ethiopian state in the name of preserving its political sovereignty and role as a leader in Africa and the black world" (205). Seife generously shared the results of her research with me.

13. For some of the details about McKay, I have relied on Tyrone Tillery, *Claude McKay: A Black Poet's Struggle for Identity* (Amherst: University of Massachusetts Press, 1992).

14. This innovative scheme apparently was approved by Cullen and Hughes but unfortunately never advanced beyond the planning stage. In the letter proposing the idea to Cullen (box 3, folder 11, ARC-TU) McKay also says, "You know I have many secret enemies."

15. Ida recalled this earlier meeting in a taped interview; the tape, recorded in May 1971, is in ARC-TU. Subsequent references are to "tape no. 2: Ida Cullen." The Cullen archive has four cassette tapes that record Ida Cullen's memories that revolve around her relationship with Cullen. Tape no. 3 is recorded over with music and contains little or no information; tape no. 4 was recorded at the American Church in Paris in May 1971. The latter is also of poor quality and contains little. Tape no. 2 contains Ida's recollections of her marriage with Cullen, and Cullen's childhood recollections that he shared with Ida. Side B of tape no. 2 contains the story of Ida's miscarriage and Cullen's last days. Tape no. 1 tells of the events dealing with *St. Louis Woman* and Cullen's last illness. All four tapes were deposited in the archive by Ida.

16. One scholar has dated the start of their relationship in 1937. See Mason Stokes, "Strange Fruits: Rethinking the Gay Twenties," *Transition* 12, no. 2 (2002): 56–79.

17. The letter of thanks is in the second folder (no. 27) of the Van Vechten–Cullen correspondence at the Beinecke, JWJ-CVV, box Cu–Dn.

18. The interview with Baldwin is in *My Soul's High Song,* 602–6.

19. Cullen mentions this in a letter but does not name the book.

20. Gillian Adams, "Missing the Boat: Countée Cullen's *The Lost Zoo," The Lion and the Unicorn* 21, no. 1, (January 1997): 40–58. Adams goes on to point out that "Cullen's children's books are not mentioned in the standard bibliographies of children's literature scholarship such as *The Oxford Companion to Children's Literature,* Linnea Hendrickson's *A Guide to Children's Literature Criticism, Children's Literature Abstracts,* and ERIC, or in the *MLA Bibliography.*" My quotations from *The Lost Zoo,* with page numbers in parentheses, are from the Silver Burdett Press reprint of 1992.

21. See Ted Shine, "Charles Sebree, Modernist," *Black American Literature Forum* 19, no. 1, Contemporary Black Visual Artists Issue (Spring 1985): 6–8. Shine refers to a 1984 interview with Sebree for his biographical information.

22. The letter is in ARC-TU and is dated August 24, 1944.

23. See the entry under Bontemps in *Encyclopedia of the Harlem Renaissance,* ed. Aberjhani and Sandra L. West (New York: Checkmark Books, 2003).

24. See Kirkland C. Jones, *Renaissance Man from Louisiana: A Biography of Arna Bontemps* (Westport, CT: Greenwood Press, 1992).

25. See "The Twenties: Harlem and Its Negritude," in *The Collected Works of Langston Hughes,* vol. 9, *Essays on Art, Race, Politics, and World Affairs,* ed. Christopher De Santis (Columbia: University of Missouri Press, 2002), 466. This reminiscence originally appeared in *African Forum* 1 (1966): 11–20.

26. See the correspondence at box 4, folder 16, ARC-TU. This folder also contains

a letter of rejection from Frank Merlin at the Little Theatre in New York City; at the time the play was going under the title *Leavin' Time*.

27. The archive for the Federal Theatre Project, a New Deal offshoot of the WPA, is in the Federal Theatre Project playscript and radioscript collection, Collection no. C0002, Special Collections and Archives, George Mason University.

28. See Langston Hughes and Zora Neale Hurston, *Mule Bone: A Comedy of Negro Life*, ed. George Houston Bass and Henry Louis Gates, Jr. (New York: Harper, 1991).

29. In *Arna Bontemps–Langston Hughes: Letters 1925–1967*, ed. Charles Nichols (New York: Paragon House, 1990), 27. All letters between Bontemps and Hughes are from this edition.

30. See the account of all the maneuvers in Arnold Rampersad, *The Life of Langston Hughes, Volume 1: 1902–1941*, (New York: Oxford University Press, 1986), 366–69.

31. Most of the details in what follows are taken from the Bontemps-Cullen correspondence, which is housed in the Special Collections Research Center at Syracuse University Library. My thanks to Mary Beth Hinton for her help in making copies available.

32. See the Bontemps-Hughes letters, 180. Isabel had just divorced Adam Clayton Powell, Jr.

33. On September 9, 1945, Cullen wrote to Locke with an invitation to attend and a list of those who were to be included.

> Thank you for your letter and for the enclosure. In deference to the flood of unwarranted criticism that is being leveled at ST. LOUIS WOMAN, I have agreed to read the script as it now stands to a representative group of Negroes on Friday evening, September 14th at half past eight at the home of Walter White, 409 Edgecombe Avenue. Walter, I believe, is inviting Judge Jane Bolin, Hubert Delaney and some others; Arna [Bontemps] has asked the Aaron Douglases, the Henry Moons, Edna Thomas and Dorothy Peterson, while I am asking you, Frank Horne (whose address I do not have but whose letter I am asking you to get to him for me) George Sc[h]uyler, Thelma Boozer, and Edward Perry. I am especially anxious to have you and Frank Horne because I want to be sure of having some sane and logical criticism (and that does not necessarily mean criticism favorable to Arna and me) to offset the purely emotional criticism that may have a tendency to prevail in some very intelligent quarters. The producer, Mr. Gross, is willing to defray the transportation expenses of both yourself and Frank Horne. Please wire me whether or not you will be able to be present, and please address the enclosed envelope to Frank. (ARC-TU)

People chosen by White, like Jane Bolin, a judge, would express conservative views, while Bontemps obviously felt those such as Aaron Douglas would adopt a more liberal approach.

34. *A Man Called White: The Autobiography of Walter White* (New York: Viking Press, 1948), 338–39.

35. The letter is dated June 30, 1945, and is in ARC-TU.

36. In *My Soul's High Song,* "Apostrophe to the Land," on page 321, and it first appeared in *Phylon* 3, no. 4 (4th Quarter, 1942): 396–97. See chapter 6, note 10.

37. This event is recounted on audiotape 4, side B, at the ARC-TU.

38. This is from the interview on audiotape 1, ARC-TU.

39. This was a part of Locke's annual survey; it is reprinted in *The Critical Temper of Alain Locke,* ed. Jeffrey Stewart (New York: Garland, 1983), 329–36.

40. The description is quoted in Hatch, *Sorrow Is the Only Faithful One,* 131–32.

41. Michael L. Lomax, "Countée Cullen: A Key to the Puzzle," in *The Harlem Renaissance Re-Examined* (New York: AMS Press, 1987), 222.

42. In "The Twenties: Harlem and Its Negritude."

Index

Extended discussions indicated by numbers in **bold**.